Lindsay Clandfield

Straightforward

Elementary **Student's Book**

D1612732

MACMILLAN

Reading	Listening	Speaking	Writing (in the Workbook)
Conversations: the first day at a new job		Guided conversation: introductions	Completing a form
	A phone call to a language school	Make a phone call to a language school **Did you know?** They aren't American!	
A conversation: talking about possessions		Game: what's this in English?	
An email from a tour company	Conversations at a welcome party	Roleplay: at a welcome party	
The expat files: article about Britons living abroad	A Briton talking about living abroad	Talk about life as an expat	A personal e-message
	A radio interview about men and women and friendship	Talk about things you do with your friends	
An Englishman's Home: Article about a man who lives with his parents		Talk about how old people are when they do certain things **Did you know?** The family in Britain	
	A phone call describing people arriving at the airport	Communication: describe famous faces past and present	
Houseswap: a website describing houses		Game: Class Houseswap	Giving directions
	A documentary about the White House	Give a virtual tour of your home **Did you know?** 10 Downing Street	
A conversation about a new flat		Communication: find differences between two rooms	
Information about Tate Modern	Conversations at the information desk of an art gallery	Roleplay: give directions in a building	
MetroNaps: Article about a nap service		Talk about daily routines	Phone messages
An interview about Nothing Day	People talking about special days	Add an extra national holiday to the calendar	
	A radio phone-in about housework	Survey: Life at work & home	
	Five phone conversations	Survey: Phones and making phone calls **Did you know?** Phone facts: North America	
Languages made easy: article about translation machines		Talk about languages Asking for clarification	Describing a holiday
	People talking about holiday photos	Talk about holiday photos **Did you know?** Top destinations for Canadian tourists	
A conversation about holiday preparations		Talk about things to take on holiday	
Two advertisements for hotels	Conversations at a hotel	Talk about a past holiday Roleplay: at a hotel	

Reading	Listening	Speaking	Writing (in the Workbook)
Blogs about celebrations		Talk about a celebration	A card for a special occasion
	Actor! Author! A television quiz show	Game: Actor! Author! **Did you know?** The Big Read: favourite books	
Crying - good for your health: article about men and crying		Game: The Dialogue Game	
	Conversations about likes and dislikes	Talk about people and things that you like and don't like	
	Exposed: A television programme about diets	Invent your own 'miracle' diet	A dish for you
Rice: article about rice		Communication: describe differences in pictures of food	
	Conversations about eating habits	Dialogue: complaining about food	
	A conversation in a restaurant	Survey: eating out Guided conversation at a restaurant **Did you know?** Eating out in America	
Fear of flying: article about flying		Questionnaire about travel	An invitation
	A traffic report on the radio	Game: In traffic **Did you know?** London's traffic law	
Tracy Dick PI: detective story		Communication: a normal day and a special day	
	Conversations about crossing London	Dialogue: suggestions	
A website about first impressions		Talk about making a good impression	Giving advice
Health: article about sitting at work	Exercise instructions	Survey: health Give instructions for an exercise	
	An interview about how people remember faces	Game: Memory test **Did you know?** Faces on coins	
	Conversations about feeling ill	Roleplay: not feeling well	
Dumb laws: article about strange laws		Make classroom 'laws' **Did you know?** Banning smoking	A city guide
	People talk about life in the capital city of their country	Talk about living in the city Roleplay: moving to another city	
Best of the best: extract from guide book about Cape Town		Talk about the best things to do in a city Give advice	
	A conversation in a souvenir shop	Roleplay: in a shop	
	Behind the scenes: television programme about jobs	Talk about work Game: Guess the job **Did you know?** The NHS	A job for the summer
Futurework: article about the future of work		Talk about your future working life	
16 before 60: article about healthy living	People talk about future plans	Talk about plans for the future	
A website discussion about love and work	Conversations about invitations	Talk about love in the workplace Dialogue: invitations	
Lifetime achievements: Article about Grammy Award winners		Talk about music Talk about a famous singer	Thanks!
	Interviews about speaking in public	Questionnaire about speaking in public **Did you know?** Person of the Year	
English in your life: brochure for a language school		A short presentation	
	Conversations at the end of the tour	Game: The Explore Tour	

Basics 1

INTERNATIONAL ENGLISH

1 Look at the international English words. Which ones do you know?

2 🔘 1.1 Listen and point to the words you hear.

3 🔘 1.2 Listen and repeat.

A HOTEL

B Hospital

C POLICE

D autostrade
Aurelia
ss 1 FIRENZE
P BUS

Bradford
P Station
Airport ✈
Armley

E

F 2×1 Pizza
free coffee
and tea

G 7·30
FOOTBALL

H TAXI

NUMBERS 1–10

1 🔘 1.3 Read and listen to the numbers.

| 1 | 2 | 3 | 4 | 5 | 6 | 7 | 8 | 9 | 10 |

2 🔘 1.3 Listen and repeat.

3 🔘 1.4 Listen and write the number you hear.

___ ___ ___ ___ ___

4 Work in pairs, A and B. Turn to page 137.

INTRODUCTIONS 1

1 🔘 1.5 Read and listen to the dialogue.

Woman: Hello.
Frank: Hi.
Woman: What's your name?
Frank: My name's Frank.
Woman: Nice to meet you.
Frank: Nice to meet you.

2 🔘 1.5 Listen and repeat.

3 🔘 1.6 Listen to two dialogues. Match the dialogues to the pictures.

A ____

B ____

4 Practise the dialogue from exercise 1.

ALPHABET

1 🔘 1.7 Read and listen to the alphabet.

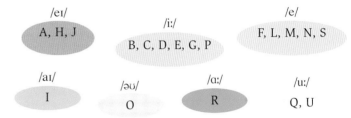

2 🔘 1.7 Listen and repeat.

3 🔘 1.8 Look at the circles. Listen to the sound and the letters.

/eɪ/
A, H, J

/i:/
B, C, D, E, G, P

/e/
F, L, M, N, S

/aɪ/
I

/əʊ/
O

/ɑ:/
R

/u:/
Q, U

4 Write the letters from the box in the correct circles.

K T V W X Y Z

5 🔘 1.9 Listen to the recording to check your answers. Repeat the letters.

6 🔘 1.10 Listen and write the letters you hear.

1 _____ 2 _____ 3 _____ 4 _____ 5 _____

INTRODUCTIONS 2

1 Put the dialogue in the correct order.

☐ Hi. My name's Katy. What's your name?
☐ L-I-N-D-S-A-Y.
☐ How do you spell that?
☐ My name's Lindsay.
☐ Hello.

2 🔘 1.11 Listen and check.

3 Work in groups. Ask other people to spell their name.

What's your name?
My name's Viktor.
How do you spell that?
V-I-K-T-O-R.

Basics 2

CLASSROOM ENGLISH 1

1 Match the pictures to the verbs in the box.

write   listen to   open   close   look at   read   talk

2 🔘 **1.12** Listen to the recording and write a word from exercise 1 in the space.

1 _____ your books.   5 _____ the picture.
2 _____ your books.   6 _____ the text.
3 _____ the words.   7 _____ the CD.
4 _____ to a partner.

3 🔘 **1.12** Listen again and check.

COLOURS

1 Match the words in the box to the colours.

red   white   green   brown   blue   black   yellow

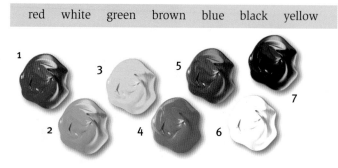

2 🔘 **1.13** Listen and repeat.

DAYS OF THE WEEK

1 🔘 **1.14** Listen to the days of the week and complete the words.

2 🔘 **1.15** Listen and repeat.

3 🔘 **1.16** Listen to five conversations. <u>Underline</u> the day of the week you hear.

1   Monday / Sunday   4   Saturday / Sunday
2   Tuesday / Thursday   5   Friday / Thursday
3   Friday / Saturday

NUMBERS 11–100

1 Match the words to the numbers.

eleven	14
twelve	11
thirteen	20
fourteen	15
fifteen	17
sixteen	19
seventeen	13
eighteen	12
nineteen	18
twenty	16

2 🔘 **1.17** Listen and repeat.

3 Write the numbers for these words.

twenty-one	_21_	seventy-five	____
thirty-three	_33_	eighty-eight	____
forty-seven	____	ninety-one	____
fifty-nine	____	one hundred	____
sixty-one	____		

THINGS AROUND YOU

1 🔘 1.18 Look at the picture and listen to the words.

> an ID card   an earring   an apple   coins   keys
> photos   a pen   sweets

2 🔘 1.19 Read and listen to the words. What things are in your classroom? Put a tick (✓) or a cross (✗).

☐ a TV   ☐ a door   ☐ a CD player
☐ a board   ☐ a window

3 🔘 1.20 Listen to words from exercises 1 and 2. Point to the object on the page or in the class and say the word.

4 What things do you have with you today? Ask a partner. Use the picture and the words to help you.

Do you have an ID card? Yes.
Do you have photos? No.
Do you have an apple? Yes.
Do you have a credit card? Yes.

GRAMMAR: *a /an*, plurals

> With singular nouns, use the article *a/an*.
> **an + vowel**
> *an* apple
> *an* ID card
>
> **a + consonant**
> *a* TV
> *a* pen
>
> To make nouns plural = noun + *s/es/ies*
> *sweets*
> *sandwiches*

> ❯ SEE LANGUAGE REFERENCE PAGE 40

1 Make the words plural.

1 wallet _____
2 bus _____
3 taxi _____
4 hotel _____
5 mobile phone _____
6 sandwich _____

2 Write *a*, *an* or nothing.

1 __ ID card   5 __ airport
2 __ bus   6 __ key
3 __ apples   7 __ hotels
4 __ taxis   8 __ hospital

CLASSROOM ENGLISH 2

1 🔘 1.21 Listen and complete the questions and sentences with a word from the box.

> say   mean   don't

1 What does *apple* _____?
2 How do you _____ *merci* in English?
3 I _____ know.
4 I _____ understand.

2 Look at the words and pictures on pages 8 and 9. Work with a partner and ask questions.

What does … mean?
How do you say … in English?

GRAMMAR TERMS

The words in bold are grammar terms used in *Straightforward* Elementary. What are they in your language?

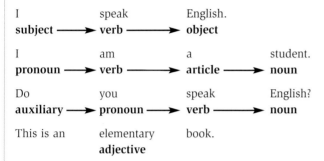

I	speak	English.
subject →	**verb** →	**object**

I	am	a	student.
pronoun →	**verb** →	**article** →	**noun**

Do	you	speak	English?
auxiliary →	**pronoun** →	**verb** →	**noun**

This is an   elementary   book.
                  adjective

PRONUNCIATION

Vowel sounds

iː	ɪ	ʊ	uː
eat	it	book	new
tree	six	pull	school
e	ə	ɜː	ɔː
very	American	her	born
any	mother	bird	awful
æ	ʌ	ɑː	ɒ
back	up	car	what
apple	does	after	on

ɪə	eɪ	ʊə	əʊ
here	face	Europe	no
ear	ate	tour	open
ɔɪ	eə	aɪ	aʊ
boy	their	hi	house
noisy	airport	eye	down

Consonant sounds

p	b	t	d	tʃ	dʒ
stop	bar	ten	desk	cheese	June
parents	job	light	red	teach	orange
k	g	f	v	θ	ð
can	go	father	very	think	the
look	bag	laugh	live	fourth	mother
s	z	ʃ	ʒ	m	n
see	zoo	she	television	make	never
rice	has	information	usually	name	ten
ŋ	h	l	r	w	j
English	hello	like	read	water	yes
sing	hand	ill	practise	where	year

A, *an*, plurals

Use *a* and *an* in front of singular nouns.

Use *a* with a consonant.
a TV
a pen
a door

Use *an* with a vowel.
an apple
an ID card
an earing

To make nouns plural add -*s*, -*es*, -*ies*.

-s
pen	pens
door	doors
apple	apples

-es
sandwich	sandwiches
bus	buses

-ies
dictionary	dictionaries
baby	babies

Do not use *a/an* with plural nouns
Not ~~a doors~~

WORD LIST

International words

airport *n* ***	/ˈeəpɔːt/
bus *n* ***	/bʌs/
coffee *n* ***	/ˈkɒfi/
football *n* **	/ˈfʊtbɔːl/
hotel *n* ***	/həʊˈtel/
hospital *n* ***	/ˈhɒspɪtl/
mobile phone *n*	/ˌməʊbaɪl ˈfəʊn/
pizza *n*	/ˈpiːtsə/
police *n* ***	/pəˈliːs/
sandwich *n* *	/ˈsænwɪtʃ/
taxi *n* ***	/ˈtæksi/
tea *n* ***	/tiː/

Numbers

one ***	/wʌn/
two ***	/tuː/
three	/θriː/
four	/fɔː/
five	/faɪv/
six	/sɪks/
seven	/ˈsevn/
eight	/eɪt/
nine	/naɪn/
ten	/ten/
eleven	/ɪˈlevn/
twelve	/twelv/
thirteen	/ˈθɜːtiːn/
fourteen	/ˈfɔːtiːn/
fifteen	/ˈfɪftiːn/
sixteen	/ˈsːkstiːn/
seventeen	/ˈsevntiːn/
eighteen	/ˈeːtiːn/
nineteen	/naɪntiːn/
twenty	/ˈtwenti/
thirty	/ˈθɜːti/
forty	/ˈfɔːti/
fifty	/ˈfɪfti/
sixty	/ˈsɪksti/
seventy	/ˈsevnti/
eighty	/ˈeɪti/
ninety	/ˈnainti/
one hundred	/wʌn ˈhʌndrəd/

Classroom English

write *v* ***	/raɪt/
listen to *v* ***	/ˈlɪsn tə/
open *v* ***	/ˈəʊpn/
close *v* ***	/kləʊz/
look at *v* ***	/ˈlʊk ət/
read *v* ***	/riːd/
talk *v* ***	/tɔːk/
book *n* ***	/bʊk/

word *n* ***	/wɜːd/
partner *n* ***	/ˈpɑːtnə/
picture *n* ***	/ˈpɪktʃə/
text *n* ***	/tekst/
CD *n* *	/siː ˈdiː/

Days of the week

Monday ***	/ˈmʌndeɪ/
Tuesday ***	/ˈtʃuːzdeɪ/
Wednesday ***	/ˈwenzdeɪ/
Thursday ***	/ˈθɜːzdeɪ/
Friday ***	/ˈfraɪdeɪ/
Saturday ***	/ˈsætədeɪ/
Sunday ***	/ˈsʌndeɪ/

Colours

black *adj* ***	/blæk/
blue *adj* ***	/bluː/
brown *adj* ***	/braʊn/
green *adj* ***	/griːn/
grey *adj* *	/greɪ/
red *adj* ***	/red/
white *adj* ***	/waɪt/
yellow *adj* ***	/ˈjeləʊ/

Things around you

apple *n* ***	/ˈæpl/
board *n* ***	/bɔːd/
CD player *n*	/siː ˈdiː pleɪə/
coin *n* ***	/kɔɪn/
door *n* ***	/dɔː/
earring *n*	/ˈɪərɪŋ/
ID card *n*	/aɪ ˈdiː kɑːd/
key *n* ***	/kiː/
pen *n* **	/pen/
photo *n* **	/ˈfəʊtəʊ/
sweet *n* **	/swiːt/
TV *n* ***	/tiː ˈviː/
wallet *n*	/ˈwɒlɪt/
window *n* ***	/ˈwɪndəʊ/

Abbreviations

n	noun	*sth*	something
v	verb	*C*	countable
adj	adjective	*U*	uncountable
adv	adverb	*pl*	plural
sb	somebody	*s*	singular

*** the most common and basic words
** very common words
*   fairly common words

1A The new person

Reading & Listening

1 Read the text.

It's Monday. This is Alyssa.
She's new. It's her first day at work.

2 Match the dialogues to the pictures.

1
Alyssa: Hello.
Charles: Good morning.
Alyssa: My name's Alyssa.
Charles: You're new. Hello, I'm Charles.
          I'm the manager.

2
Charles: Good morning, Julian.
Julian: Good morning, Charles.
Charles: Julian, this is Alison. She's new.
Julian: Nice to meet you, Alison.
Alyssa: I'm not Alison.
Julian: What?
Alyssa: My name isn't Alison. It's Alyssa.
Julian: Nice to meet you, Alyssa.
Charles: Sorry.

3
Eric: Alyssa!
Alyssa: Hello, Eric!
Eric: How are you?
Alyssa: I'm fine, thanks. How are you?
Eric: Fine. Good to see you. Goodbye.
Alyssa: Yeah. Bye.

4
Margaret: She's new.
Carla: What's her name?
Margaret: Alyssa.
Carla: Alyssa? How do you spell that?
Margaret: I don't know.

Useful language

Good morning: < 12:00 pm
Good afternoon: 12:00 pm – 6:00 pm
Good evening: > 6:00 pm

3 🔘 **1.22** Listen to the recording to check
your answers.

4 Work in pairs. Repeat the dialogues.

VOCABULARY: objects 1

1 🔘 **1.23** Listen and repeat the words.

> a desk   a computer   a chair   a pen
> a coffee   a piece of paper   a phone
> a book

2 Find the things on page 12.

3 🔘 **1.24** Listen to Alyssa and Margaret. Tick (✓) the words from exercise 1 you hear.

GRAMMAR: verb *to be*; possessive adjectives

> I'm *new.*
> They **are** *Charles and Julian.*
> She **isn't** *Alison. She's Alyssa.*
>
> **Possessive adjectives**
> **Her** *name is Margaret.*
> *What's* **your** *name?*
> **Their** *names are Eric and Carla.*

> ❯ SEE LANGUAGE REFERENCE PAGE 20

1 Complete the sentences with *is/are/am.*

1 Her name ___ not Alison.
2 Her name ___ Alyssa.
3 You ___ new.
4 I ___ the manager.
5 They ___ in the office.
6 He ___ in the hotel.
7 Eric and Julian ___ not managers.
8 I ___ fine, thanks.

2 Say the sentences in exercise 1 with contractions.

3 Underline the correct word.

1 This is *your / his* pen.

2 This isn't *my / your* sandwich!

3 *His / Her* name is George.

4 They're *her / their* earrings.

5 It's *my / our* computer.

6 *His / Her* name is Elizabeth.

SPEAKING

1 Work in groups of three, A, B and C. Write a dialogue. Look at the diagram below and the dialogues 1 and 2 on page 12 to help you.

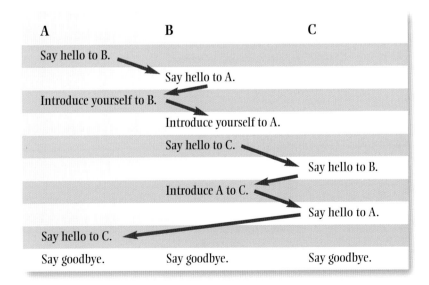

A	B	C
Say hello to B.		
	Say hello to A.	
Introduce yourself to B.		
		Introduce yourself to A.
	Say hello to C.	
		Say hello to B.
	Introduce A to C.	
		Say hello to A.
Say hello to C.		
Say goodbye.	Say goodbye.	Say goodbye.

2 Change roles and repeat the conversation.

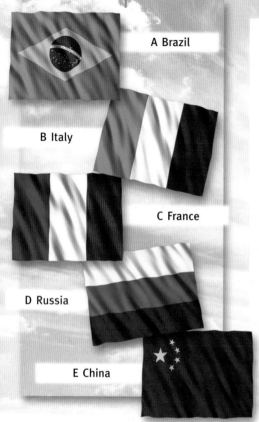

A Brazil

B Italy

C France

D Russia

E China

F Japan

G Poland

H Turkey

I Britain

J Greece

The **number 1** language practice system for Russian students, English students, Spanish students, French students, Italian students, Japanese students, Chinese students, German students, Arab students ...

Language Link
for international language students!

Language Link is simple
1 Register at Language Link.
2 Create your Language Link profile.
3 Choose a language you want to practise.
4 Link with a student who wants to practise your language. Link via email, video conference or telephone.

Jobs for language teachers too!

Be a member!
Visit our website www.languagelink.org
Or telephone 0800 429 7126

VOCABULARY: countries & nationalities

1 Match the sentence to the correct flag or flags.

1 The British and Russian flags are red, white and blue. ☐ ☐
2 The Chinese flag is red and yellow. ☐
3 The Italian flag is red, white and green. ☐

2 Write the nationalities for these countries in the correct column.

| Brazil | ~~Greece~~ | Germany | Poland | Turkey | France | Ireland |
| Japan | Italy | ~~Britain~~ | ~~Russia~~ | ~~China~~ | | |

-(i)an	-ish	-ese	other
Russian	British	Chinese	Greek

3 🔘 1.25 Listen to the recording to check your answers. Listen and repeat.

4 Describe the other flags in the picture. Use the words from exercise 1.

5 Work in pairs. Where are you from? What's your nationality? Tell a partner.

Where are you from? I'm from Poland.
What's your nationality? I'm Polish.

LISTENING

1 Look at the advertisement. What is Language Link?

2 🔘 1.26 Listen to a telephone call to Language Link. Underline the correct answer.

1 Mark is a *language teacher / language student*.
2 Mark is a(n) *German / English* student.
3 Mark's first language is *German / English*.
4 He is *26 / 25* years old.
5 He is *American / Australian*.
6 The woman is from *London / Sydney*.

3 🔘 **1.26** Listen again. Complete the form for Mark.

Language Link – Personal Profile

First name: _Mark_   Sex: male ☐ female ☐
Last name: _____
                            Age:
Language student ☐   13-16 ☐
Language teacher ☐   17-25 ☐
Language of study: _German_ 26-35 ☐
First language: _English_   36-45 ☐
Nationality: _____   46-55 ☐
Email address: _mark@mail.com_ over 55 ☐

GRAMMAR: verb *to be* – negative & questions

With the verb *to be*, change the position of the subject and the verb to make a question.
   You **are** a student.

   Are you a student?

In English there are two kinds of questions:
Wh- questions = questions with a question word
   Where are you from?
Yes/no questions = questions with no question word
   Are you a student?

Yes/no questions have a short answer.
   Yes, I **am**.   **No**, I'm **not**.

> SEE LANGUAGE REFERENCE PAGE 20

1 Read about another Language Link member. Make questions and answers.

Ben Stark is a language student at university. He's 21 years old. He studies Chinese and Korean. Ben is from Los Angeles, in the USA.

1 / Canadian?
   Is he Canadian? No, he isn't.
2 / American?
   Is he American? Yes, he is.
3 / his last name Stark?
4 / from New York?
5 / a language student?
6 / 43 years old?

2 Rearrange the words to make questions.

1 name what's your ?
2 last what's name your ?
3 language teacher you are a ?
4 you are a language student ?
5 are you old how ?
6 you are from where ?

3 🔘 **1.27** Listen to the recording to check your answers. Repeat the questions.

SPEAKING

1 Work in pairs, A and B.

A: You want to be a member of Language Link.
B: You work at Language Link.

Read the conversation.

B: *Good afternoon, Language Link.*
A: *Hello, I want to be a member.*
B: *Of course. What's your name?*
A: *…*

2 Continue the conversation. Use the questions in Grammar exercise 2 to help you.

DID YOU KNOW?

1 Read the text about nationalities.

Cate Blanchett
Jim Carrey

They aren't American!
Hollywood stars from other countries.

Jim Carrey is from Newmarket in the province of Ontario, Canada. Charlize Theron is from the small town of Benoni, South Africa. She's South African. Russell Crowe is from Wellington, New Zealand. Nicole Kidman and Cate Blanchett are Australian. Kidman is from Sydney and Blanchett is from Melbourne. Pierce Brosnan is Irish. He's from Drogheda, Ireland.

2 Work in pairs. Discuss these questions.

- How many of these people do you know?
- Do you know other Hollywood stars who aren't American? Where are they from?

1c | Personal possessions

VOCABULARY: objects 2

1 Look at the pictures. How many things can you say in English? Make sentences with words in the box.

> umbrella   mobile phone   keys   alarm clock
> bottle of water   pens   camera   glasses
> newspaper   book

It's a …
It's an …
They're …
I don't know what this is.

2 🔘 1.28 Listen and check your answers. Repeat the sentences.

LISTENING

1 🔘 1.29 Listen and tick the objects you hear.

2 Check your answers with the tapescript on page 140.

3 Work with a partner. Read the dialogues on page 140.

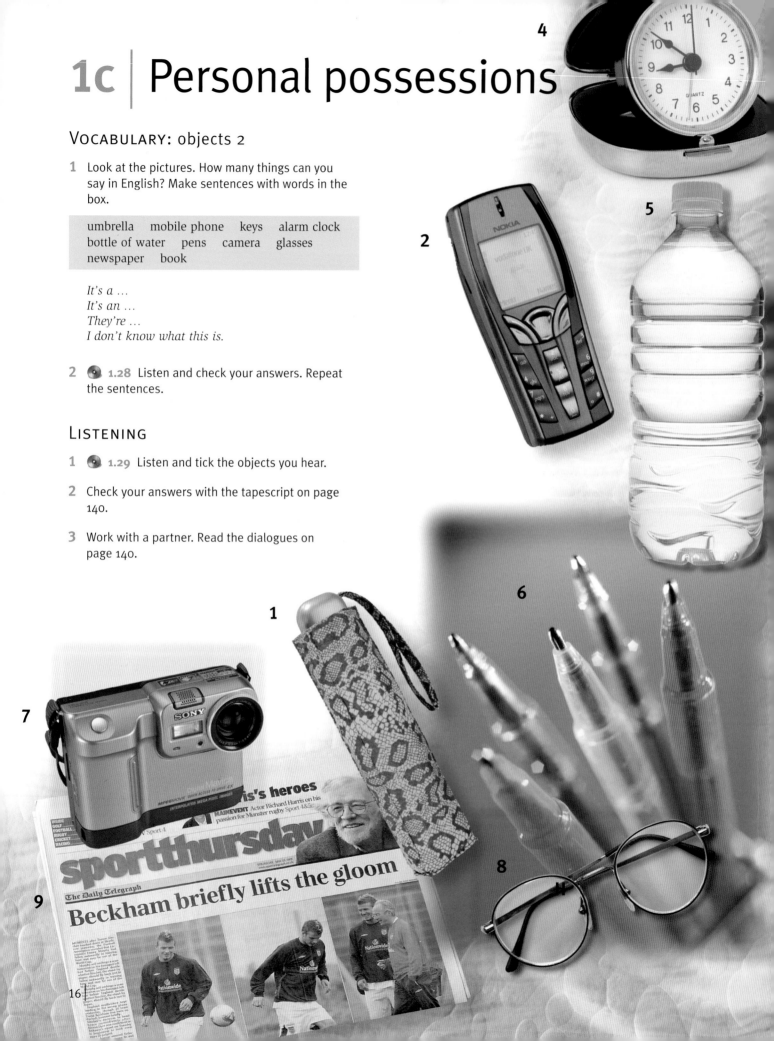

GRAMMAR: *this, that, these, those*

this (pen)

that (pen)

these (pens)

those (pens)

> SEE LANGUAGE REFERENCE PAGE 20

1 Underline the correct word in the dialogues.

1 What's *those / this*?
It's my private book!

2 Wait a minute. Is *that / those* a camera?
Yes. Just one photo please!

3 I think *these / this* are your keys.
Yes, they are!

4 Is that the alarm clock?
No, *that / these* is my mobile phone.

5 Are *those / that* your glasses?
Yes, they are.

10

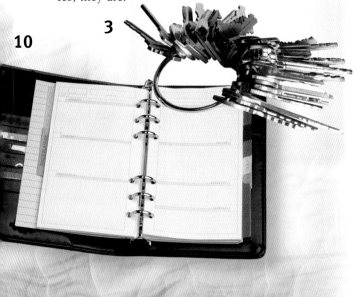

3

2 Complete with *this/that/these/those*.

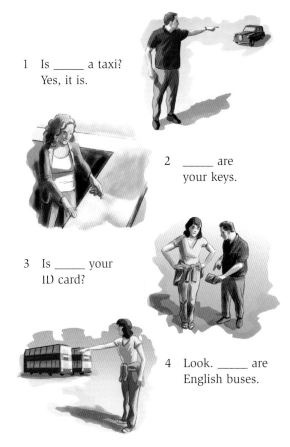

1 Is _____ a taxi?
Yes, it is.

2 _____ are
your keys.

3 Is _____ your
ID card?

4 Look. _____ are
English buses.

3 🔘 1.30 Listen to the recording to check your answers. Say the sentences.

SPEAKING

1 Play What's this in English? Work in groups of three. Each person puts three personal possessions from their bag on the table.

2 One person starts. Ask questions.

For things in the classroom, ask
What's that in English? What are those in English?
For things on the table, ask
What's this in English? What are these in English?

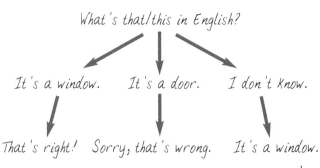

What's that/this in English?

It's a window.   It's a door.   I don't know.

That's right!   Sorry, that's wrong.   It's a window.

READING

1 Read the email. What is it about?

2 Read again and answer the questions.

1 What is Explore London?
2 Who is Valerie?
3 Where is the welcome party?
4 When is the welcome party?

LISTENING

1 🔘 1.31 Listen. Where are the conversations? Underline the correct place for each conversation.

1 reception   bar   hotel room
2 reception   bar   hotel room
3 reception   bar   hotel room
4 reception   bar   hotel room
5 reception   bar   hotel room
6 reception   bar   hotel room

2 🔘 1.31 Listen again. Is the underlined information correct? Put a tick (✓) or a cross (✗).

1 Rob and Meg are in reception.
2 They are in room 24.

3 They are in the bar.
4 He has tea and she has a beer.

5 Her name is Sam Moore.
6 Valerie is the tour guide.

7 Sam isn't in his room.
8 Sam is in the bar.

9 Herb and Hannah Curtis are from America.
10 Rob and Meg are from Britain.

11 Rob has a coffee.
12 Meg has a beer.

From: Valerie Hudson <v.hudson@explorelondon.org>
To: Mr and Mrs Curtis <herbcurtis@americainternet.com>
Subject: Welcome party
Date: Mon, May 8 2006 09:15:53

Dear Mr Curtis,
My name is Valerie and I am your tour guide for the Explore London tour.

Explore London Tours would like to invite you to a welcome party at the Regent Hotel, London on Sunday, May 14 at 7:30 p.m. Come for a drink and meet the other people on your tour.

If you have any questions about your tour, please email me or phone our head office in London on 0207 954 6178.

We look forward to seeing you,

Valerie Hudson
Explore London Tours "London … In Style"

VOCABULARY: drinks

1 Match the words in the box to the pictures.

> tea   coffee   wine   (orange) juice
> mineral water   beer

2 🔘 1.32 Listen and repeat the words.

3 Work in pairs. Cover the words. Test your partner.

What's this in English?
Coffee.
That's right.

FUNCTIONAL LANGUAGE: offers & responses

1 Complete the words in the box to make phrases.

Offers
Would you l___ a drink?

Responses
Yes, p_____.

No, t_____ you. No, t_____.

> SEE LANGUAGE REFERENCE PAGE 20

2 🔘 1.33 Listen to the recording to check your answers.

3 🔘 1.34 Listen to the words and make offers.

a coffee   Would you like a coffee?

4 Work in pairs, A and B.

A: Offer things to B.   B: Respond.

Roleplay

5 Work in groups of three. You are at the welcome party in the lounge of the Regent Hotel. One person is the tour guide, the other two people are on the tour. Prepare a conversation. Use the menu and the useful language below to help you.

6 Present your conversations to other groups in the class.

DRINKS MENU

Coffee
Tea

Beer
Glass of red wine
Glass of white wine

Orange juice
Apple juice

Mineral water

Useful language

Greetings	Hello. Good afternoon …
Introductions	My name's … Nice to meet you.
Personal information	Where are you from? I'm from …
Offers	Would you like …?
Responses	Yes, please. No, thank you.

1 | Language reference

GRAMMAR
Verb *to be*: present simple

Affirmative

Full form			Contraction	
I	am		I'm	
He/She/It	is	from Canada.	He's/She's/It's	fine.
You/We/They	are		You're/We're/They're	

To make the verb *to be* negative, add *not* (or *n't*) to the verb.

Negative

Full form	Contraction
I am not from Spain.	I'm not from Spain.
He/She/It is not a teacher.	He/She/It isn't a teacher.
You/We/They are not in class.	You/We/They aren't in class. or You're/We're/They're not in class.

To make questions with the verb *to be*, put the verb before the subject.

verb subject
Are   you   married?

Question

Am	I	
Is	he/she/it	30 years old?
Are	you/we/they	

Short answer

	I	am. / 'm not.
Yes, No,	he/she/it	is. / isn't.
	you/we/they	are. / aren't.

Possessive adjectives

I	my	It's my book.
you	your	What's your name?
he	his	It's his mobile phone.
she	her	Is it her pen?
it	its	What's its name?
we	our	It's our class.
they	their	I am their teacher.

Possessive adjectives go before a noun.

This, these, that, those
Use *this/these* to talk about things that are here.

Use *that/those* to talk about things that are there.

FUNCTIONAL LANGUAGE
Hello & goodbye

Hello
Hello.
Hi.
Good morning/afternoon/evening.

Goodbye
Goodbye.
Bye.
See you tomorrow/Monday/Tuesday.

Offers & responses

Would you like a …?
Yes, please.
No, thank you.
No, thanks.

WORD LIST

Objects

alarm clock *n*	/əˈlɑːm klɒk/
bottle of water *n*	/ˈbɒtl əv ˈwɔːtə/
camera *n* ***	/ˈkæm(ə)rə/
chair *n* ***	/tʃeə/
computer *n* ***	/kəmˈpjuːtə/
desk *n* ***	/desk/
glass *n* ***	/glɑːs/
newspaper *n* ***	/ˈnjuːspeɪpə/
paper *n* ***	/ˈpeɪpə/
phone *n* ***	/fəʊn/
umbrella *n*	/ʌmˈbrelə/

Countries & nationalities

Brazil	/brəˈzɪl/
Brazilian	/brəˈzɪliən/
Britain	/ˈbrɪtn/
British	/ˈbrɪtɪʃ/
China	/tʃaɪnə/
Chinese	/tʃaɪˈniːz/
France	/frɑːns/
French	/frentʃ/
Germany	/ˈdʒɜːməni/
German	/ˈdʒɜːmən/
Greece	/griːs/
Greek	/griːk/
Ireland	/ˈaɪələnd/
Irish	/ˈaɪrɪʃ/
Italy	/ˈɪtəli/
Italian	/ɪˈtæljən/
Japan	/dʒəˈpæn/
Japanese	/dʒæpəˈniːz/
Poland	/ˈpəʊlənd/
Polish	/ˈpəʊlɪʃ/
Russia	/ˈrʌʃə/
Russian	/ˈrʌʃn/
Turkey	/ˈtɜːki/
Turkish	/ˈtɜːkɪʃ/

Drinks

beer *n* *	/ˈbɪə/
coffee *n* ***	/ˈkɒfi/
(orange, apple) juice *n* **	/dʒuːs/
tea *n* ***	/tiː/
(mineral) water *n* ***	/ˈwɔːtə/
wine *n* ***	/waɪn/

Other words & phrases

afternoon *n* ***	/ɑːftəˈnuːn/
age *n* ***	/eɪdʒ/
bar *n* ***	/bɑː/
country *n* ***	/ˈkʌntri/
email *n* ***	/ˈiːmeɪl/
evening *n* ***	/ˈiːvnɪŋ/
glass *n* ***	/glɑːs/
guide *n* **	/gaɪd/
invite *v* ***	/ɪnˈvaɪt/
language *n* ***	/ˈlæŋgwɪdʒ/
meet *v* ***	/miːt/
morning *n* ***	/ˈmɔːnɪŋ/
nationality *n* *	/næʃ(ə)ˈnælɪti/
new *adj* ***	/njuː/
party *n* ***	/ˈpɑːti/
practise *v* **	/ˈpræktɪs/
reception *n* *	/rɪˈsepʃn/
room *n* ***	/ruːm/
telephone *n* ***	/ˈtelɪfəʊn/
tour *n* **	/tʊə/

2A | The expat files

VOCABULARY: common verbs 1

1 Write a verb from the box in the space.

live	eat	drink	have	speak	work	read	go

1 _____ in a house/in a flat
2 _____ tea/coffee
3 _____ to school/to work
4 _____ chocolate/bread
5 _____ a newspaper/a book
6 _____ English/French
7 _____ in an office/in a shop
8 _____ a cat/friends

2 Put these words with the correct verb in exercise 1.

a dog   water   hamburgers
in a hospital   Italian   in Britain

3 🔊 **1.35** Listen to someone talk about her life in Britain. <u>Underline</u> the words from exercises 1 and 2 that you hear.

READING

1 Read the article and answer the questions about the people.

1 Where are they from?
2 Where are they now?
3 Are they happy ☺?

THE EXPAT FILES

These people are British, but they don't live in Britain anymore. They live in other countries. They are British expatriates, or expats. The Expat Files look at the lives of different British expats around the world.

Name: Sandra   From: London
Job: Student   New home: USA

HOW IS YOUR LIFE DIFFERENT?
I go to an American university in Seattle. I have a very American life now. I have a big car and a big house. I live there with three friends. I eat a lot of Mexican-American fast food. I have friends from here and from South America.

HOW IS YOUR LIFE SIMILAR?
I drink lots of tea. The Americans say I'm typically English in that way! I have my dog, Chelsea. That isn't very different because lots of people here have dogs.

Your opinion: ☺ ☺ *I like it!*

Name: Carl and Anna Eder   From: Liverpool
Job: Retired   New home: Spain

HOW IS YOUR LIFE DIFFERENT?
We don't work now. We're retired. We don't live in a house. We live in a flat in Malaga. We drink red wine with lunch, that's different. We love Spanish food and Spanish wine. We don't have our cats here.

HOW IS YOUR LIFE SIMILAR?
Lots of English people live here. We have English shops and we read English newspapers. We watch the BBC on satellite television. We don't have an English garden, but we have plants on the balcony. We speak a little Spanish. We go to language classes every Thursday.

Your opinion: ☺ ☺ ☺ *We love it!*

2 Read the article again and answer the questions. Write 'Sandra' or 'Carl and Anna' in the space.

1 _____ don't work.
2 _____ lives in a house.
3 _____ has friends from different countries.
4 _____ drink red wine.
5 _____ has a dog.
6 _____ go to language classes.

3 Close your books. Choose Sandra or Carl and Anna. Make notes about them. Compare your notes with your partner. Who remembers most?

4 Work in pairs. Would you like to live in a different country? Tell a partner.

LISTENING

1 🔘 1.36 Listen to David. Underline the correct information.

Name: David McKinnon / MacKinnon
From: Ireland / Scotland
New home: Istanbul / Edinburgh
Job: Teacher / Student

Opinion: I like it. / I don't like it.

2 🔘 1.36 Listen again and decide if the sentences are true (T) or false (F).

1 He lives in a house.
2 He eats Scottish food.
3 He doesn't read the English newspapers.
4 He goes to football matches.
5 He speaks Turkish.
6 He works at the university.

3 Work in pairs. Discuss these questions.

• Do you know any expats?
• Where do they live?

GRAMMAR: present simple affirmative & negative

Use the present simple to talk about things that are generally true.
*I **go** to an American university.*
*We **live** in a flat in Malaga.*

For *he, she, it* add *-s* to the verb.
*He **speaks** Turkish.*
*She **eats** fast food.*

Make negatives with *don't/doesn't* + infinitive
*I **don't** live in England.*
*He **doesn't have** Scottish friends.*

⏵ SEE LANGUAGE REFERENCE PAGE 30

1 Make sentences in the present simple.

1 She / work / in Germany.
2 We / live / in a big flat.
3 I / no speak English.
4 He / have / a dog.
5 They / no eat / a lot of pizza.
6 He / go / to an American school.

2 Complete the text. Put the verbs in brackets into the present simple.

Rosa (1)___ (*be*) an Italian expat. She (2)___ (*be*) from Rome and (3)___ (*live*) in Brighton, a town in England. She (4)___ (*be*) a nurse, and (5)___ (*work*) in a hospital. She (6)_____ (*live*) with an English family. The family (7)_____ (*not speak*) Italian. Rosa (8)_____ (*drink*) lots of tea now.

3 Complete the sentences with a positive or negative verb so that they are true for you.

1 I _____ in a house.
2 I _____ coffee.
3 I _____ in an office.
4 I _____ a dog.
5 I _____ a car.
6 I _____ Spanish.

4 Work in pairs. Compare your sentences. What's the same? What's different?

SPEAKING

1 Read about an American expat. Where is he?

I'm American. I live in a flat. I drink coffee and I eat lots of French bread. I go to the Champs Elysées and the Eiffel Tower every day. I don't have a car. I read the newspaper *Le Monde*. I speak French. I like it.

2 Imagine you are an expat. Prepare a similar text about your new life. Don't say the country.

3 Work in pairs. Tell your partner about your new life. Guess your partner's country.

4 Introduce your partner to another student. Give information about your expat.

He's American. He lives in a flat …

2B | Typical friends

VOCABULARY: common verbs 2

1 Match each picture A–D to a phrase from the box.

> watch TV   go to the cinema   go dancing
> play sports   study   go shopping
> go to restaurants   listen to music   travel

2 Work in pairs. Ask and answer these questions.

- Which activities in exercise 1 do you do?
- What activities do you usually do alone?
- What activities do you usually do with friends?

I don't go to restaurants.
I play sports with friends.
I study alone.

He goes to the cinema alone.

LISTENING

1 Read the webpage. What is it about?

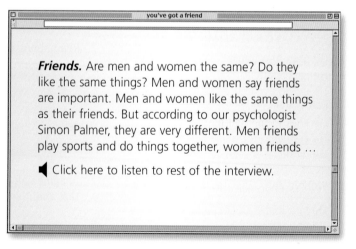

> **you've got a friend**
>
> ***Friends.*** Are men and women the same? Do they like the same things? Men and women say friends are important. Men and women like the same things as their friends. But according to our psychologist Simon Palmer, they are very different. Men friends play sports and do things together, women friends …
>
> ◀ Click here to listen to rest of the interview.

2 🔘 1.37 Listen to the interview. Tick (✓) the words you hear.

> sports   football   feelings   personal   tennis   movies
> fashion   television   politics

3 🔘 **1.37** Listen again. Are the sentences about men (M), women (W), or both (MW)?

1 They like the same things.	_MW_
2 They play sports.	_M_
3 They talk about sports.	____
4 They talk about personal things.	____
5 They talk about their feelings.	____
6 They listen more to their friends.	____
7 They don't know a lot about their friends.	____

4 What do you think? Put a tick (✓) if you agree and a cross (✗) if you disagree.

5 Work in pairs. Compare your answers.

Language note

man (singular) _men_ (plural)
woman (singular) _women_ (plural)

GRAMMAR: present simple questions & short answers

Make questions with _do/does_ + subject + infinitive.
Do you have a lot of friends?
Does he play sports with his friends?

Use the subject and _do/does/doesn't_ in short answers.
No, **they don't**.
Yes, **he does**.

> SEE LANGUAGE REFERENCE PAGE 30

1 Make questions in the present simple.

Part 1

1 he / have a lot of friends?
   Does he have a lot of friends?
2 they / play sports? _Do they play sports?_
3 they / talk about personal things?
4 he / have women friends?

Part 2

5 she / have a lot of friends?
6 they / talk about personal things?
7 they / do things together?
8 she / have men friends?

2 🔘 **1.38** Listen to a man and a woman talk about their friends. Mark the questions in exercise 1 yes (✓) or no (✗).

3 Work in pairs. Ask and answer the questions in exercise 1.

Does he have a lot of friends?
No, he doesn't.
Does she have a lot of friends?
Yes, she does.

4 Work in pairs. Ask and answer the questions.

you / have a lot of friends?
Do you have a lot of friends?

you / have more men friends or women friends?
you / know a lot about your friends?

PRONUNCIATION: word stress 1

1 🔘 **1.39** Listen to the words in the chart.

☐	☐ ☐	☐ ☐ ☐
sports	travel	personal
watch	shopping	politics
go	music	cinema
play	football	hospital
live	study	
	restaurant	

2 🔘 **1.40** Listen and put the words into the chart in exercise 1.

hamburger   have   English   newspaper   coffee   friend

3 Say the words in the chart. Pay attention to the word stress.

SPEAKING

1 Look at the words and phrases. What things do you do with your friends?

- Talk about personal things
- Watch TV
- Travel
- Speak English
- Eat at restaurants
- Go shopping
- Play sports
- Go to work

2 Work in pairs. Interview your partner about what they do with friends. Make questions with the words in exercise 1.

Do you talk about personal things?

3 Are you a 'typical' man friend or a 'typical' woman friend?

2c | He still lives with his parents

SPEAKING

1 Work in pairs. Discuss these questions about your country.

- How old are people when they leave the family home?
- How old are people when they get married?

READING

1 Read the article about the Castle family. What is the problem?

2 Read the article again and <u>underline</u> the correct word.

1 Andy *is* / *isn't* 32 years old.
2 Andy *has* / *doesn't have* a car.
3 His mother *wants* / *doesn't want* Andy to live at home.
4 Emily *lives* / *doesn't live* with Andy.
5 Andy *is* / *isn't* married.
6 His father *loves* / *doesn't love* Andy.
7 Andy *likes* / *doesn't like* his house.

3 What's your opinion? Answer the questions in the article. Do you know a person in Andy's situation?

> ### Useful language
>
> *It's not a problem.* *It's a problem.*
> *It's fine.* *It's not right.*

An Englishman's home . . . is his Castle!

THE CASTLE FAMILY
Andy Castle lives in Brighton. He's not married. He has a nice car and a good job. Andy Castle lives with his parents, in his parents' house. He's thirty-seven years old.

His mother's opinion

It isn't a problem. Andy is a very good boy. He doesn't have parties in the house.

Why does Andy live at home?

Because he likes it here. He helps me around the house. It's not a problem. I have a daughter Emily, but she doesn't live at home. Andy is my only son.

His father's opinion

It's not right. His mother says he's a good boy ... well, he's a man! And a thirty-seven-year old man doesn't live with his mother and father. What about a family for Andy? I want to be a grandfather!

Why does Andy live at home?

I don't understand. He has money, he's a handsome young man. I love him, but it's better for Andy if he has his own house or flat.

Andy's opinion

It's fine. My father isn't very happy, but that's his problem. I don't have a girlfriend right now. When I meet the right girl, I'll get married and leave home.

Why do you live at home?

I have great parents, and I'm very happy to live with them. I like my house. A lot of my friends live at home.

■ ■ ■

What do YOU think of the situation?
Why does Andy live at home?
Send your answers to yourview@pointofview.co.uk

VOCABULARY: the family

1 Find all the family words in the text. What are they in your language?

parents, mother

2 Work in pairs, A and B. You are going to complete Emily's family tree.

A: Turn to page 134. B: Turn to page 136.

GRAMMAR: *Wh-* questions & possessive's

What, where, when, who, why and *how* are question words. Put them at the beginning of the question.

Where *are you from?*   **Who** *does he live with?*
What *is his name?*   **Why** *does he live at home?*

Use *'s* to show possession.
Andy's mother   His parents' house.

SEE LANGUAGE REFERENCE PAGE 30

1 Complete the questions with a question word from the box.

| who   why   what   how   where |

1 _____ is he from?   Brighton, England.
2 _____ does he live with?   With his parents.
3 _____ does he live at home?   Because he likes it.
4 _____ old is he?   Thirty-seven.
5 _____ is his name?   Andy.

2 Rearrange the words to make questions.

1 live do where you ?
2 with who live you do ?
3 their what names are ?
4 old they how are ?

3 Work in pairs. Ask and answer the questions in exercise 2.

4 Add *'s* or *'* to make possessives.

1 our sons__ names   4 Andy__ books
2 John__ cousin   5 his brother__ birthday
3 the teachers__ room   6 those families__ houses

5 Work in groups of three, A, B and C.

A: Close your eyes.
B and C: Put objects on the table.
A: Open your eyes and make sentences about the objects.

This is Ana's pen.   This is Enzo's book.

PRONUNCIATION: final -*s*

1 🔘 1.41 Listen to the pronunciation of the final -*s* in these words. Sometimes the final -*s* is pronounced as an extra syllable.

no extra syllable	extra syllable
go goes	watch watches
computer computers	house houses
	class classes

2 🔘 1.41 Listen again and repeat.

3 Say these words. Is there an extra syllable in the second word?

do does   Charles Charles'
listen listens   bus buses
study studies   sandwich sandwiches

4 🔘 1.42 Listen to the recording to check your answers.

DID YOU KNOW?

1 Read the text about the family in Britain.

The Family in Britain

Women now have an average of 1.62 children. It is normal now for a British woman to have her first child when she is 29 years old. 31% (per cent) of parents are not married. 23% of children live with one parent, usually the mother. **On average, 40% of marriages end in divorce.**

2 Work in pairs. Discuss these questions.

- How many children do women have in your country?
- Is divorce common in your country?
- How many people live in the family house or flat?
- Are the statistics for Britain similar in your country?

2D | Tour group

VOCABULARY: adjectives

1 Match the adjectives in the box to the pictures and complete the sentences.

> young   short   tall   fat   thin
> old   beautiful   handsome   ugly
> fair   dark

1   Height

He's _tall_. He's ____.

2   Age

She's ____. She's ____.

3   Weight

He's ___. He's ____.

4   Looks:

He's ___. She's ____. They're _____.

5   Hair

She has ____ hair. He has ____ hair.

2   🔊 1.43 Listen to the recording to check your answers. Say the sentences.

3   Are these adjectives for height, age or looks? Put them in the right category.

> middle-aged   medium height   average-looking   pretty

GRAMMAR: adjectives

> Adjectives go before the noun in English.
> *He's a **handsome** man.* ~~He's a man handsome.~~
> Adjectives don't have a plural form.
> *They are **young** children.* ~~They are youngs children.~~

> ❯ SEE LANGUAGE REFERENCE PAGE 30

1   Think of a famous person for each category. Write their names on a piece of paper.

A handsome film star   An ugly politician

A young film star   A fat man

A beautiful singer   A thin woman

A handsome film star   Brad Pitt

2   Work in pairs, A and B.

A: Say a name.   A: *Brad Pitt.*
B: Say the category.   B: *Is he a handsome film star?*
                            A: *Yes, he is.*

Change roles. Say the other names.

LISTENING

1   Valerie and Brian work with Explore London Tours. Look at the pictures and describe them.

2 🔘 **1.44** Listen to the conversation. Answer the questions.

1 Where is Brian?
2 What does Valerie talk to Brian about?

3 🔘 **1.44** Listen again. Match the people to the pictures. There is one extra picture.

Delilah Williams – from New Zealand
Patti Owen – from New Zealand
Dave Matthews – from Canada

A

B

C

D

FUNCTIONAL LANGUAGE: describing people

Asking about people

What   *does ... look like?*

How   *old is ...?*
       tall is ...?

What colour *hair* *does ... have?*
          eyes

Describing people

He's	*tall/young/handsome.*
She has	*fair/dark/brown/black hair.*
He has	*blue/green/brown eyes.*
She has	*glasses.*
She's (about)	*thirty years old.*

▶ SEE LANGUAGE REFERENCE PAGE 31

1 🔘 **1.45** Listen to the words and make sentences with *She is* or *She has*.

1 glasses   *She has glasses.*
2 tall   *She's tall.*

2 Correct the questions and sentences.

1 What do they look?
2 Delilah is short pretty.
3 How old she?
4 Patti is around 30 years.
5 What he look like?
6 He has dark and glasses.
7 She blue eyes.

3 Work in pairs, A and B.

A: Choose a person in the class. Don't tell B.
B: Ask questions. Use the words below.
A: Answer the questions. Use the words below to help you.

What colour hair ... have?
Blonde/brown/dark/red.

What colour eyes ... have?
Blue/brown/green

How old ...?
He's young/old/about thirty/about twenty-five.

How tall ...?
She's about 1 metre 50/1 metre 73.

Where is he/she from ...?
He's from Brazil.

SPEAKING

1 Work in pairs, A and B.

A: Turn to page 132.
B: Turn to page 135.

GRAMMAR

Present simple

Use the present simple to talk about things which are generally true.

*I **go** to an American university.*
*We **live** in Malaga.*

Affirmative		
I	speak	
He/She/It	speaks	English.
You/We/They	speak	

The form of the verb is the same except for *he/she/it*. For *he/she/it*, add *-s*.

Spelling: present simple verbs with *he/she/it*
For most verbs: add *-s*.

work – works   eat – eats   like – likes   play – plays

For verbs ending in consonant + *y*: *y – ies*.

study – studies

For verbs ending in *-ch, -sh, o*: add *-es*.

do – does   watch – watches

Note: *have – has*

Make the negative with *don't* + infinitive or *doesn't* (for *he/she/it*) + infinitive.

subject	auxiliary + *not*	infinitive	
I	*don't*	*live*	*in Britain.*
She	*doesn't*	*have*	*a boyfriend.*

Negative			
I	don't		
He/she/It	doesn't	live	in a house.
You/We/They	don't		

For questions, put *do/does* before the subject and the infinitive after the subject.

auxiliary	subject	infinitive	
Do	*you*	*speak*	*English?*
Does	*he*	*listen*	*to music?*

Answer these questions with short answers.

*Do you speak English? **Yes, I do.***
*Does he have a big family? **No, he doesn't.***

Question		
Do	I	
Does	he/she/it	work?
Do	you/we/they	
Short answer		

Yes, No,	I	do. don't.
	he/she/it	does. doesn't.
	you/we/they	do. don't.

Wh- questions

What, where, when, who, why and *how* are question words. Put them at the beginning of the question.

***How** are you?*
***Where** are you from?*
***What** is his name?*
***Who** does he live with?*
***Why** does he live at home?*

Possessive *'s*

Use *'s* to show possession.

*John**'s** cousin*
*my son**'s** bedroom*

If the word ends in an *-s*, add *'*.

*His parents**'** house.*   *The babies**'** rooms.*

Not ~~the room of my son, the house of his parents~~.

Adjectives

Adjectives go before the noun.

*a **black** cat*
*the **big** house*

Adjectives also go after the verb *to be*.

*Nancy is **tall**.*
*Her hair is **long**.*

Adjectives do not have a plural form.

The old men.

Not ~~The olds men~~.

Plurals

Plurals of words that end in -y

> family = families
> baby = babies

Irregular plurals

> child = children
> man = men
> woman = women
> person = people

FUNCTIONAL LANGUAGE

Asking about people

What	does …	look like?
How	old is …?	
	tall is …?	
What	hair	does … have?
colour	eyes	

Describing people

He's	tall/young/handsome.
She has	fair/dark/brown/black hair.
He has	blue/green/brown eyes.
She has	glasses.
She's (about)	thirty years old.

WORD LIST

Common verbs

drink v ***	/drɪŋk/
eat v ***	/iːt/
go v ***	/gəʊ/
have v ***	/hæv/
live v ***	/lɪv/
read v ***	/riːd/
speak v ***	/spiːk/
study v ***	/ˈstʌdi/
travel v ***	/ˈtrævl/
work v ***	/wɜːk/

Free time activities

go dancing v	/gəʊ ˈdɑːnsɪŋ/
go shopping v	/gəʊ ˈʃɒpɪŋ/
go to restaurants v	/ˌgəʊ tə ˈrestrɒnts/
go to the cinema v	/ˌgəʊ tə ðə ˈsɪnəmə/
listen to music v	/ˈlɪsn tə ˈmjuːzɪk/
play sports v	/pleɪ ˈspɔːts/
watch TV v	/ˌwɒtʃ tiː ˈviː/

Family

aunt n **	/ɑːnt/
brother n ***	/ˈbrʌðə/
child n ***	/tʃaɪld/
cousin n **	/ˈkʌzn/
daughter n ***	/ˈdɔːtə/
father n ***	/ˈfɑːðə/
grandchild n	/ˈgræntʃaɪld/
granddaughter n	/ˈgrændɔːtə/
grandfather n *	/ˈgrænfɑːðə/
grandmother n *	/ˈgrænmʌðə/
grandparent n *	/ˈgrænpeərənt/
grandson n	/ˈgrænsʌn/
husband n ***	/ˈhʌzbənd/
mother n ***	/ˈmʌðə/
parent n ***	/ˈpeərənt/
sister n ***	/ˈsɪstə/
son n ***	/sʌn/
uncle n *	/ˈʌŋkl/

Descriptions

age n ***	/eɪdʒ/
average-looking adj **	/ˈæv(ə)rɪdʒˌlʊkɪŋ/
beautiful adj ***	/ˈbjuːtɪfl/
dark adj ***	/dɑːk/
fair adj ***	/feə/
fat adj **	/fæt/
glasses n	/ˈglɑːsɪz/
hair n ***	/heə/
handsome adj **	/ˈhænsəm/

height n ***	/haɪt/
medium height adj	/ˈmɪdiəm haɪt/
middle-aged adj	/ˈmɪdlˌeɪdʒd/
old adj ***	/əʊld/
pretty adj *	/ˈprɪti/
short adj ***	/ʃɔːt/
tall adj ***	/tɔːl/
thin adj ***	/θɪn/
ugly adj *	/ˈʌgli/
weight n ***	/weɪt/
young adj ***	/jʌŋ/

Other words & phrases

boy n ***	/bɔɪ/
bread n ***	/bred/
cat n ***	/kæt/
chocolate n **	/ˈtʃɒklət/
different adj ***	/ˈdɪf(ə)rənt/
divorce n *	/dɪˈvɔːs/
fashion n **	/ˈfæʃn/
feelings n ***	/ˈfiːlɪŋz/
flat n **	/flæt/
friend n ***	/frend/
get married	/get ˈmærɪd/
girl n ***	/gɜːl/
home n ***	/həʊm/
house n ***	/haʊs/
leave v ***	/liːv/
life n ***	/laɪf/
love v ***	/lʌv/
man n ***	/mæn/
office n ***	/ˈɒfɪs/
per cent n ***	/pə ˈsent/
personal adj ***	/ˈpɜːsənəl/
point of view n	/ˌpɔɪnt əv ˈvjuː/
politics n ***	/ˈpɒlətɪks/
problem n ***	/ˈprɒbləm/
same adj ***	/seɪm/
sports n ***	/spɔːts/
thing n ***	/θɪŋ/
university n ***	/ˌjuːnɪˈvɜːsɪti/
woman n ***	/ˈwʊmən/

3A | Houseswap

VOCABULARY: places to live

1 Match the adjectives in A to their opposites in B.

A	B
big	quiet
new	small
noisy	old
lovely	horrible

2 🔘 **1.46** Listen to someone talking about where she lives. <u>Underline</u> the words that you hear.

> I live in a small / big flat on Herbert Street. It's in the centre of Dublin. It's a lovely / horrible flat, but the street is noisy/quiet. I don't like / like it.

3 Work in pairs. Tell your partner about where you live. Use the words in exercises 1 and 2 to help you.

> I live in a _____ on _____. It's in _____. It's a _____ _____. I like / don't like it.

READING

1 Read the introduction to the Houseswap webpage. What does *swap* mean?

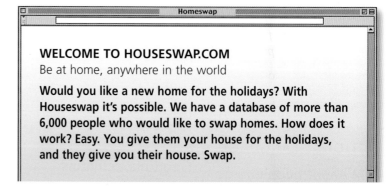

> **Homeswap**
>
> **WELCOME TO HOUSESWAP.COM**
> Be at home, anywhere in the world
>
> **Would you like a new home for the holidays? With Houseswap it's possible. We have a database of more than 6,000 people who would like to swap homes. How does it work? Easy. You give them your house for the holidays, and they give you their house. Swap.**

2 Read about some of the homes on Houseswap. Match each home to a picture. There is one extra picture.

3 Read the texts again and decide if the sentences are true (T) or false (F).

1 Ann's house is in Cambridge.
2 Ann's house is very big.
3 Sean's house is in England.
4 Sean's house isn't in the mountains.
5 Michael and Catherine's house isn't very big.
6 Hugh's flat is in the city centre.
7 Hugh's flat is not close to the shops.
8 Gerard's flat is very quiet.

4 Work in pairs. Which of the five homes on Houseswap would you like for the holidays? Tell your partner.

---

1 This is my home. I live in a small, white house. It's in Cambridge. It's next to an old restaurant and it's close to the university.
Email Ann ann@houseswap.com

2 This is my home. It's a small house in Scotland. It's beautiful here and very quiet. The cottage is in the mountains. It's far from other people and noisy cities!
Email Sean sean@houseswap.com

**3 We have a lovely big family house on the beach. It's in Santa Monica, California. It is a very good area to see Hollywood stars. The famous Hollywood letters are near our house!
Email Michael and Catherine mikecathy@houseswap.com**

4 I live with two friends in the centre of London. The flat is in Notting Hill. It's a little noisy. It's behind a market. It's close to a hospital and 30 minutes from Heathrow Airport.
Email Hugh hugh@houseswap.com

5 My wife and I have a big flat at the end of the Champs Elysées in Paris. It's a little noisy, but it's beautiful. We are opposite the Arc de Triomphe.
Email Gerard gerard@houseswap.com

GRAMMAR: prepositions of place

in [diagram] on [diagram] at [diagram]

Other prepositions of place are:
close to/near to   *far from*
next to   *in front of*
behind   *opposite*

Prepositions of place go in front of a noun.
in London   **close to** the school   **behind** the market

> SEE LANGUAGE REFERENCE PAGE 40

1 Find and underline the prepositions of place and the nouns after them in the texts.

2 Complete the texts with prepositions.

This is our home. It's (1)___ New York. We are (2)___ the centre of Manhattan. It's a flat (3)___ Fifth Avenue.

I have a very small house (4)___ the beach. It's (5)___ Vancouver, Canada. The house is (6)___ front of a school and close (7)___ the hospital and shops. Good for families. It's a little far (8)___ the city centre, but it's quiet.

3 Choose a person in the class. Complete the sentences with information about that person.

1 I sit close to/far from the teacher.
2 I sit next to …
3 I sit in front of …
4 I sit behind …

4 Work in pairs. Read the sentences in exercise 3. Guess who the person is.

SPEAKING

1 Play Class Houseswap. On a piece of paper, write your name and a description of your home. Look at the webpage to help you.

2 Walk around the class. Tell other students in the class about your home. Find someone who wants to swap homes with you. Swap papers.

3 Tell other students about your new home.

Useful language

This is my home. It's …
Would you like my house for the holidays?
Yes, OK.
No, thanks.

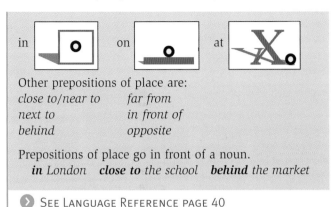

3B | 1600 Pennsylvania Avenue

LISTENING

1 Look at the photos of the house at 1600 Pennsylvania Avenue. What do you know about this house? Answer the questions.

☐ How old is it?
☐ What is the name of the house?
☐ Who lives there?
☐ Are there public visits?
☐ How many rooms are there?
☐ Where is it?

2 🔘 1.47 Listen to the beginning of a documentary about the house at 1600 Pennsylvania Avenue. Put the questions in exercise 1 in the order you hear them.

3 🔘 1.47 Listen again and complete the sentences with the numbers from the box.

    4   10   32   7   200

1 There are ____ names for the house at 1600 Pennsylvania Avenue.
2 It's more than ____ years old.
3 There are 16 family bedrooms, 3 kitchens and ____ bathrooms.
4 There are also 6 floors, ____ staircases, 3 elevators, 147 windows and 412 doors.
5 Public visits are available for groups of ____ people or more.

4 Work in pairs. Would you like to visit this famous house? Tell your partner.

VOCABULARY: parts of a house

1 🔘 1.48 Listen and repeat the words in the box. Match each word to a number on the map.

    living room   hall   kitchen   balcony
    bedroom   bathroom   dining room

2 🔘 **1.49** Listen to the recording to check your answers.

3 Work in pairs. Ask and answer the questions.

In your house or flat …

1 Where do you watch TV?
2 Where do you eat?
3 Where do you study?
4 Where do you sleep?

GRAMMAR: *there is / there are*; *How many*

Affirmative
There is *a tennis court.*
There are *three kitchens.*

Negative
There isn't *a restaurant.*
There aren't *any public telephones.*

Question and short answer
Is there *a bathroom?* Yes, **there is**. No, **there isn't**.
Are there *any offices?* Yes, **there are**. No, **there aren't**.

Use *How many* to ask questions.
How many *bedrooms are there?* *There are 16 bedrooms.*

❯ SEE LANGUAGE REFERENCE PAGE 40

1 Make sentences about the White House. Use (+) *There's …/There are …*, (-) *There isn't …/There aren't any … .*

1 a small cinema (+) *There's a small cinema.*
2 public bathrooms (-) *There aren't any public bathrooms.*
3 two swimming pools (+)
4 a restaurant (-)
5 three kitchens (+)
6 seven lifts (+)
7 public telephones (-)

2 Make questions using the words in the table.

Is	there	a	bathroom dining room restaurant windows telephones	at your school? in your classroom? in your bedroom? in your house?
Are		any		

3 Work in pairs. Ask and answer the questions from exercise 2.

4 Make questions. Use *How many.*

1 bedrooms / your house
How many bedrooms are there in your house?
2 students / class today
3 bathrooms / your house
4 teachers / your school
5 books / your bag today

5 Work in pairs. Ask and answer the questions in exercise 4.

SPEAKING

1 Draw a map of your house or flat. Prepare a short presentation of your home. Use the words from the lesson and the useful language to help you.

Useful language

So, this is my home.
There are … rooms. This is the bedroom/living room/kitchen …
There's a bathroom/bedroom/study here.

DID YOU KNOW?

1 Read about 10 Downing Street.

Number 10 Downing Street, also called Number 10, is the official residence of the Prime Minister of Britain. It is in the centre of London, in Westminster. It's a small house, and inside there are offices and a flat for the Prime Minister's family. There is one entrance through a black door on Downing Street. A policeman always stands outside the door. There aren't any public visits to Number 10, but thousands of tourists come every year to visit the street and look at the door.

2 Work in groups and discuss these questions.

- Does the President or Prime Minister of your country have a famous house? Where is it?
- Are there any other famous houses or flats in your country? Where are they?

35

3c | My first flat

VOCABULARY: furniture

1 Look at the pictures. What rooms are they?

Flat A

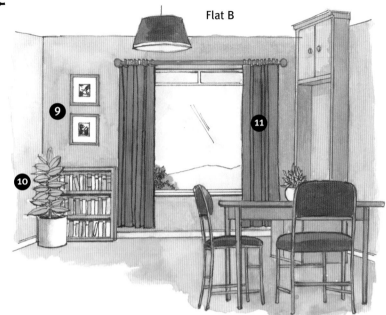

Flat B

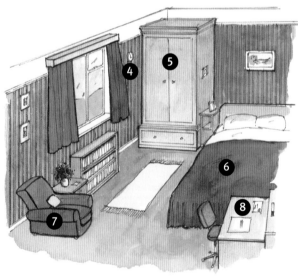

Flat B

Flat A

2 Match the words to the numbers in the pictures.

a fridge __   a clock __   a desk __   pictures __
a stereo __   a sofa __   plants __   a bed __
a chair __   a television __   a wardrobe __
curtains __   a cupboard __   a cooker __

3 🔘 1.50 Listen and say the words.

4 🔘 1.51 Shelly and Claudia are students. They want to rent a flat.
Listen. Which flat do they rent?

36

Reading & listening

1 🔘 1.52 Read and listen to the dialogue. Answer the questions.

1 Does Shelly like her flat?
2 Where is Claudia from?
3 Does Shelly want to see her parents?

Shelly: Hello?
Father: Hello, Shelly?
Shelly: Oh, hi, Dad.
Father: How are you?
Shelly: I'm fine. Fine.
Father: How's your new flat? Do you like it?
Shelly: Yes, I do. It's ... perfect.
Father: Well, tell me about it. Is it big?
Shelly: Yes, it is.
Father: And what about furniture? Is there any furniture?
Shelly: Yes, I have a desk and a bed in my room.
Father: Would you like a lamp? We have an extra lamp at home.
Shelly: No, thanks, Dad. Claudia has a lamp for the living room.
Father: Who's Claudia?
Shelly: She's my flatmate. She's Italian. Don't worry, there aren't any boys here.
Father: Good. Your mother has some old curtains. Do you want them?
Shelly: No, that's fine. We have curtains.
Father: Really?
Shelly: Yes.
Father: Oh. So, when do we come and see the flat?
Shelly: This week isn't good. We don't have any chairs.
Father: No chairs? What does that mean, no chairs?
Shelly: I don't know. Sorry, that's the door. Talk to you later, OK, Dad? Bye.

2 Shelly doesn't tell the truth about her flat. Look at the pictures again. Read the text again and underline the false information.

3 Work in pairs. Read the dialogue.

Grammar: *a, an, some* & *any*

> Use *a/an* with single nouns.
> *I have **a desk** in my room.*
> Use *some* with plural nouns with positive verbs.
> *There are **some lamps** here.*
> Use *any* with plural nouns in questions.
> *Do you have **any curtains**?*
> Use *any* with plural nouns with negative verbs.
> *There **aren't any boys** here.*

> ⊙ See Language Reference page 40

1 Look at Shelly's bedroom. Complete the sentences with *some/any* or *a*.

1 She doesn't have _____ chairs in her room.
2 There's _____ bed.
3 There are _____ papers on the bed.
4 There's _____ pizza on the floor.
5 Does she have _____ CDs? Yes, she does.
6 There are _____ pictures on the wall.
7 Is there _____ wardrobe? No, there isn't.
8 There aren't _____ plants.

2 Make true sentences about your classroom. Use the words in the box.

There	are is aren't isn't	any some a	student(s) whiteboard(s) teacher(s) window(s) door(s) CD player(s) plant(s) cupboard(s) television(s) picture(s)	in the classroom.

Speaking

1 Work in pairs, A and B.

A: Turn to page 132.
B: Turn to page 136.

3D | Tate Modern

READING

1 Read the text and look at the pictures. What is Tate Modern?

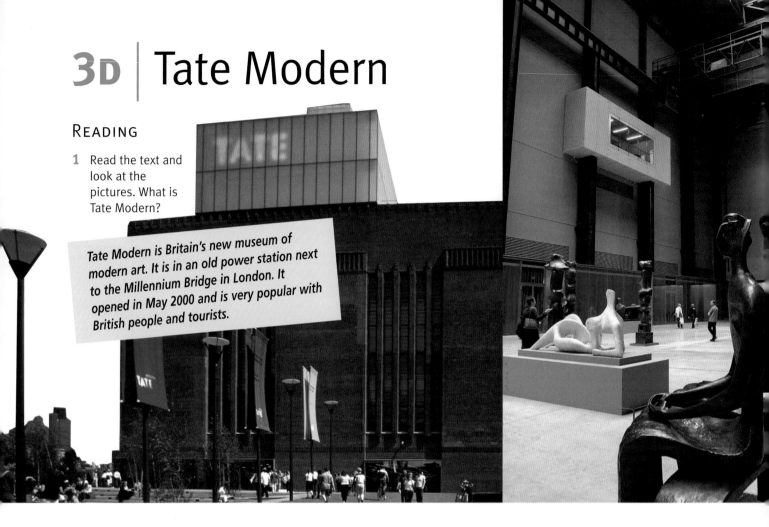

Tate Modern is Britain's new museum of modern art. It is in an old power station next to the Millennium Bridge in London. It opened in May 2000 and is very popular with British people and tourists.

2 Work in pairs. Answer the questions.

1 Where is Tate Modern?
2 What do people see there?

3 Work in pairs. Ask and answer these questions.

- Do you like modern art?
- Are there any famous museums in your town or city?

VOCABULARY: ordinal numbers

Language note

We use ordinal numbers to say the order or sequence of things.

1 Match the words to the ordinal numbers.

1st 2nd 3rd 4th 5th 6th 7th 8th 9th 10th

| third | fifth | seventh | ninth | fourth | second | first |
| eighth | tenth | sixth |

2 🔘 1.53 Listen and <u>underline</u> the word you hear. Practise saying the words.

1 1   1st   3 7   7th   5 10th 10   7 2nd 3rd
2 3rd 3   4 9th 9   6 5th   5   8 5th 4th

3 Look at the diagram of Tate Modern. Make questions about these places.

café   What floor is the café on?
        It's on the second floor.
education centre   members' room
bar   exhibition
shop

7   Restaurant
    Bar

6   Members Room

5   Collection 2004

4   Exhibitions
    Espresso Bar
    Shop

3   Collection 2004
    Studio C

2   Café, Untitled Gallery
    Starr Auditorium
    Seminar Room

1   Shop, Cloakroom,
    Clore Education Centre,
    McAulay Studios
    Turbine Hall

a Clore Information Room
b Clore Education Centre
c McAulay Studios
● Free Guided Tours
■ Architecture Audio Tour
▪ Tickets/Information/
   Members/ Tate Audio

LISTENING

1 Look at the map and match the words to the symbols.

> public telephone   men's toilets   information
> lift   women's toilets   baby changing room   café

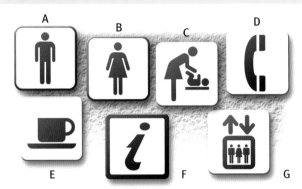

2 🔘 1.54 Listen to the recording to check your answers. Say the words.

3 🔘 1.55 The Explore London tour group is at the Tate Modern. Listen to five conversations at the information desk and tick (✓) the words from exercise 1 you hear.

4 🔘 1.55 Listen again and match each sentence to a place in exercise 1.

1 It doesn't accept coins.   _____
2 You need a card.   _____
3 Look, the brown doors.   _____
4 It's next to the women's toilets. _____
5 It's behind you.   _____
6 It's on the second floor.   _____

FUNCTIONAL LANGUAGE: directions

1 Complete the directions with a word from the box.

> left   up   down   right   along

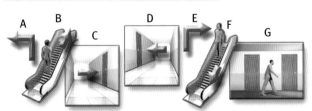

Giving directions
A turn _____   B go _____   C on the _____   D on the left

E turn right   F go _____   G go _____

Asking for directions
Excuse me, where is the ...?
Is there a ... near here?

⊙ SEE LANGUAGE REFERENCE PAGE 40

2 🔘 1.56 Listen and complete the sentences with a word or words.

1 Where ____ the café?
2 It's on the second floor. Go ___ the stairs and ___ right.
3 Where ____ the men's toilets?
4 They're over there. They're on the ___, next to the lift.
5 It's next to the stairs. It's on the ___.
6 Go ___ these stairs here. Then turn ___ and go ___ the hall.

3 Look at tapescript 1.56 on page 141 to check your answers.

4 Work in pairs. Read the dialogues in the tapescript.

SPEAKING

1 Work in pairs, A and B. Look at the map of the Modern Art Museum.

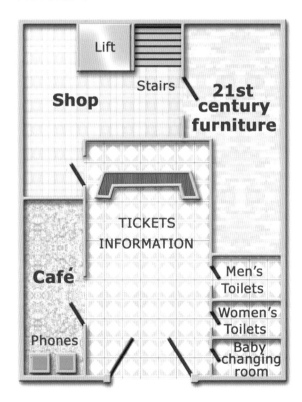

A: You work at the information desk. Listen to B's questions and give directions. Start each conversation with *Can I help you?*
B: You are a visitor to the museum. Choose a place on the floor plan and ask A for directions.

2 Swap roles and continue.

GRAMMAR

Prepositions of place

Other prepositions of place are:

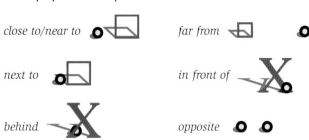

Prepositions of place go in front of a noun.

> **in** London   **close to** the school   **behind** the market

> I live **close to**/**near to** the city centre.
> I live **far from** the city centre.
> They live **next to** my house.
> Her house is **in front of** the school.
> There's a big garden **behind** the house.
> The flat is **opposite** the hospital.

> I work **at** home.
> Not I work ~~in home~~.

There is/there are

Affirmative		
There	is	a tennis court.
	are	three kitchens.

Negative		
There	isn't	a restaurant.
	aren't	any public telephones.

Question & short answer				
Is	there	a bathroom?	Yes, No,	there is. there isn't.
Are		any offices?	Yes, No,	there are. there aren't.

Use *How many* to ask questions:

> **How many** bedrooms are there?   There are 32 bedrooms.

A, an, some & any

a/an
Use *a/an* with single nouns.

> I have **a** desk in my room.

some
Use *some* with plural nouns and positive sentences.

> There are **some** lamps here.

any
Use *any* with plural nouns in questions and with plural nouns and negative sentences.

> Do you have **any** curtains?
> There aren't **any** boys here.

FUNCTIONAL LANGUAGE

Asking for directions

Excuse me, where is the ...?
Is there a ... near here?

Giving directions

Turn right/left.
Go right/left/straight on.
It's on the right/left.

WORD LIST

Places to live

city *n* ***	/ˈsɪti/
city centre *n*	/ˈsɪti ˈsentə/
flat *n* **	/flæt/
house *n* ***	/haʊs/
town *n* ***	/taʊn/
village *n* ***	/ˈvɪlɪdʒ/

Parts of a house

balcony *n*	/ˈbælkəni/
bathroom *n* **	/ˈbɑːθruːm/
bedroom *n* **	/ˈbedruːm/
dining room *n*	/ˈdaɪnɪŋ ruːm/
door *n* ***	/dɔː/
hall *n* ***	/hɔːl/
kitchen *n* ***	/ˈkɪtʃɪn/
living room *n*	/ˈlɪvɪŋ ruːm/
staircase *n*	/ˈsteəkeɪs/
window *n* ***	/ˈwɪndəʊ/

Furniture

bed *n* ***	/bed/
bookcase *n*	/ˈbʊkkeɪs/
chair *n* ***	/tʃeə/
clock *n* ***	/klɒk/
cooker *n*	/ˈkʊkə/
cupboard *n* *	/ˈkʌbəd/
curtain *n* ***	/ˈkɜːtn/
desk *n* ***	/desk/
fridge *n* *	/frɪdʒ/
lamp *n* **	/læmp/
picture *n* ***	/ˈpɪktʃə/
plant *n* ***	/plɑːnt/
sofa *n*	/ˈsəʊfə/
stereo *n*	/ˈsterɪəʊ/
television *n* ***	/ˈteləvɪʒn/
wardrobe *n*	/ˈwɔːdrəʊb/

Ordinal numbers

first ***	/fɜːst/
second ***	/ˈseknd/
third	/θɜːd/
fourth	/fɔːθ/
fifth	/fɪfθ/
sixth	/sɪksθ/
seventh	/ˈsevnθ/
eighth	/eɪtθ/
ninth	/naɪnθ/
tenth	/tenθ/

Other words & phrases

art *n* ***	/ɑːt/
baby *n* ***	/ˈbeɪbi/
big *adj* ***	/bɪg/
café *n* **	/ˈkæfeɪ/
easy *adj* ***	/ˈiːzi/
elevator *n*	/ˈeləveɪtə/
entrance *n* ***	/ˈentrəns/
famous *adj* ***	/ˈfeɪməs/
film star *n*	/ˈfɪlm stɑː/
floor *n* ***	/flɔː/
horrible *adj* *	/ˈhɒrəbl/
information *n* ***	/ɪnfəˈmeɪʃn/
lift *n* *	/lɪft/
lovely *adj*	/ˈlʌvli/
modern *adj* ***	/ˈmɒdn/
museum *n* ***	/mjuˈzɪəm/
new *adj* ***	/njuː/
noisy *adj* *	/ˈnɔɪzi/
official *adj* ***	/əˈfɪʃl/
old *adj* ***	/əʊld/
outside *adj* ***	/ˈaʊtsaɪd/
policeman *n*	/pəˈliːsmən/
quiet *adj* ***	/ˈkwaɪət/
residence *n* *	/ˈrezɪdəns/
school *n* ***	/ʃɒp/
shop *n* ***	/skuːl/
stand *v* ***	/stænd/

4A | MetroNaps

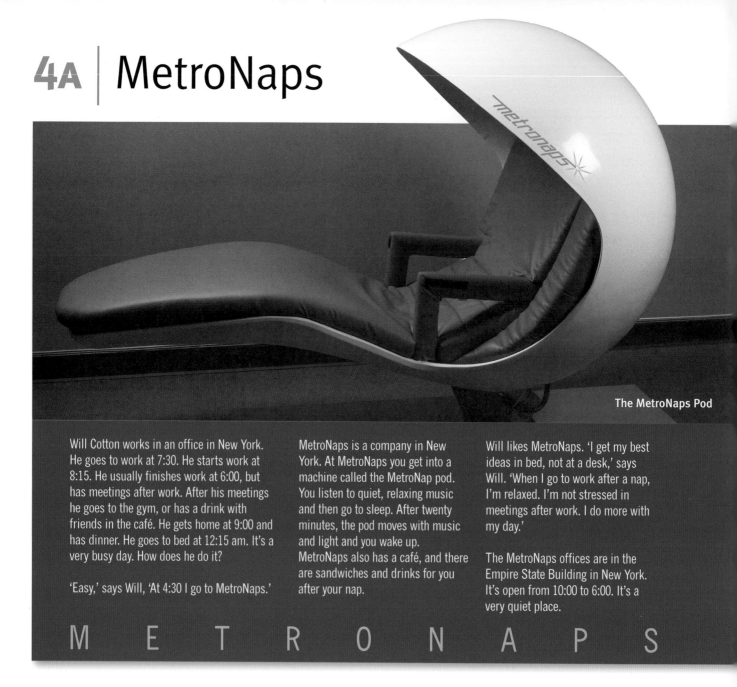

The MetroNaps Pod

Will Cotton works in an office in New York. He goes to work at 7:30. He starts work at 8:15. He usually finishes work at 6:00, but has meetings after work. After his meetings he goes to the gym, or has a drink with friends in the café. He gets home at 9:00 and has dinner. He goes to bed at 12:15 am. It's a very busy day. How does he do it?

'Easy,' says Will, 'At 4:30 I go to MetroNaps.'

MetroNaps is a company in New York. At MetroNaps you get into a machine called the MetroNap pod. You listen to quiet, relaxing music and then go to sleep. After twenty minutes, the pod moves with music and light and you wake up. MetroNaps also has a café, and there are sandwiches and drinks for you after your nap.

Will likes MetroNaps. 'I get my best ideas in bed, not at a desk,' says Will. 'When I go to work after a nap, I'm relaxed. I'm not stressed in meetings after work. I do more with my day.'

The MetroNaps offices are in the Empire State Building in New York. It's open from 10:00 to 6:00. It's a very quiet place.

M E T R O N A P S

READING

1 Look at the picture of a MetroNaps pod. Which activity do you think people do at MetroNaps?

go to sleep   have a shower   watch TV

2 Read the article to check your answer.

3 Read the article again. Answer the questions.

1 Where does Will Cotton work?
2 What time does he start work?
3 What time does he finish work?
4 What is a *nap*?
5 Where is MetroNaps?
6 Why does Will like MetroNaps?
7 What time does MetroNaps open and close?
8 How many hours is it open?

4 Put the events in order for a typical MetroNap.

☐ You have a sandwich and a drink.
☐ You get into the MetroNap pod.
☐ The MetroNap pod moves.
1 You go to MetroNaps.
☐ You listen to quiet music.
☐ You wake up.
☐ You go to sleep.

5 Work in pairs. Do you have a nap during the day? Would you like a MetroNap? Tell your partner.

FUNCTIONAL LANGUAGE: telling the time

He gets home at	*nine thirty/half past nine.*
He goes to bed at	*twelve fifteen/a quarter past twelve.*

Asking the time	**Saying the time**
What time is it?	*It's four forty-five/a*
What's the time?	*quarter to five.*

⊙ SEE LANGUAGE REFERENCE PAGE 50

1 Say the times for the clocks.

1   2   3   4   5

2 ⊙ **1.57** Listen to Will's conversations and complete the clocks.

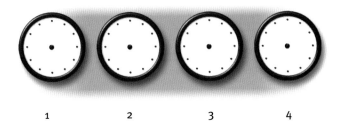

1   2   3   4

3 Look at tapescript 1.57 on page 141 to check your answers. Practise the conversations, but change the times.

VOCABULARY: collocations *have, go & get*

1 Find these words in the text and put them in the correct circles.

to work/to the gym   meetings   a drink   dinner
to bed   to sleep   ideas   a nap

have   *get*

go

2 Put these words in the circles.

a shower   dressed   breakfast   classes   a break
lunch

3 What is the difference between the underlined phrases? What are they in your language?

I <u>go home</u> at 6:00 and I <u>get home</u> at 6:15.
I <u>wake up</u> at 7:00 and I <u>get up</u> at 7:05.

PRONUNCIATION: vowels 1

1 ⊙ **1.58** Listen and repeat the sounds and the words.

/æ/ h**a**ve	/e/ g**e**t	/eɪ/ w**a**ke	/əʊ/ g**o**

2 Put these words in the correct column in exercise 1.

nap   break   home   bed   desk   make   seven
eight   any   day   flat   lamp   no

3 ⊙ **1.59** Listen to the recording to check your answers. Repeat the words.

SPEAKING

Language note

Use the present simple to talk about daily routines and habits.
   I wake up at 6:00.
To make questions, remember the word order.
Question word + auxiliary (*do/does*) + subject + verb
What time do you get up in the morning?

1 Work in pairs, A and B.

A: Turn to page 133.
B: Turn to page 136.

2 What do you do at these times? Tell your partner.

1 8:00   2 12:00   3 6:00   4 10:00

A day off

VOCABULARY: months

1 💿 1.60 Listen to the pronunciation of these months.

January	March	April	July	September
☐☐☐☐	☐	☐☐	☐☐	☐ ☐ ☐

2 Write the following months in the correct column in exercise 1.

February   May   June   August
October   November   December

3 💿 1.61 Listen to the recording to check your answers. Repeat the months.

4 Work in pairs. What is your favourite month? Why? Tell your partner.

LISTENING

1 💿 1.62 Listen to people talking about special days that they like. Match the speakers 1–4 to the pictures A–D.

☐ A   ☐ B   ☐ C   ☐ D

2 💿 1.62 Listen again. What months are these special days in?

3 Work in pairs. Do you have these days in your country? Do people work on these days? What do they do? Tell your partner.

A   International Women's Day

B   Teacher's Day

C   May Day

D   New Year's Eve

FUNCTIONAL LANGUAGE: the date

We write the date:
1ˢᵗ May, 2006 or *1 May 2006* or *1/5/06* or *01/05/06*
We say the date:
the first of May two thousand and six or *May the first two thousand and six*

We ask the date:
What's the date today? *What date is it today?*

> SEE LANGUAGE REFERENCE PAGE 50

1 Say the dates.

1 13/10/2006   3 14/09/2000   5 21/03/2008   7 22/03/2008
2 03/07/1999   4 11/09/2000   6 30/10/2006   8 31/07/1999

2 Write five important dates for you on a piece of paper. Work in pairs. Ask your partner about his or her important dates.

Why is 5ᵗʰ March important for you?
Because it's my birthday!

READING & LISTENING

1 Read the interview with Christina East. Match the questions to the answers.

When is Nothing Day?   Why Nothing Day?
What do people do on Nothing Day?   What is Nothing Day?

Christina East *is a British mental health specialist. She thinks it's time for a new special holiday, called Nothing Day.*

(1)_____
The idea comes from Harold Coffin, an American journalist. It's a day for nothing. No parties, no gifts, no cards. It's a time to have a break, to sit and do nothing.

(2)_____
It's on January 16ᵗʰ. The first Nothing Day was in 1973.

(3)_____
Because there are special days for everything. In March we have Mother's Day and in June we have Father's Day. In October there's United Nations Day and Halloween and in April there's Earth Day.

(4)_____
Ideally, people do nothing. But that's very difficult. Here are some suggestions.
In the morning, wake up when you like. Have a relaxing breakfast. Do nothing.
In the afternoon, go for a walk. Sit in a park. Do nothing.
At night, telephone an old friend and talk. Read a book, or go to bed. Do nothing.

2 **1.63** Listen to the interview and check your answers.

3 **1.63** Read and listen again and decide if the sentences are true (T) or false (F).

1 The idea for Nothing Day comes from the United States.
2 Nothing Day is on 6ᵗʰ January.
3 United Nations Day is in April.
4 On Nothing Day, people do nothing.

GRAMMAR: prepositions of time *in*, *at*, *on*

Use the prepositions *in*, *on* and *at* to talk about time.
in + months, years, the morning/afternoon/evening
    in March, *in the morning*
on + days, dates
    on Monday, on 16ᵗʰ January
at + time of day
    at four o'clock at night

> SEE LANGUAGE REFERENCE PAGE 50

1 Complete the sentences with a preposition and a time word so that they are true for you.

1 I usually relax …
2 I watch television …
3 People in my country go on holiday …
4 My birthday is …
5 My English class is …
6 The next day off is …

2 Work in pairs. Read your sentences to your partner. Ask *What about you?*

SPEAKING

1 Work in groups. The government wants to create three new holidays. Decide on three new holidays and what dates they are. What do people do on these days?

2 Present your ideas for new holidays to the class. Which are the most interesting?

Our idea for a new holiday is Student's Day. It's on 3ʳᵈ June. On this day people …

4c | Do the housework!

VOCABULARY: verb collocations (housework)

1 Match the pictures to the phrases.

> do the shopping   do the dishes   wash the clothes
> make the bed   clean the bathroom   take out the rubbish

2 Work in pairs. Which activities in exercise 1 do you do at home? Which activities don't you do at home?

LISTENING

1 You are going to hear part of a radio show phone-in. Look at the newspaper headline and listen. What is today's show about?

75% of British men DON'T do the housework

2 🔘 1.64 Listen to the radio show and tick (✓) the phrases you hear from section vocabulary exercise 1.

3 🔘 1.64 Who does it? Listen again and tick (✓) the correct column.

Name	Ralph	Ralph's mother	Tom	Tom's wife
Does the shopping once a week.				
Is always on the phone.				
Uses the washing machine.				
Always does all the housework.				

GRAMMAR: frequency adverbs & phrases

> There are two ways to talk about how often we do things:
> Use frequency adverbs.
> > *How **often** do you do the housework?*
> > *I **often** do the dishes.*
> > *He's **always** on the phone.*
>
> | always | often | usually | sometimes | hardly ever/rarely | never |
> |---|---|---|---|---|---|
> | 100% | | | | | 0% |
>
> Use phrases like *every day/month/year, once a week/month/year*.
> > *I make the bed **every morning**.*
> > ***Once a year** he washes the clothes.*

⊙ SEE LANGUAGE REFERENCE PAGE 50

1 🔘 **1.65** Read and listen to the sentences, then make an answer using the words in brackets.

1 You never do the dishes.
That's not true. *I often do the dishes!*
(often)
2 You don't clean the bathroom.
That's not true._____ (always)
3 You're always in front of the television.
That's not true. _____
(hardly ever)
4 I always wash your clothes.
That's not true. _____ (often)
5 This flat's always dirty.
That's not true. _____ (rarely)
6 You're usually on the telephone.
That's not true. _____
(sometimes)

2 Put an adverb of frequency in the sentence so that it's true for you. Then write two more similar sentences.

1 I am late for English class.
2 I work on Saturdays.
3 I watch English films.
4 I have coffee in the morning.
5 I go to bed before 10:00 pm.
6 I am tired in the morning.

3 Rewrite the sentences with one of the phrases.

twice a week   once a year   every day
three times a year   once a week

1 I read the newspaper on Mondays, Tuesdays, Wednesdays, Thursdays, Fridays, Saturdays and Sundays.
2 I go on holiday in August.
3 On Saturdays and Sundays I have a nap in the afternoon.
4 I see my grandparents at Christmas, at Easter and on my birthday.
5 I do the shopping on Saturdays.

4 Choose two sentences from exercise 2 and two sentences from exercise 3. Make questions with *How often*.

How often do you watch English films?

5 Work in pairs. Ask and answer the questions.

PRONUNCIATION: vowels 2

1 🔘 **1.66** Listen and repeat the sounds and the words.

/aɪ/	/aʊ/	/uː/	/ʌ/
h**i**	h**ou**se	r**oo**m	**u**p

2 Which word sounds different? Underline the different word.

1 time   hi   drink   wife
2 house   aunt   brown   now
3 son   bread   bus   some
4 blue   new   June   good

3 🔘 **1.67** Listen to the recording to check your answers. Say the words.

SPEAKING

1 Work in groups of three or four. Do the *Life and work at home* survey. Make questions with *How often* ...? Ask and answer the questions. Make notes of the answers.

2 Compare your survey results with other groups in the class.

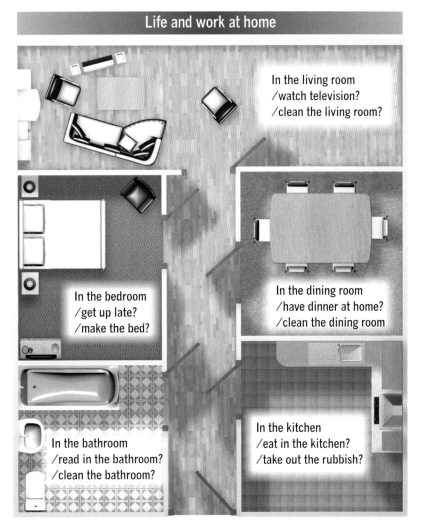

Life and work at home

In the living room
/watch television?
/clean the living room?

In the bedroom
/get up late?
/make the bed?

In the dining room
/have dinner at home?
/clean the dining room

In the bathroom
/read in the bathroom?
/clean the bathroom?

In the kitchen
/eat in the kitchen?
/take out the rubbish?

4D | I'm on the phone

SPEAKING

1 Work in pairs.
Do the phone survey.

PHONE SURVEY

How many phones do you have in your house?

Where are they?

Do you have a mobile phone?

How often do you use the phone?

Do you use the phone in the car?

How many phone calls do you make every day?

How many phone calls do you get every day?

PRONUNCIATION: phone numbers

1 🔊 1.68 Listen to two phone numbers.

- How do you say 0 in phone numbers?
- How do you say two numbers together?

  0802 788 743
  416 928 2212

2 🔊 1.68 Listen again and repeat.

3 🔊 1.69 Listen and <u>underline</u> the phone number you hear. Then say the phone numbers.

1 1 455 635 0403 / 1 455 635 0413

2 639 099 088 / 639 099 098

3 0802 788 743 / 0802 728 743

4 011 513 992 0732 / 011 516 992 0732

4 What's your phone number? Ask four other people in the class.

LISTENING

1 🔊 1.70 Listen to three phone conversations. <u>Underline</u> the correct word *makes* or *gets*.

1 Dave *makes* / *gets* a phone call.
2 Sam Moore *makes* / *gets* a phone call.
3 Valerie *makes* / *gets* a phone call.

2 🔊 1.70 Listen again and decide if the sentences are true (T) or false (F).

1
1 Angie wants to talk to Dave.
2 Dave wants to talk to Angie.

2
1 Sam calls the airport.
2 Sam talks to Mr Green.

3
1 The man wants to talk to Simon.
2 The man calls the wrong number.

3 1.71 Listen to two more phone conversations. Complete the notes.

Message for Rob
Call Ms _____ Kerr.
Phone number:

_____

Flight confirmation details for Mr and Mrs Curtis

Flight number _____ to Dallas USA.
Terminal: 2
Date: Thursday, _____ _____
Time: 8:45 am

FUNCTIONAL LANGUAGE: on the phone

1 There is one mistake in each of these phrases. Correct the mistake.

1 Just minute.
2 can call you back.
3 I'd like to say to Mr Green.
4 Would you like to leave message?
5 Please tell him to call I.
6 Is Simon here, please?
7 Sorry, you have the number wrong.
8 Hi, I'm Rob.

2 Look at tapescripts 1.70 and 1.71 on page 142 to check your answers.

3 Read and complete these four telephone dialogues with the correct sentence.

Hi, Sarah. How are you?
No, he isn't. Can I take a message?
Good morning, Acme Company.
Is that 1823 556 0211?

1
Hello.
Hello, it's Sarah.
(1)_____

2
(2)_____ Can I help you?
Good morning, can I speak to Mr James?
Yes. Just a minute.

3
Hello, is David there?
(3)_____
Please tell him to call me.
What's your phone number?
It's 662 4043.

4
Hello, is that Michelle?
I'm sorry, you have the wrong number.
(4)_____
No, it isn't.
Oh, sorry.

4 1.72 Listen to the recording to check your answers.

5 Work in pairs. Roleplay the dialogues from exercise 3, but use information about you.

DID YOU KNOW?

1 Read these facts about phones and phone numbers in North America.

Phone facts: North America

The international code for North America (Canada and the United States) is 1.

All phone numbers have 10 digits. The first three digits are the area code.

The phone number for emergencies is 911.

The phone number for information is 411. This is free.

In North American films and television shows, all the phone numbers begin with 555.

Numbers which begin with 1-800, 1-888, 1-866 or 1-877 are free.

2 Work in pairs. Discuss the question.

• What phone information is important for visitors to know in your country?

GRAMMAR

Prepositions of time: *in*, *at*, *on*

Use the prepositions *in*, *on* and *at* to talk about time.

in + months, years, the morning/afternoon/evening
  in *March,* **in** *the morning*
on + days, dates
  on *Monday,* **on** *January 16th*
at + time of day; also *at night*
  at *four o'clock*

We use *at* with *night, the weekend*:

  at *night,* **at** *the weekend*

We use *at* with some special holidays:

  at *Christmas,* **at** *Easter*

Frequency adverbs & phrases

Use frequency adverbs to say how often you do something.

  *How **often** do you do the housework?*
  *I **never** do the housework.*

always	often	usually	sometimes	hardly ever/rarely	never
100%					0%

Frequency adverbs go before the verb (except *to be*).

  *He **never** makes the bed.*

Frequency adverbs go after the verb *to be*.

  *He's **always** on the phone.*

You can also use phrases like:

  every day/month/year
  once a week/month/year

These phrases go at the beginning or end of a sentence.

  *I make the bed **every morning**.*
  ***Once a year** he washes the clothes.*

FUNCTIONAL LANGUAGE

Telling the time

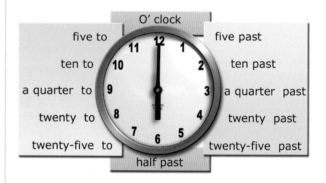

Use *It's* + time to say the time in English.

  It's eight o'clock.
  It's a quarter past five.
  It's half past eleven.
  It's ten to nine.

We can say the time in two ways:

  It's twenty to six.
  It's five forty.

We can also use *about* + time. We use *about* when we don't know the exact time.

  It's about half past three.

We can ask the time in two ways:

  What's the time?
  What time is it?

The date

Write the date:

  1st May, 2006 or *1 May 2006* or *1/5/06* or *01/05/06*

Say the date:

  the first of May two thousand and six or
  May the first two thousand and six

Ask the date:

  What's the date today?
  What date is it today?

We use ordinal numbers to say the date in English. For more on ordinal numbers, see lesson 3D.

Talking on the phone

Just a minute.
Can I call you back?
I'd like to speak to Mr Green.
Would you like to leave a message?
Please tell him to call me.
Is (Simon) there please?
I'm sorry, you have the wrong number.
(Jerry) can't answer the phone right now.
Can I take a message?
Hi, it's (Rob).

WORD LIST

Phrases with *have*, *go* & *get*

have breakfast/dinner/lunch	/hæv 'brekfəst, 'dɪnə, lʌntʃ/
have a drink/a coffee/	/hæv ə 'drɪŋk, ə 'kɒfi,
a sandwich	ə 'sænwɪtʃ/
have a break	/hæv ə 'breɪk/
have a nap	/hæv ə 'næp/
get dressed	/get 'drest/
get up	/get 'ʌp/
get home	/get 'həʊm/
go home	/gəʊ 'həʊm/
go to bed	/gəʊ tə 'bed/
go to sleep	/gəʊ tə 'sliːp/

Months

January ***	/dʒænjəri/
February ***	/'februəri/
March ***	/mɑːtʃ/
April ***	/'eɪprl/
May ***	/meɪ/
June ***	/dʒuːn/
July ***	/dʒəˈlaɪ/
August ***	/'ɔːgəst/
September ***	/sepˈtembə/
October ***	/ɒkˈtəʊbə/
November ***	/nəʊˈvembə/
December ***	/dɪˈsembə/

Housework

do the shopping	/duː ðə 'ʃɒpɪŋ/
clean the bathroom	/'kliːn ðə bɑːθruːm/
make the bed	/ˌmeɪk ðə 'bed/
wash the clothes	/ˌwɒʃ ðə 'kləʊðz/
do the dishes	/duː ðə 'dɪʃɪz/
take out the rubbish	/ˌteɪk aʊt ðə 'rʌbɪʃ/

Other words & phrases

breakfast *n* **	/'brekfəst/
card *n* ***	/kɑːd/
class *n* ***	/klɑːs/
closed *adj* **	/kləʊzd/
dinner *n* ***	/'dɪnə/
Earth *n* ***	/ɜːθ/
finish *v* ***	/'fɪnɪʃ/
gym *n*	/dʒɪm/
Halloween *n*	/hæləʊ'iːn/
idea *n* ***	/aɪˈdɪə/
lunch *n* ***	/lʌntʃ/
meeting *n* ***	/'miːtɪŋ/
nap *n*	/næp/
nothing *prn* ***	/'nʌθɪŋ/
open *adj* ***	/'əʊpn/
shower *n* *	/'ʃaʊə/
special *adj* ***	/'speʃl/
United Nations *n*	/juːˌnaɪtɪd 'neɪʃnz/

5A | Languages made easy!

SPEAKING

1 Work in pairs. Discuss these questions.

- What languages do you speak?
- Do you have any of these things?
  an English dictionary
  a bilingual dictionary
  a phrasebook
  an electronic dictionary
- How often do you use them?

READING

1 Look at the pictures of two language machines. Before you read, guess what they do. Use the phrases in the box to help you.

> you type a word   has a microphone
> has a clock   you hear the translation
> knows lots of languages
> has a calculator

The phraselator has a microphone.
You type a word with the ...

2 Read the article to check your answers.

3 Read the article again. Are these sentences about Lingo Global 29 (LG) or the Phraselator (P)? Write LG or P in the space.

1 It knows 29 languages.   ____
2 To use the machine, you type words or phrases.   ____
3 It has a clock.   ____
4 It has a microphone.   ____
5 You hear the translation of the phrase.   ____
6 To use the machine, you say phrases.   ____
7 It can tell the time in different cities.   ____
8 It says words or phrases.   ____

4 What do you think of the Lingo Global 29 and the Phraselator? What does your teacher think of them?

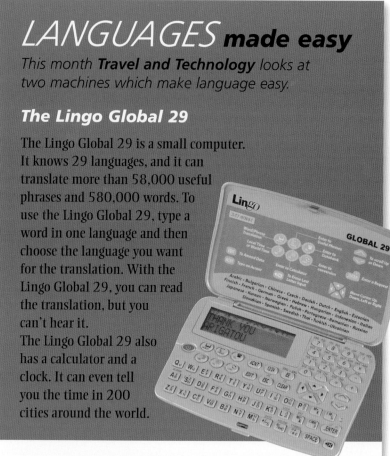

LANGUAGES *made easy*

*This month **Travel and Technology** looks at two machines which make language easy.*

The Lingo Global 29

The Lingo Global 29 is a small computer. It knows 29 languages, and it can translate more than 58,000 useful phrases and 580,000 words. To use the Lingo Global 29, type a word in one language and then choose the language you want for the translation. With the Lingo Global 29, you can read the translation, but you can't hear it. The Lingo Global 29 also has a calculator and a clock. It can even tell you the time in 200 cities around the world.

The Phraselator

The Phraselator is a translation machine. It can translate phrases from one language into another language. But the Phraselator is different, because it can *hear* a phrase and then *say* the translation for that phrase in a different language. It's easy to use the Phraselator. First, say your phrase into the microphone. The computer inside the Phraselator translates the phrase and then says the phrase in the other language. You can hear the new phrase. Today the Phraselator can translate English to other languages, but it can't translate other languages to English.

GRAMMAR: *can/can't*

> Use *can/can't* to talk about ability.
> The Phraselator **can** *translate phrases from English to another language.*
> It **can't** *translate other languages to English.*
> You **can** *read the word but you* **can't** *hear it.*

> ❯ SEE LANGUAGE REFERENCE PAGE 60

1 Complete the English Language Ability Survey with *can/can't* so that it's true for you.

English Language Ability Survey –
Can you do it?

1 I _____ spell my first name and last name.
2 I _____ introduce myself and another person.
3 I _____ give my address and phone number.
4 I _____ understand the words in English songs.
5 I _____ talk about the people in my family.
6 I _____ describe someone in the class.
7 I _____ talk about where I live.
8 I _____ give simple directions.
9 I _____ answer the phone and leave a message in English.
10 I _____ speak on the telephone for a long time in English.

2 Work in pairs, A and B.

A: Turn to page 134.
B: Turn to page 136.

PRONUNCIATION: *can/can't*

1 🔘 **1.73** Listen how the words *can/can't* are pronounced in these sentences.

It can translate.
It can't translate.

In sentences and questions, *can* is pronounced /kən/.
In negatives, *can't* is pronounced /kɑːnt/.

2 🔘 **1.74** Listen and <u>underline</u> the word you hear. Then repeat the sentences.

1 It *can / can't* translate phrases.
2 It *can / can't* hear an English phrase.
3 You *can / can't* read it.
4 It *can / can't* translate other languages.
5 It *can / can't* tell the time.

SPEAKING

1 🔘 **1.75** Listen to two dialogues. Match them to the pictures A and B.

A

B

2 Work in pairs. Look at tapescript 1.75 on page 142 to check your answers. Practise the dialogues with your partner.

3 Prepare a similar dialogue for the other picture.

C

> ### *Useful language*
> *Excuse me, can you repeat that please?*
> *Can you write it for me on a piece of paper?*
> *I'm sorry, I don't understand. Do you speak Spanish/French/Polish …?*
> *I only speak a little English.*
> *Can you speak more slowly please?*

5B | Cross Canada trip

VOCABULARY: the weather

1 Look at the weather map of Canada. Complete the sentences with the names of the cities.

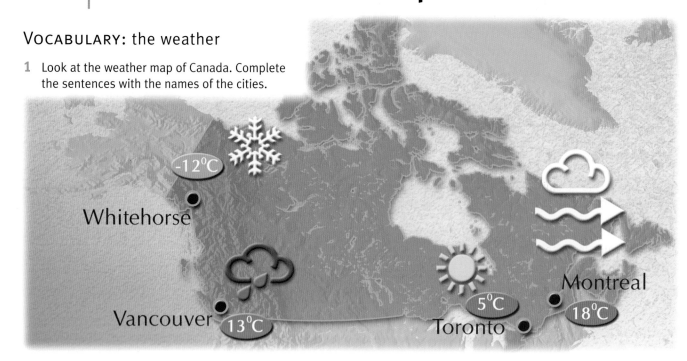

1 In _____ today it's **cloudy** and **windy**, but **warm**.
2 It's **cold** and **snowy** in _____, with temperatures of minus 12.
3 In _____ it's **sunny** and **cold**, 5 degrees.
4 You need your umbrellas in _____ today. It's **rainy** and **cool**.

2 🌐 1.76 Listen to the recording to check your answers. What are the words in bold in your language?

Language note

Use the pronoun *it* to talk about the weather.
  It's rainy and cold. It's sunny and warm.
To ask about the weather.
  What's the weather like?

3 Work in pairs. Ask and answer these questions.

• What's the weather usually like on your birthday?
• What's your favourite weather?
• What weather don't you like?

LISTENING

1 🌐 1.77 Listen to two people talk about their holiday in Canada. Put the photos in the order you hear them. There is one extra photo.

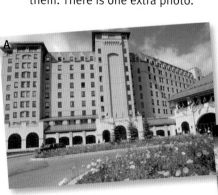

☐ Montreal jazz

B

☐ Toronto

A

☐ Our hotel in Banff

☐ Canoeing in the Rockies

D

☐ Train in Halifax

E

2 🔘 **1.77** Listen again and tick (✓) the words and expressions you hear.

1 it was rainy all the time
2 the airport
3 the houses were lovely
4 bar
5 two days
6 city has great jazz concerts
7 shops weren't open
8 it was cloudy
9 it was cold
10 perfect place to go skiing
11 Jacuzzi in our room
12 go swimming

3 Work in pairs. Imagine this was your Cross Canada trip. Use the words in exercise 2 to talk about the photos.

4 Would you like to visit these places?

GRAMMAR: past simple *was/were*

The past tense of the verb *be* is *was/were*.
*Our holiday **was** lovely.*
*We **were** in Canada.*

The negative is *wasn't/weren't*.
*I **wasn't** very happy.*
*The shops **weren't** open.*

⊘ SEE LANGUAGE REFERENCE PAGE 60

1 Read the sentences. Then make answers with the words in brackets.

1 We were in Dublin. (Glasgow) *No, we weren't. We were in Glasgow.*
2 The hotel was expensive. (cheap)
3 It was in a noisy part of town. (quiet)
4 It was sunny and warm. (rainy and cold)
5 Our tour guide was an Irish man. (Scottish man)
6 We were there for a week. (ten days)

2 Complete the dialogue with *was/wasn't*, *were/weren't*.

Lara: This is Toronto. You can see the CN Tower there. The shops (1)_____ (-)open that day. So we (2)_____ in the park. I (3)_____(-) very happy.
Tom: No, you (4)_____ (-). You (5)_____ miserable.
Lara: It (6)_____ snowy! And cold!
Tom: How many days (7)_____we in Toronto?
Lara: We (8)_____ there for two days.

3 Work in pairs. Read the dialogue.

DID YOU KNOW?

1 Read the information about Canadian tourist destinations.

TOP DESTINATIONS FOR CANADIAN TOURISTS

Canada is one of the most popular countries for tourists from other countries, but where do Canadians go on holiday? Every year, more than 17 million Canadians go to other countries for tourism. Here are the top ten countries that Canadians like to visit.

10 **Spain**
9 **the Netherlands**
8 **Italy**
7 **Germany**
6 **the Dominican Republic**
5 **Cuba**
4 **France**
3 **the United Kingdom**
2 **Mexico**
1 **the United States**

2 Work in pairs. Discuss these questions.

• Do people in your country travel to other countries often?
• What are the popular destinations for tourists from your country?
• Do you know any other countries? Which ones?
• Would you like to visit any of the top ten countries on the list?

5c | Travel essentials

SPEAKING

1 Look at the picture. What can you see? How many things can you say in English?

2 Work in pairs. Imagine you are going on a last minute holiday to Washington. It's time to pack your bag. You can only take five things from the picture. What do you take?

Useful language

I think the ... is a good idea.
I agree. We can take the ... and the ... .
I don't agree. I think the ... is more important.

READING & LISTENING

1 🔘 1.78 The Thompsons are going to the airport. Read and listen to their conversation. Who packed the bags – Walter or Thelma Thompson?

Walter: Come on!
Thelma: I'm here. I'm here.
Walter: Did you turn off the lights?
Thelma: Yes, I did. I turned off the lights and your computer.
Walter: Good. Did you pack my digital camera?
Thelma: Yes, I did. It's in the black bag with your mobile phone and book.
Walter: Which book?
Thelma: The book that was on the table next to your bed.
Walter: Oh. I didn't want a book. I wanted the ipod.
Thelma: Well I didn't know!
Walter: We don't have the ipod then.
Thelma: No, we don't.

Walter: Do you have the guide book?
Thelma: Just a minute.
Walter: Oh no, you didn't remember the guide book.
Thelma: Yes, I did. Here it is!
Walter: Plane tickets?
Thelma: I remembered. They're here.
Walter: Good. Good. Well, darling, we're on holiday.
Thelma: We can finally relax.

2 Read the text again. Put a tick (✓) next to the things they have in the car.

| computer | digital camera | mobile phone |
| book | ipod | guide book | plane tickets |

3 Work in pairs. Read the dialogue.

4 🔘 1.79 Listen to Walter and Thelma at the airport. What is the problem?

GRAMMAR: past simple regular verbs

> The past tense of regular verbs is verb + ed.
> *I **wanted** the ipod.*
> The past simple negative is *didn't* + verb.
> *She **didn't remember** the ipod.*
> The past simple question form is *did* + subject + verb.
> ***Did you pack** my digital camera?*

> SEE LANGUAGE REFERENCE PAGE 60

1 Complete the sentences. Put the verbs in brackets into the past simple.

1 They _____ (*remember*) the tickets but they _____ (*not remember*) the passports.

2 He _____ (*want*) a book but he _____ (*not want*) that book.

3 They _____ (*visit*) Washington but they _____ (*not visit*) the White House.

4 They _____ (*enjoy*) the city but they _____ (*not enjoy*) the weather.

5 They _____ (*like*) the hotel but they _____ (*not like*) the food.

2 Work in pairs, A and B. Look at the picture in Speaking exercise 1 on page 56. Write down the names of five things on a piece of paper. Don't show your partner.

A: Ask B questions and guess what B packed.
B: Answer.

A: *Did you pack the ipod?*
B: *Yes, I did. / No, I didn't.*

When you finish, swap roles.

3 Make questions about last night. Use the words in the box.

| use | play | watch | study | cook | take out |

1 you/television?
Did you watch television?

2 you/the internet?

3 you/dinner?

4 you/English?

5 you/the rubbish?

6 you/football?

4 Work in pairs. Ask the questions in exercise 3. Answer *Yes, I did* or *No, I didn't*.

PRONUNCIATION: past simple regular verbs

1 🔘 1.80 Listen to the verbs and the past tense forms. What is different between group A and group B?

A		B	
pack	packed	want	wanted
open	opened	end	ended
watch	watched		

2 Complete the rule about pronouncing past tense endings using a) or b).

If the past simple verb ends in *-ted* or *-ded* then
a) pronounce the *-ed* as an extra syllable /ɪd/.
b) don't pronounce the *-ed* as an extra syllable /ɪd/.

3 How do you pronounce the verbs in these sentences?

1 I **liked** it.
2 He **closed** the door.
3 They **remembered** it.
4 We **visited** her.
5 You **cooked** dinner.
6 English class **started** in September.

4 🔘 1.81 Listen to the recording to check your answers.

SPEAKING

1 Make questions in the past simple.

Last year …

1 /travel by plane? Where?
2 /visit another country? Where?
3 /stay in a hotel? How was it?
4 /study English? In what school?
5 /play a sport? What sport?
6 /live in a different house or flat? Where?

2 Work in pairs, A and B.

A: Ask B questions from exercise 1.
B: Answer. Tell a lie about ONE thing that A asks.
A: Guess the lie.
You lied about question 2.
That's right.
That's wrong. That was the truth.

3 Swap roles and repeat the activity.

5D | Bed & breakfast

SPEAKING

1 Complete the sentences with information about you.

1 I often/sometimes/hardly ever/never stay in hotels.
2 The last time I stayed in a hotel was _____.
3 The hotel was in _____.
4 The hotel was very good/good/OK/ not very good.
5 I was there for _____ nights.

2 Work with a partner. Compare your answers.

READING

1 Read the advertisements for two hotels in Stratford. Which hotel would you like to stay in?

2 Read the advertisements again. Write S for the Shakespeare Guest House, C for the Stratford Central Hotel or SC if the sentence is true for both hotels.

1 It's an old house. ____
2 It's good for business travellers. ____
3 You can have breakfast in the hotel. ____
4 You can have dinner in the hotel. ____
5 It is open every day. ____
6 Children can play in the garden. ____
7 You can smoke in the hotel. ____

3 Complete the definitions with a word from the advertisements.

1 Someone who is f_____ is nice and helpful to other people.
2 If something is w_____ it is hot in a comfortable, pleasant way.
3 If something is c_____ then it's free.
4 A m_____ is a time when you eat, such as breakfast, lunch or dinner.
5 If something is a_____ then you can use, take or get it.

The Shakespeare Guest House

Happy, friendly 18th century guest house located near the famous town of Stratford-on-Avon. Open all year round (including Christmas and New Year). Clean, warm rooms and traditional English breakfast every morning. There is an excellent selection of restaurants and tea houses near the guest house, which we can book for you.

There is a pretty garden with garden furniture and a barbecue area, a separate play area for children and parking. This is a quiet, rural location with lots of walks nearby, and excellent views.

Animals welcome. Please note: the guest house is non-smoking.

The Stratford Central Hotel

Our professional, modern hotel is in the centre of Stratford-on-Avon. We are open all year round and are only minutes away from shops, cinemas and discos. All our 81 rooms have a bathroom with shower, complimentary tea and coffee, internet access and modern furniture and design. Our hotel is perfect for business travellers and families. A continental breakfast is included with the price of your room and is served in the breakfast lounge. There is also a restaurant for your evening meals.

Children welcome. We have smoking and non-smoking rooms available.

Free parking for guests.

LISTENING

1 🔘 **1.82** The Explore London tour is on a trip to Stratford. Listen to the conversation. Which hotel do they visit?

2 🔘 **1.83** Listen to four conversations at the hotel. Match each conversation to a sign.

A This phone is NOT for guests

B Beware of Dog!

C Sorry we do not take American Express

D Baggage Service £2.00

3 🔘 **1.83** Listen to the conversations again and complete the dialogues with the correct word from the box.

> public   credit card   fifteen   mobile phone
> dangerous   private   take   bags   sorry   four

Hannah: I'm (1)_____. I was only looking. What's his name?
Owner: Rex.
Hannah: Can I touch him?
Owner: I'm afraid you can't. He's very (2)_____.

Herb: Hi. Excuse me, but could I use your phone? My (3)_____ doesn't work here.
Owner: I'm afraid we don't have a phone for the (4)_____.
Herb: What do you mean, no phone! What about that phone?
Owner: Sorry, it's (5)_____.

Herb: I'd like to pay the bill. Can I pay by (6)_____?
Owner: Of course. Visa? Mastercard?
Herb: American Express.
Owner: Oh no, I'm sorry but we don't (7)_____ American Express.

Herb: One more thing. Our bus leaves at a quarter past (8)_____. Is it OK to leave our bags here please?
Owner: Certainly. It's £2 an hour.
Herb: But it's only for (9)_____ minutes!
Owner: I'm sorry, it's £2 minimum to keep (10)_____.

4 Look at tapescript 1.83 on page 143 to check your answers.

FUNCTIONAL LANGUAGE: asking for permission

Asking for permission

Can I Could I May I	use your phone? smoke here?	(please).
Is it OK if I/Is it OK to	(+ infinitive)	

Responding

☺		☹	
(Yes)	Of course. Go ahead. Sure.	(No)	I'm sorry (but …) I'm afraid not.

> ❯ SEE LANGUAGE REFERENCE PAGE 61

Language note

It's very common to use *please* when we ask for permission.

1 Rearrange the words to make questions. Then ask the teacher the questions.

1 your   please   phone   I   may   use ?
2 to   the   go   toilet   please   can   I ?
3 alright   it   is   if   now   go   I ?
4 please   I   can   pen   your   use ?

2 Work in pairs. Take turns. Ask the questions in exercise 1. Respond to the questions ☺ or ☹.

Roleplay

3 Work in pairs, A and B.

A: You are a guest at the Stratford Central Hotel. You are at reception. You want to do different things. Use the ideas on page 132 to help you. Ask permission at reception.

B: You are the receptionist at the Stratford Central Hotel. Answer A's questions. Use the ideas on page 138 to help you.

4 Swap roles. Then change partners and repeat the roleplay.

GRAMMAR

Can/can't

Can is a modal auxiliary verb. This means:

- it goes with the infinitive without *to*.
- it has the same form for all subjects.
- the negative is with *not* (*n't*).
- to make a question, put *can* before the subject and the infinitive after the subject.

Affirmative		
I You He/She/It We They	can	speak another language.

Negative		
I You He/She/It We They	can't	speak another language.

I can speak French.
Not ~~I can to speak French~~.

I can't understand.
Not ~~I don't can understand~~.

Question & short answer			
Can	I you he/she/it we they	repeat that, please?	
	Yes,	I you he/she/it we they	can.
	No,		can't.

Can you hear me?
Not ~~Do you can hear me?~~

Can has different uses.
Use *can* to talk about ability.

> *I can speak English.*

Use *can* to ask for permission.

> ***Can** I use your phone?*

Past simple *was/were*

The past simple of *to be* is *was/were*.

> *I **was** in Canada.*
> *We **weren't** in a lovely hotel.*

Affirmative & negative		
I He/She/It	was wasn't	on holiday.
You We They	were weren't	

Question		
Was	I he/she/it	in Toronto?
Were	you/we/they	

Short answer		
Yes, No,	I he/she/it	was. wasn't.
	you/we/they	were. weren't.

Past simple - regular verbs

For most regular verbs, add *-ed* to the verb for the past simple.

> *He **closed** the door.*
> *He **walked** to work.*
> *He **started** work at nine o'clock.*

Affirmative		
I You He/She/It We They	packed	our bags.

For negatives, use the auxiliary *did* and *did not* (*didn't*) and the infinitive.

Negative			
I You He/She/It We They	didn't	visit	the museum.

For questions, use the auxiliary *did*. Put the auxiliary before the subject and the infinitive after the subject.

Question			
Did	I you he/she/it we they	remember	the passports?

FUNCTIONAL LANGUAGE

Asking for permission

Can I + infinitive?
Could I + infinitive?
May I + infinitive?

Is it OK if I + infinitive?
Is it OK to + infinitive?

Responses

Yes, of course.
Go ahead.
Sure.

No, I'm sorry but …
No, I'm afraid not.

WORD LIST

Things to take on holiday

alarm clock *n*	/əˈlɑːm klɒk/
guide book *n*	/ˈgaɪd bʊk/
passport *n* *	/ˈpɑːspɔːt/
phrasebook *n*	/ˈfreɪzbʊk/
sunglasses *n*	/ˈsʌnglɑːsɪz/
ticket *n* ***	/ˈtɪkɪt/

The weather

cloudy *adj*	/ˈklaʊdi/
cold *adj* ***	/kəʊld/
cool *adj* ***	/kuːl/
rainy *adj*	/ˈreɪni/
snowy *adj*	/ˈsnəʊi/
sunny *adj*	/ˈsʌni/
warm *adj* ***	/wɔːm/
windy *adj*	/ˈwɪndi/

Other words & phrases

animal *n* ***	/ˈænɪməl/
available *adj* **	/əˈveɪləbl/
barbecue *n*	/ˈbɑːbɪkjuː/
bilingual *adj*	/baɪˈlɪŋgwəl/
clean *adj* ***	/kliːn/
complimentary *adj*	/ˌkɒmplɪˈment(ə)ri/
concert *n* **	/ˈkɒnsət/
continental breakfast *n*	/ˌkɒntɪnentl ˈbrekfəst/
cook *v* ***	/kʊk/
design *n* ***	/dɪˈzaɪn/
destination *n* *	/destɪˈneɪʃn/
dictionary *n*	/ˈdɪkʃnri/
draw *v* ***	/drɔː/
drive *v* ***	/draɪv/
electronic *adj* **	/ɪlekˈtrɒnɪk/
establishment *n* **	/ɪsˈtæblɪʃmənt/
exchange rate *n*	/ɪksˈtʃeɪndʒ ˌreɪt/
go skiing *v*	/gəʊ ˈskiːɪŋ/
hear *v* ***	/ˈhɪə/
ipod *n*	/aɪpɒd/
jazz *n*	/dʒæz/
machine *n* ***	/məˈʃiːn/
money *n* ***	/ˈmʌni/
play chess/tennis *v*	/pleɪ ˈtʃes, ˈtenɪs/
sing *v* ***	/sɪŋ/
swim *v* **	/swɪm/
torch *n*	/tɔːtʃ/
translate *v* *	/trænzˈleɪt/
translation *n* *	/trænzˈleɪʃn/
type *v*	/taɪp/
unnecessary *adj* *	/ʌnˈnesəri/
view *n* ***	/vjuː/

6A | Celebrations

VOCABULARY & SPEAKING: celebrations

1 Look at the different cards. Match each card to a celebration in the box.

> a retirement party   a birthday
> a wedding   a new baby

2 Work in pairs. Discuss these questions.

- Do you celebrate the events in exercise 1?
- What do you do?

READING

1 Read the blogs*. Match each blog to a card from Speaking exercise 1.

2 Read the blogs again and put the sentences a–c in the gaps 1–3.

a Anyway, we sat and talked for a long time.
b This year it was at my best friend's house.
c He didn't know anything about it.

3 Read the sentences and decide if they are true (T) or false (F).

1 Patrick got a watch at the party.
2 Richard was with the company in 1975.
3 Kyle and Sue didn't have a big wedding.
4 Kyle and Sue got married in an Indian restaurant.
5 The birthday party was outside.
6 People danced at the birthday party.

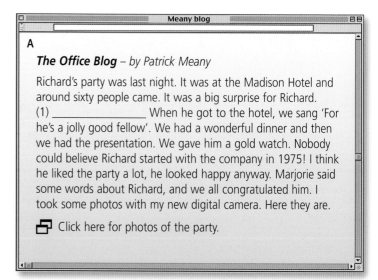

Meany blog

A

The Office Blog – by Patrick Meany

Richard's party was last night. It was at the Madison Hotel and around sixty people came. It was a big surprise for Richard. (1) _____ When he got to the hotel, we sang 'For he's a jolly good fellow'. We had a wonderful dinner and then we had the presentation. We gave him a gold watch. Nobody could believe Richard started with the company in 1975! I think he liked the party a lot, he looked happy anyway. Marjorie said some words about Richard, and we all congratulated him. I took some photos with my new digital camera. Here they are.

⊡ Click here for photos of the party.

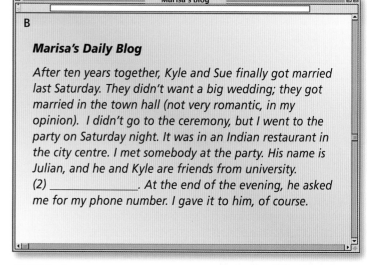

Marisa's blog

B

Marisa's Daily Blog

After ten years together, Kyle and Sue finally got married last Saturday. They didn't want a big wedding; they got married in the town hall (not very romantic, in my opinion). I didn't go to the ceremony, but I went to the party on Saturday night. It was in an Indian restaurant in the city centre. I met somebody at the party. His name is Julian, and he and Kyle are friends from university. (2) _____. At the end of the evening, he asked me for my phone number. I gave it to him, of course.

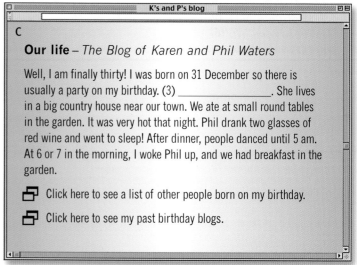

K's and P's blog

C

Our life – The Blog of Karen and Phil Waters

Well, I am finally thirty! I was born on 31 December so there is usually a party on my birthday. (3) _____. She lives in a big country house near our town. We ate at small round tables in the garden. It was very hot that night. Phil drank two glasses of red wine and went to sleep! After dinner, people danced until 5 am. At 6 or 7 in the morning, I woke Phil up, and we had breakfast in the garden.

⊡ Click here to see a list of other people born on my birthday.

⊡ Click here to see my past birthday blogs.

* a blog is the short form of 'web log'. Many people have a diary on their blog which other people can read.

GRAMMAR: past simple irregular verbs

There are two kinds of verbs in the past simple.
Regular verbs end in –ed in the affirmative form of the past simple.

Irregular verbs have a different form in the past simple affirmative.

eat – ate   go – went   make – made
see – saw   have - had

You can see a list of irregular past simple verbs on page 159.

The rules for questions and negatives are the same for regular and irregular past simple verbs.

Did you go to Richard's party? Yes, we did.
We didn't go to a disco.

> SEE LANGUAGE REFERENCE PAGE 70

1 Look at the texts in Reading exercise 1. <u>Underline</u> twelve different irregular past tense affirmative verbs. Write the past form and the infinitive.

got – get

2 Complete the text. Put the verbs in brackets into the past simple.

Scott's blog

Scott's Millennium Blog

On December 31, my friend and I (1)_____ (be) on a train from Switzerland to Spain. We (2)_____ (have) a compartment for two people, some champagne and nice food. We (3)_____ (want) to be on a train for the new millennium. The train (4)_____ (not stop) at midnight, but it (5)_____ (stop) twenty minutes later. We (6)_____ (drink) our champagne and (7)_____ (look) out of the window. We (8)_____ (not sleep) all night, we (9)_____ (sit) and (10)_____ (talk). We (11)_____ (get) home to Barcelona at 8 am in the morning on January 1st. It (12)_____ (be) a good New Year's Eve.

---

3 Make questions in the past with the words and with *you*.

1   where / go?
2   what / do?
3   who / be with?
4   what / eat?
5   what / drink?
6   what time / go to bed?

4 Work in pairs. Choose one of the following celebrations and interview your partner with the questions in exercise 3.

- A birthday party
- A wedding
- A New Year's Eve party
- Other (you choose)

SPEAKING

1 Work in pairs, A and B. You are going to tell a story of a celebration.

A: Begin. Complete sentence 1 with an idea of your own.
B: Continue the story with sentence 2.

1   Last night we went to a _____ party.
2   It was in a _____.
3   It started at _____.
4   _____ and _____ were at the party.
5   We ate _____,
6   and we drank _____.
7   At the party we met _____.

2 Continue the story in turns. Choose phrases from the list below to give you ideas.

- called for a pizza
- had a coffee
- washed the dishes
- the music was loud and noisy
- danced in the street
- went out to the street
- the police arrived
- had a nap

3 Finish the story.
At _____ we went home. It was an interesting party!

6B | Actor! Author!

VOCABULARY & SPEAKING: films & books

1 Match the words to the pictures.

> comedy   horror   love story/romance
> science fiction   cartoon   western   thriller

2 Work in pairs. Think of a film or book you know for each category. Write their names.

3 Work with another pair. Read out the names of the films or books. Can the other pair say what the category is?

4 Work in pairs, A and B.

A: Turn to page 138.
B: Turn to page 135.

LISTENING

1 🔘 **2.1** Listen to the beginning of the television show *Actor! Author!* What are the rules?

2 🔘 **2.2** Listen to the show. Can you guess the famous actor or author before Mike or Steph?

3 🔘 **2.2** Listen again. <u>Underline</u> the correct word/s.

Actor : (1)_____
He was born in Manhattan in *1952 / 1962*.
He fell off *a horse / a house* twelve years ago.
He died in *2005 / 2004*.

Author: (2)_____
He is *Canadian / American*.
His books are translated into more than *14 / 40* languages.
He wrote a famous *thriller / love story*.
It's about symbols in the art of a famous *German / Italian* painter.

Author: (3)_____
She's from *England / Ireland*.
She taught *Spanish / English* in Portugal more than ten years ago.
There are more than *six / nine* books in the series.

Actress: (4)_____
She was born in *1967 / 1976*.
She's from *Australia / America*.
She won an Oscar for the film *The House / The Hours*.

GRAMMAR: past simple irregular verbs; past time expressions

> Past simple irregular verbs
> He **wrote** a thriller.
> She **taught** in Portugal.
>
> Past time expressions
> I saw Gladiator on DVD **last night**.
> I read that book **two years ago**.
>
> ⟫ SEE LANGUAGE REFERENCE PAGE 70

1 Look at tapescript 2.1 on page 143. Find the past simple of these verbs.

1 write _____   3 win _____   5 read _____
2 teach _____   4 fall _____   6 make _____

2 Rearrange the words to make sentences.

1 weekend last a DVD I watched .
2 last didn't television I watch night .
3 bought ago two months I a book .
4 I didn't the Oscars last year watch .
5 this read newspaper I the morning .
6 use didn't I the internet email or yesterday .

3 Change the sentences in exercise 2 so that they are true for you.

PRONUNCIATION: past simple irregular verbs

1 🔘 2.3 Listen to these verbs and their irregular past simple forms.

think thought understand understood say said
speak spoke swim swam make made

2 🔘 2.3 Listen again and repeat.

3 Complete the table with an irregular past simple form from exercise 1.

/əʊ/	/ʊ/	/ɔː/	/e/	/eɪ/	/æ/
wrote	could	taught	read	ate	drank
woke	took	bought	went	gave	had

4 🔘 2.4 Listen to the recording to check your answers. Say the verbs.

SPEAKING

1 Work in groups of three. Write down the names of two famous actors and two famous authors. Don't show your names to the others.

2 Prepare clues for your actors and authors.

   He/she was born in …
   He/she won an Oscar.
   He/she wrote …
   He/she acted in …

3 Play Actor! Author! One person gives clues, the others guess.

4 Swap roles.

DID YOU KNOW?

1 Read the text about books.

The Big Read

In 2003, the BBC had a television show and competition to discover Britain's favourite books. More than 750,000 people voted for the book they liked the most. Here is the list of the top ten books in Britain.

1 **The Lord of the Rings**, J R R Tolkien
2 **Pride and Prejudice**, Jane Austen
3 **His Dark Materials**, Philip Pullman
4 **The Hitchhiker's Guide to the Galaxy**, Douglas Adams
5 **Harry Potter and the Goblet of Fire**, J K Rowling
6 **To Kill a Mockingbird**, Harper Lee
7 **Winnie the Pooh**, A A Milne
8 **Nineteen Eighty-Four**, George Orwell
9 **The Lion, the Witch and the Wardrobe**, C S Lewis
10 **Jane Eyre**, Charlotte Brontë

2 Work in pairs. Discuss these questions.

• Do you know any of these books?
• What are the titles in your language?
• What are the favourite books in your country, do you think?

6c | They cry easily

Vocabulary: feelings

1 Match the sentences to the people.

1 She is happy. ___ ☐
2 He is nervous. ___ ☐
3 He is angry. ___ ☐
4 She is bored. ___ ☐
5 He is sad. ___ ☐

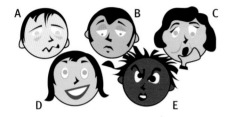

2 🔊 **2.5** Listen to the people at an important sports event. How do they feel? Put the sentences from exercise 1 in the correct order.

3 Work in pairs. Imagine you are in these situations. How do you feel? Tell your partner.

You are in an exam.
It's a beautiful sunny day and you have the day off.
It's your birthday.
It's Friday night and you finish work.
You are at an important football match.
You are at the airport. Your plane is three hours late.
You can't find an important piece of paper.

Reading

1 Look at the photos. How do these people feel?

2 Read the article. Choose the best title.

Men never cry
Crying – it's a man's thing
Crying – good for your health
Men and sports

Men don't cry, or do they? British psychologists and researchers say that men cry easily, more easily than we think. One in three British men cry once a month, and in America, men cry on average 1.4 times a
5 month.

Why do men cry more now? In Britain and America it is more acceptable for men to cry today. Two recent US presidents, Bill Clinton and George W Bush, cried quietly on television in front of millions of people.
10 Football star David Beckham cried when he took his children to school the first time. And British Olympic athlete Matthew Pinsent cried when he won a gold medal at the Athens Olympics in 2004.

In a survey on crying, men said that they often cry
15 when they are sad or when they feel bad. They said they don't cry when they are angry. But men cry a lot more than women when they are happy. For example, many British men cry when their favourite football team plays very well and wins a cup.

20 Doctors say that crying is good for your body. Most people say that they usually feel better after crying. So the next time you want to cry, go ahead. It's good for you!

3 Read the sentences and decide if they are true (T) or false (F).

1 It's difficult for British men to cry.
2 American men cry more often than British men.
3 Two American presidents cried in public.
4 David Beckham cried when he won a gold medal.
5 Men cry when they are angry.
6 British men cry at sports, especially football.

4 Work in pairs. Discuss these questions.

• Is it common for people to cry in your country?
• Who cry more, men or women?
• Do you cry at sports events?
• Do you cry easily?
• When was the last time you cried?

GRAMMAR: adverbs of manner

We use adverbs of manner to say how we do something.
*Bill Clinton cried **quietly**.*
*The football team played **well**.*

⟩ SEE LANGUAGE REFERENCE PAGE 70

1 Find and underline the adverbs of manner in the article.

2 Complete the sentences with the correct form of the word in brackets.

1 He explained the rules very _____. (careful)
2 The winner at Wimbledon this year played tennis _____. (beautiful)
3 The manager of the football team answered the question _____. (angry)
4 Formula One cars go very _____. (fast)
5 She goes to the swimming pool every day, and she swims very _____. (good)

3 Underline the correct word.

1 He speaks very *quietly / quiet*. I can't hear him.
2 It's a very *sadly / sad* film.
3 My boyfriend cries very *easy / easily*.
4 It was a *well / good* party.
5 This is a very *hard / hardly* test.
6 He sat and ate his pizza *noisy / noisily*.

4 Work in pairs. Can you think of a famous sports person who …

• drives very fast?
• plays football very well?
• speaks English badly?

PRONUNCIATION: word stress 2, intonation 1

1 🔘 **2.6** Listen and repeat the adverbs of manner. Underline the stressed syllable in these adverbs.

angrily   happily   nervously   slowly
carefully   quietly   noisily

2 🔘 **2.7** Listen to four dialogues. Which adverb describes each dialogue?

SPEAKING

1 Play the Dialogue Game. Your teacher will explain the rules.

6D | I'm not crazy about it

SPEAKING

1 Work in pairs. Look at the different things to do in
London. Imagine you have a free day/evening in the city.
Choose three things that you would like to do.

Have some free time?

EXPLORE LONDON
recommends ...

- go shopping in London's most
  famous shopping districts
  (Oxford Street, Knightsbridge)
- see a film at one of London's many cinemas
- go to a Chelsea or Arsenal football match
- a nightclub
- Kew Gardens
- a boat ride on the Thames
- St Paul's Cathedral
- the London Aquarium
- a tour round London on an open top bus
- the Tower of London

2 Compare your answers with another pair in
the class.

VOCABULARY: adjectives of opinion

1 🔘 **2.8** Listen and <u>underline</u> the word you hear.
Say the sentences.

1 It was an *awful / excellent* film.
2 The shopping is *good / bad* here.
3 The boat ride was *great / terrible*.
4 The gardens are *nice / horrible*.
5 The football match was *good / terrible*.

2 Put the adjectives into the correct column.

| ~~good~~ ~~bad~~ nice lovely awful |
| great excellent terrible horrible |

Positive adjectives	Negative adjectives
good	bad

3 Work in pairs. Give examples of:

- excellent weather
- terrible weather
- a nice hotel
- an awful hotel
- a good film
- an awful film
- a great place to visit on holiday
- a terrible place to visit on holiday

LISTENING

1 2.9 The Explore London tour had a free day and evening yesterday. Listen to the conversations and decide which activities from Speaking exercise 1 on page 68 they are talking about.

2 2.9 Listen again and tick (✓) the phrases you hear in the conversations.

1 I can't stand it. ☐
2 I love football. ☐
3 I'm not crazy about it. ☐
4 It was OK. ☐
5 It was awful. ☐

FUNCTIONAL LANGUAGE: talking about likes & dislikes

1 Complete the table with words from Listening exercise 2 above.

> ☺☺
> I really like football.
> I (1)_____ rock music.
> I think London is wonderful/great/excellent.
> ☺☺
> I like the hotel.
> I think the food is good.
> ☺
> I don't mind sport.
> It's (2)_____.
> ☹
> I don't like football.
> I'm not (3)_____ the hotel.
> ☹☹
> I hate the food.
> I (4)_____ the weather.
> I think the book is/terrible/awful/horrible.

 SEE LANGUAGE REFERENCE PAGE 70

2 Rearrange the words to make questions.

1 you of think do what rock music ?
2 do you films what like ?
3 you do like football ?
4 of think what do you English class ?

3 Work in pairs. Discuss the questions in exercise 2.

SPEAKING

1 Write the names of real people or things that you like.

• An actor from your country
• An American actor
• A restaurant in your city
• A TV programme
• A film
• A singer/group

2 Work in small groups. Ask other people in your group about the things they wrote in exercise 1. Use the different expressions in the functional language box to answer questions.

A: *What do you think of Antonio Banderas?*
B: *I think he's OK.*
A: *What about you? Do you like Antonio Banderas?*
C: *Yes, I do. I think he's great.*

3 Find two people or things that everybody in the group likes. Report back to the rest of the class.

We all like …

Grammar

Past simple - irregular verbs

Many common verbs are irregular in the past simple.

> *eat – ate   go – went   make – made   see – saw*
> *have – had*

There is a list of past simple irregular verbs on page 159.

Affirmative		
I You He/She/It We They	went	to the party.

The rules for the negative and question are the same as past simple regular verbs. See Language reference 5, page 60.

Past time expressions & *ago*

Use the following expressions with the past tense.
yesterday, last night/week/Saturday/month/year

These expressions go at the beginning or end of a sentence.

> *I saw a film **last night**.*
> ***Yesterday** I had English class.*

We also use periods of time + *ago* with the past tense. It usually goes at the end of a sentence.

> *I saw the film **two weeks ago**.*
> *They booked their tickets **six months ago**.*

Adverbs of manner

Use adverbs of manner to say how we do something.

> *Bill Clinton cried **quietly**.*
> *The football team played **well**.*

Adverbs of manner usually go at the end of the sentence.

To make an adverb of manner, you usually add -*ly* to the adjective.

> *quiet – quietly   slow – slowly   bad – badly*

For adjectives that end in -*y*, change *y* to -*ily*.

> *easy – easily   noisy – noisily*

There are some adverbs that do not change.

> *late – late   fast – fast   hard – hard   early –early*

The adverb for *good* is *well*.

> *They are **good** players. They play **well**.*

Functional language

Talking about likes/dislikes

☺ ☺
I really like …
I love …
I think … is wonderful/great/excellent.

☺
I like …
I think … is good.

😐
I don't mind …
It's OK.

☹
I don't like …
I'm not crazy about …

☹ ☹
I hate …
I can't stand …
I think … is/are terrible/awful/horrible.

WORD LIST

Celebrations

birthday *n* **	/ˈbɜːθdeɪ/
ceremony *n* *	/ˈserəməni/
champagne *n*	/ʃæmˈpeɪn/
congratulate *v* *	/kənˈɡrætʃuleɪt/
New Year's Eve *n*	/njuː jɪəz ˈiːv/
retirement *n*	/rɪˈtaɪəmənt/
wedding *n* **	/ˈwedɪŋ/

Films & books

cartoon *n*	/kɑːˈtuːn/
comedy *n* *	/ˈkɒmədi/
horror *n*	/ˈhɒrə/
love story *n*	/ˈlʌv stɔːri/
romance *n*	/rəʊˈmæns/
science fiction *n*	/saɪəns ˈfɪkʃn/
thriller *n*	/ˈθrɪlə/
western *n*	/ˈwestən/

Feelings

angry *adj* ***	/ˈæŋɡri/
bored *adj* **	/bɔːd/
happy *adj* ***	/ˈhæpi/
nervous *adj* **	/ˈnɜːvəs/
sad *adj* **	/sæd/

Adjectives of opinion

awful *adj* **	/ˈɔːfl/
bad *adj* ***	/bæd/
excellent *adj* ***	/ˈeksələnt/
good *adj* ***	/ɡʊd/
great *adj* ***	/ɡreɪt/
horrible *adj* *	/ˈhɒrɪbl/
lovely *adj*	/ˈlʌvli/
nice *adj* ***	/naɪs/
terrible *adj* **	/ˈterɪbl/
wonderful *adj* **	/ˈwʌndəfl/

Other words & phrases

acceptable *adj* *	/əkˈseptəbl/
act *v* ***	/ækt/
actor *n* ***	/ˈæktə/
athlete *n*	/ˈæθliːt/
author *n* **	/ˈɔːθə/
boat ride *n*	/ˈbəʊt raɪd/
buy *v* ***	/baɪ/
cry *v* ***	/kraɪ/
fall *v* ***	/fɔːl/
favourite *adj* **	/ˈfeɪv(ə)rɪt/

feel *v* ***	/fiːl/
health *n* ***	/helθ/
horse *n* ***	/hɔːs/
medal *n*	/ˈmedl/
president *n* ***	/ˈprezɪdənt/
psychologist *n*	/saɪˈkɒlədʒɪst/
stress *n* *	/stres/
symbol *n* *	/ˈsɪmbəl/
was born *v*	/wəz ˈbɔːn/
weekend *n* ***	/wiːˈkˈend/
win *v* ***	/wɪn/

7A | Miracle diets?

VOCABULARY: food 1

1 Match the words to the pictures.

fish   chicken   potatoes   lettuce
ice cream   bananas   bread
apples   milk   eggs   cake

2 Complete the information for the *Nutrition Reference Guide* with words from exercise 1. Check you know the meaning of the other food words.

Nutrition Reference Guide

1 _____
  pasta

  steak
2 _____
3 _____

  carrots
4 _____
  tomatoes
5 _____

6 _____
  oranges
7 _____
  lemons

8 _____
  cheese
  milk

  chocolate
9 _____
10 _____

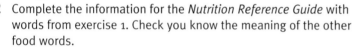

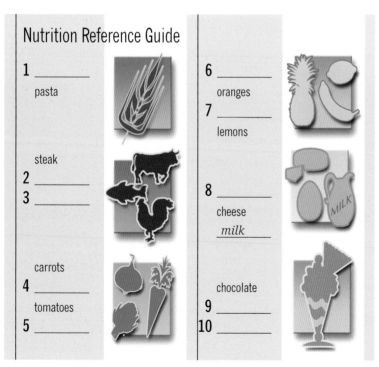

3 🔘 2.10 Listen to the recording to check your answers. Say the words.

4 Work in pairs. Find out what food your partner likes. Ask questions.

Do you like pasta?
Yes, I do.
Do you like eggs?
No, I don't.

LISTENING

1 Read the extract from a TV magazine. What is the show about?

EXPOSED!

Film stars talk about them, doctors don't always believe them, and people pay a lot of money for them. Reporter Daniel Barber investigates the world of Miracle Diets. Do they work? Find out tonight at 9:15 pm on Channel 5.

2 🔘 2.11 Listen to part of the programme. What three diets does Daniel talk about? <u>Underline</u> the correct name.

Diet 1:   *The Two Fs diet / The Two Ss diet*
Diet 2:   *The High C diet / The Low C diet*
Diet 3:   *The Soup diet / The Fish diet*

3 🔘 2.11 Listen again. Complete Daniel Barber's notes. Underline the correct word in Daniel Barber's notes

> Diet 1
> For breakfast, have some (1) fruit / milk.
> Don't eat any (2) meat / bread or drink any coffee.
> You can eat fish and (3) potatoes / tomatoes at lunch.
> Don't have any wine or beer, but fruit juice is OK.
> Lose (4) 2 or 3 / 5 or 6 kilos in a week.
>
> Diet 2
> Eat lots of fish, meat and (5) pasta / chicken.
> Eggs are OK too.
> Don't eat any bread, pasta or (6) soup / fruit.
> You can eat some lettuce, but not any
> (7) potatoes / cheese or carrots.
> 'Amazing results' - famous people use this diet?
>
> Diet 3
> Couldn't speak to a representative.
> Website says you can eat all foods, but in soup form.
> For example, fish soup, (8) pasta soup / chicken soup
> and banana and (9) apple / chocolate soup?!?
> Lose (10) 9 / 5 kilos in a week (?)

4 What do you think? Are these good diets? Do you know any miracle diets?

GRAMMAR: countable & uncountable nouns

Nouns can be countable or uncountable. Countable nouns have a plural form.
  *You can eat **eggs** with this diet.*
Uncountable nouns do not have a plural form.
  *Don't eat any **pasta**.*

Some/any
We use *some/any* with plural countable nouns and uncountable nouns. Use *some* in affirmative sentences and *any* in questions and negatives.

🔘 SEE LANGUAGE REFERENCE PAGE 80

1 Mark the foods on page 72 countable (C) or uncountable (U).

2 Underline the correct word in the sentences.

1 I had some *coffee / coffees* for breakfast.
2 I don't have *any / some* beer at home.
3 I like *a French bread / French bread*.
4 I have *an / any* orange in my bag.
5 I ate some *pastas / pasta* yesterday.

3 🔘 2.12 Listen to the recording to check your answers. Repeat if it's true for you.

4 Daniel Barber interviewed Susan Jeffreys about her experience with the *Two Fs* diet. Complete the dialogue with *some* or *any*.

Daniel: So, did the diet work for you?
Susan: No, it didn't. Every morning I had three apples, two bananas and (1)___ water for breakfast. I didn't eat (2)___ bread or drink (3)___ coffee or tea. I was tired all day!
Daniel: What else did you eat? Did you eat (4)___ fish?
Susan: Yes, I did. On Monday I ate (5)___ fish. On Tuesday I ate (6)___ fish. On Wednesday I ate (7)___ tomato salad but I didn't eat (8)___ fish. On Thursday I ate (9)___ fish again, with tomatoes.
Daniel: Did you eat (10)___ meat, or vegetables?
Susan: No, I didn't. Only fish, fish, fish! At the end of the week I was tired of it!
Daniel: What do you think of the Two Fs diet?
Susan: I didn't lose one kilogram! It's an awful diet!

5 Work in pairs. Read the dialogue.

SPEAKING

1 Work in pairs. Invent your own 'miracle diet'. Make a list of foods you can eat and a list of foods you can't eat. Give a name to your diet.

2 Work with another pair. Talk about your diet. Ask questions about the other diet.

> **Useful language**
>
> *In the ... diet*
> *You can eat ...   Eat lots of ...*
> *You can eat some ...*
> *You can't eat any ...*
> *Don't eat any ...*
> *The results are amazing/incredible. You can lose 10 kilos in a week.*
> *Can I eat any ...?*

7B | Rice

SPEAKING

1 Work in pairs. Discuss these questions.

- Do you like rice?
- Did you eat any rice this week?
- What do you eat rice with?

READING

1 Read a magazine article about rice. Match the paragraphs 1–3 to the headings a–d below. There is one extra heading.

a Rice in danger
b Rice – an important food
c Why I like rice
d Why is rice so popular?

2 Read the article again and answer the questions.

1 How much rice do Europeans eat every year?
2 How much rice does a person in Myanmar eat every day?
3 How much rice does the world produce every year?
4 Where can you grow rice?
5 How many different types of rice are there?
6 What can you make with rice?
7 Why is rice important for poor people?

3 Look at the article and <u>underline</u> two facts you didn't know before. Compare with a partner.

1 _____

Rice is life for millions of people around the world. It is the most important food for 50% of the world's population. Almost every country has rice in their diet. Europeans don't eat much rice, perhaps three kilograms per year. But in Myanmar, for example, each person eats half a kilogram of rice every day. Rice and fish is a popular combination in many Asian countries; rice and vegetables are important dishes in the Middle East and Southern Europe; and rice and beans is very popular in Latin America (in Colombia it is the national food).

2 _____

Every year the world produces more than 500 million tonnes of rice. Rice is a popular food because it grows almost everywhere. You can grow rice on wet land and dry land, in tropical rainforests and in deserts. Scientists think that there are more than 140,000 different types of rice in the world. Rice also has lots of uses. You can make paper, wine, bread, beer, sweets, cosmetics and even toothpaste with rice.

3 _____

Rice is in danger in many parts of the world, because of wars, environmental problems and pollution. Many of the poorest people in the world need rice to survive. For these reasons, the United Nations declared 2004 the International Year of Rice and started many development projects connected to rice production and distribution. These programmes continue today.

GRAMMAR: *how much/how many*

Use *How much* and *How many* to ask about quantities.
How much + uncountable nouns
  How much rice do people eat?
How many + countable nouns
  How many countries grow rice?

To talk about quantities, we use
a lot (of) / lots (of)
some
(not) much
(not) many

  Rice is in **a lot of** national dishes.
  People do**n't** eat **much** rice in Europe.

> SEE LANGUAGE REFERENCE PAGE 80

1 Make questions using the words in the table.

How much How many	people water coffee rice hours eggs bread	do you buy every week? do you drink every day? are there in your English class? did you sleep last night? did you eat yesterday?

2 Work in pairs. Ask the questions from exercise 1. Answer *a lot, not much, not many* or *none*.

  How much coffee do you drink every day? A lot!

VOCABULARY: food 2

1 🔊 2.13 Read and listen to descriptions of two rice dishes. Underline all the food and drink words. What are they in your language?

This is a dish I learnt in Mexico. It's called rice and beans. It's simple – it has rice, beans and corn. I like it for breakfast, with eggs and a large cup of coffee with lots of sugar. Delicious!

There are lots of different kinds of paella in Spain. For this paella you need rice, different kinds of shellfish, Spanish sausages, an onion, some garlic, tomatoes, salt, pepper and a lemon. It's wonderful with red wine on a hot summer day.

2 Which words are countable and which are uncountable? Write C or U. Say the words.

PRONUNCIATION: word stress 3

1 💿 2.14 Listen and read the three shopping lists. How many syllables do the words have in each list?

Will's shopping list
cheese
bread
milk

Jenny's shopping list
sugar
sausage
onion

Samantha's shopping list
banana
oranges
tomatoes

2 Who buys what? Put the words below into the correct shopping lists in exercise 1.

  rice   potatoes   ice cream   lettuce   cake   sausages

3 💿 2.15 Listen to the recording to check your answers. Add more words to each list.

4 Work in pairs. Read your lists to your partner.

SPEAKING

1 Work in pairs, A and B. Find six differences in the pictures.

  A: Turn to page 133.
  B: Turn to page 134.

7c | Fussy eaters

spinach

SPEAKING & VOCABULARY: describing food

1 Work in pairs. What do you think of these dishes?

What do you think of sushi?
I like it / I hate it / I think it's ... I don't know it.

sushi

curry

chips

brownies à la mode

2 🔘 2.16 Listen and match the adjectives to the dishes in exercise 1. Say the words. What are these words in your language?

salty	spicy	sweet	raw	cooked	hot	cold

3 Work in groups. Find someone who ...

- likes spicy food.
- doesn't like raw vegetables.
- likes sweet coffee.
- likes cold soups.
- always eats cooked vegetables.
- doesn't eat salty food.

Do you like spicy food?   Yes, I do. No, I don't.

LISTENING

1 Read the definition of fussy eater.
Do you know a fussy eater? Who is it? Why?

> **A fussy eater is a person who eats only some types of food. They don't like trying new food.**

My brother is a fussy eater. He doesn't eat onions, vegetables or fruit.

2 🔘 2.17 Listen to four conversations. Put the food and drink words in the order you hear them. There are three extra words.

hamburgers	rice	pasta	fish	wine
beer	cake			

3 🔘 2.17 Listen again and decide if the sentences are true (T) or false (F).

1 The woman's brother is a fussy eater.
2 The man likes the wine.
3 The woman doesn't want the cake.
4 The boyfriend can only eat salty food.

4 Work in pairs. Discuss these questions.

- What foods don't *you* like?
- Are you a fussy eater?

Grammar: *too*

Too + adjective means 'more than we want'
*It's **too spicy**.*

Too + adjective and *very* + adjective are different.
*The tea was **too hot**. I couldn't drink it.*
*The tea was **very hot**, but I could drink it.*

> See Language Reference page 80

1 Match the sentences in column A to the sentences in column B.

A		B	
1	There's a lot of sugar in this coffee.	a	You're too late.
2	I can't eat Mexican food.	b	He's too short.
3	We can't move in this kitchen.	c	It's too small.
4	Our baby needs to eat more.	d	It's too spicy.
5	He can't reach the shelf.	e	It's too sweet.
6	The film started ten minutes ago.	f	He's too thin.

2 Rearrange the words to make sentences.

1 in too it's here hot .
2 tired very not I'm .
3 easy too this is class .
4 very food is expensive in country my .
5 too for me chocolate is sweet .
6 cloudy it's today very .

3 2.18 Listen to the recording to check your answers. Repeat if it's true for you.

Speaking

1 2.19 Read and listen to the dialogue.

Man: Excuse me, waiter?
Waiter: Yes sir.
Man: I can't eat this soup. It's too cold.
Waiter: I'm sorry, sir.
Man: I hate cold soup!

2 Match the dialogue to one of the pictures.

3 Work in pairs. Choose one of the other pictures. Write a similar dialogue.

4 Present your dialogue to another pair.

SPEAKING & READING

1 Read the sentences below in the 'Eating Out' survey. For each sentence, write a number 1 to 3 (1=usually; 2=sometimes; 3=hardly ever).

• • • EATING OUT SURVEY • • • • • •

☐ I have breakfast in a café or restaurant.
☐ I go to restaurants with my family.
☐ I go to restaurants with friends.
☐ I go to restaurants alone.
☐ I eat at a cafeteria at work or school.
☐ I go to fast food restaurants.

2 Work in pairs. Compare your results. Then calculate your points. Who has more points? Who eats out more?

VOCABULARY: eating out

1 Match the words in column A to the words in column B to make sentences.

A		B	
1	We asked for a table	a	what we wanted to eat.
2	We looked	b	for two in the non-smoking section.
3	The waiter/waitress* asked us	c	for the waiter/waitress.
4	We had fish	d	for the main course.
5	We ate some chocolate cake	e	at the menu.
6	When we finished the meal	f	for dessert.
7	We left a tip	g	we asked for the bill.

* waiter = man   waitress = woman

2 🔘 2.20 Listen to the recording to check your answers. Say the sentences.

LISTENING

1 🔘 2.21 Herb and Hannah go to the Bella Pizza restaurant. Tick (✓) the food they order on the menu.

MENU for BELLA PIZZA

Salads
Tomato and onion salad
Lettuce, tomato, onion and
corn salad

Pasta
Spaghetti with tomato sauce
Four cheese pasta
Vegetarian lasagne

Risottos
Seafood risotto
Mushroom risotto
Vegetable risotto

Pizzas
Marguerita
(tomato sauce and cheese)
Vegetarian (tomato sauce,
onion, green pepper, mushroom)
Mexican spicy (tomato sauce,
beef, corn, beans)

Drinks
Cola
Mineral water
(sparkling or still)
House wine (red or white)
Beer

2 🔘 **2.21** Listen again. Complete the dialogues with a word or words.

1 Herb: Table for _____, please.
  Waiter: Smoking or non smoking?
  Herb: _____, please.

2 Waiter: Anything to _____?
  Herb: Yes. A beer, please.

3 Herb: Could we have the ____ too, please?
  Waiter: Of course.

4 Waiter: Are you _____ to order?
  Herb: Yes, we are.

5 Hannah: No coffee for me, thank you. Just
    the _____.
  Waiter: Of course. Here you are.

3 🔘 **2.22** Listen to the end of the meal. What happens?

FUNCTIONAL LANGUAGE: in a restaurant

Customer
Can I have	fish/the menu/the bill,	
Could I/we have	a table for two	please?
Can I pay	by credit card/by cheque	

Waiter/waitress
Can I help you?   Are you ready to order?
Here you are.   That's X pounds, please.

> ❯ SEE LANGUAGE REFERENCE PAGE 80

1 Correct the mistakes in the sentences.

1 I can help you?   *Can I help you?*
2 Here are you.
3 That are £15 please.
4 Could I has the fish, please?
5 Can I pay by the credit card?
6 Anything for drink?
7 Can we have a bill, please?

PRONUNCIATION: word linking 1

1 🔘 **2.23** Listen to six sentences. How many words do you hear in each sentence? (contractions=2 words)

2 Look at tapescript 2.23 on page 144 to check your answers.

3 🔘 **2.23** Listen to the sentences again and repeat.

SPEAKING

1 Work in pairs, A and B.

A: You are the waiter at Bella Pizza.
B: You are a customer at Bella Pizza.

Follow the directions below.

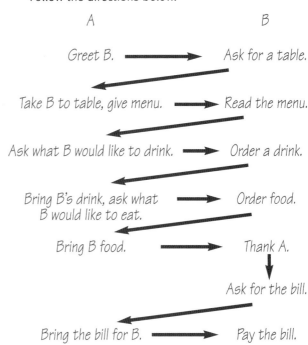

2 Change roles and repeat.

DID YOU KNOW?

1 Read the text about eating out in America.

Eating out in America

Eating out in America is a lot more common now than in the past. Eight out of ten American families eat out once a month, and fifty per cent of families eat out once a week. August is the most popular month to eat out, and Saturday is the most popular day of the week.

The top five reasons that families eat in restaurants are:

1. Because they like doing it
2. Birthdays
3. Special occasions
4. Good work at school or school achievements
5. Parents don't want to or are too busy to cook

2 Work in pairs. Discuss these questions.

- Are these facts similar for your country?
- When do you eat out?
- Why do you eat out?

GRAMMAR

Countable & uncountable nouns

Nouns can be countable or uncountable.

Countable nouns	Uncountable nouns
• have a plural form *This dish has five eggs.* • use *a/an* or *the* for the singular *Can I have an orange?* • use *some* with plural nouns and affirmative sentences *I'd like some carrots.* • use *any* with plural nouns in negatives/questions *Does it have any chocolate in it?* • in the dictionary, countable nouns are marked with a C *pen (n/C)*	• do not have a plural form, they are always singular *I love fruit.* • do not use *a/an* • use *some* with uncountable nouns in affirmative sentences *She drank some water.* • use *any* with uncountable nouns in negatives/questions *Don't eat any bread.* • in the dictionary, uncountable nouns are marked with a U *salt (n/U)*

Some nouns can be countable or uncountable, but they mean different things.
beer (U) = *the drink*
a beer (C) = *a glass or bottle of beer*
Other nouns like this are *coffee, juice.*

How much / how many

Use *how much* and *how many* to ask about quantities.

How much + uncountable nouns
   How much rice do people eat?
How many + plural countable nouns
   How many countries make rice?

Use words like *lots, much, some* to talk about quantities. These words go before the noun.

a lot (of) / lots (of)

some

not much (with uncountable nouns)
not many (with countable nouns)

*He has **lots of** friends.*
*They don't make **much** money.*

Too

Too + adjective means 'more than we want'.
   *It's **too** spicy.*

Too + adjective and *very* + adjective are different.
   *The tea was **too** hot. I couldn't drink it.*
   *The tea was **very** hot, but I could drink it.*

Can I have + noun, *please?*
Could I/we have + noun?
Can I pay by credit card/by cheque?

Can I help you?
Are you ready to order?
Here you are.
You're welcome.
That's X pounds, please.

WORD LIST

Food

apple n C/U ***	/ˈæpl/
banana n C/U	/bəˈnɑːnə/
bean n C	/biːn/
bread n U ***	/bred/
butter n U **	/ˈbʌtə/
cake n C/U **	/keɪk/
carrot n C/U	/ˈkærət/
cheese n C/U **	/tʃiːz/
chicken n C/U **	/ˈtʃɪkɪn/
chips n U ***	/tʃɪps/
chocolate n C/U **	/ˈtʃɒk(ə)lət/
corn n U	/kɔːn/
curry n C/U	/ˈkʌri/
diet n C **	/ˈdaɪət/
egg n C/U ***	/eg/
fish n U ***	/fɪʃ/
fruit n C/U ***	/fruːt/
garlic n U	/ˈgɑːlɪk/
ice cream n U	/aɪs ˈkriːm/
lemon n C/U	/ˈlemən/
lettuce n C/U	/ˈletɪs/
milk n U ***	/mɪlk/
nutrition n U	/njuˈtrɪʃn/
onion n C	/ˈʌnjən/
orange n C **	/ˈɒrɪndʒ/
pasta n C/U	/ˈpæstə/
pepper n U	/ˈpepə/
potato n C/U **	/pəˈteɪtəʊ/
rice n U *	/raɪs/
salt n U *	/sɒlt/
sausage n C/U	/ˈsɒsɪdʒ/
shellfish n C/U	/ˈʃelfɪʃ/
soup n C/U *	/ˈspɪnɪdʒ/
spinach n U	/suːp/
steak n C/U	/steɪk/
sugar n U **	/ˈʃʊgə/
tomato n C	/təˈmɑːtəʊ/
vegetable n C ***	/ˈvedʒəˈtəbl/
water n U ***	/ˈwɔːtə/
wine n C/U ***	/waɪn/

Describing food

cold adj ***	/kəʊld/
cooked adj	/kʊkt/
delicious adj *	/dɪˈlɪʃəs/
hot adj ***	/hɒt/
raw adj *	/rɔː/
salty adj	/ˈsɒlti/
spicy adj	/ˈspaɪsi/
sweet adj **	/swiːt/

Eating out

bill n C ***	/bɪl/
dessert n C *	/dɪˈzɜːt/
main course n C	/meɪn ˈkɔːs/
meal n C ***	/miːl/
menu n C *	/ˈmenjuː/
tip n C *	/tɪp/
waiter n C	/ˈweɪtə/
waitress n C	/ˈweɪtrəs/

8A | I hate flying

SPEAKING

1 Work in pairs. Ask and answer these questions about air travel.

- Did you travel to another country last year?
- Did you travel by plane?
- When did you travel?
- Where did you go?

READING

1 Read the magazine article and put the events in the correct order.

☐ The writer talked to a psychologist.
☐ The writer visited her brother in Hong Kong.
☐ The writer went on a course for people afraid of flying.
☐ The writer talked to a pilot.

2 Read the article again and answer the questions.

1 How many Americans hate flying?
2 Did the writer travel by plane before the course?
3 Why was the writer's phobia a problem?
4 Who taught the writer how to relax on a plane?
5 What did the people do when the flight started?
6 What did the writer do after her flight?

3 Work in pairs. What about you? What do you think of flying? Do you know someone who is afraid of going on a plane?

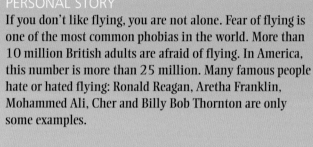

FEAR OF FLYING

PERSONAL STORY

If you don't like flying, you are not alone. Fear of flying is one of the most common phobias in the world. More than 10 million British adults are afraid of flying. In America, this number is more than 25 million. Many famous people
5 hate or hated flying: Ronald Reagan, Aretha Franklin, Mohammed Ali, Cher and Billy Bob Thornton are only some examples.

I hated flying. I knew that planes were very safe, that they were safer than cars (about 29 times safer), and the chance
10 of being in a plane accident were about 0.0000000004%. But every time I was at the airport, I felt terrible. I couldn't get on the plane. The only problem was that I loved travelling. And if you love travelling and hate flying, that is a problem.

15 After many years, I decided to do something. A friend told me about a special course for people like me. It was a one-day course at the airport. There were more than 100 people on this course. The first part of the course was a class with a pilot. He explained exactly how a
20 plane works, and showed us all the different parts. I liked that because it helped me a lot. Then we had a long talk with a psychologist. She gave us information about phobias and taught us a relaxation technique.

Then we had the most difficult part, a 45-minute
25 flight. We were all still very nervous. Some people held hands, and some people cried. But we all did it. At the end of the flight I felt nervous, tired but very happy. I could get on a plane and survive. The next day I booked a ticket to see my brother in Hong Kong.
30 It was the first time I visited him.

That was three years ago, and I don't mind flying now. But I don't like eating on planes, and no course can help me with that.

GRAMMAR: verb + *-ing*

> After the verbs *like, hate, love,* we use the verb + *-ing.*
> *Many famous people **hate flying**.*
> *I **don't like eating** on planes.*

> ⟩ SEE LANGUAGE REFERENCE PAGE 90

1 Put the words in the correct order on the line.

like   hate   don't like   love   don't mind

_____

☺☺   ☺   ☺   ☹   ☹☹

2 Find examples of the verbs in exercise 1 in the article. <u>Underline</u> them and the verbs that go with them.

3 Here are some of the reasons why the writer doesn't like travelling on planes. Complete the sentences with a word from the box. Use the *–ing* form.

wait   go   sit   talk   eat

1 I don't like _____ through security, it makes me nervous.
2 I hate _____ next to other people on planes. The seats are too small.
3 I don't like _____ to a stranger on a plane.
4 I don't like _____ for a long time at the airport.
5 I hate _____ airline food.

4 Work in pairs, A and B. Find out each other's likes and dislikes.

A: Turn to page 134.
B: Turn to page 136.

VOCABULARY: transport

1 Look at the words in the box. Put them into two groups.

car   airport   car park   plane   boat
motorbike   railway station   train   bicycle
bus   underground   bus stop   port   on foot

A Places connected to transport
B Kinds of transport

2 💿 2.24 Listen to the recording to check your answers. Say the words.

> *Language note*
>
> With the verb *go* and kinds of transport, use the preposition *by* + transport.
> *I went **by car**. They go to work **by train**.*

3 Work in pairs. Ask and answer the questions.

How do you get from your home to …	the city centre? English class? another city in your country? the sea? the USA?

PRONUNCIATION: /ŋ/

1 💿 2.25 Listen and repeat the words.

waiting   young   flying   eating   think   English

2 💿 2.26 Listen and complete the sentences.

1 I _____ flying.   3 I _____ watching horror films.
2 I _____ speaking English.   4 I _____ writing exams.

3 Complete the sentences with *like/don't like/hate* etc so they are true for you. Say the sentences.

SPEAKING

1 Do the *Travel* questionnaire below.

Do you hate flying?   Yes, I do.
Why?   Because I'm afraid of planes.

NAIRE **TRAVEL QUESTIONNAIRE** TRAVEL QUES

Find someone who …

Air
hates flying. Why?
takes planes often. For work or holidays?

Car
likes listening to music while they drive.
  What kind of music?
doesn't have a car.
  How do you get to class?

Boat & Train
takes the train or underground often.
  How often?
would like to make a long journey by boat.
  Where to?

8B | Traffic jam

LISTENING

1 🔊 **2.27** Listen to the traffic report. Match the pictures A–D to the stories 1–4.

2 🔊 **2.27** Listen again. What is the problem in each picture?

A

B

C

D

3 🔊 **2.27** Listen again and decide if the sentences are true (T) or false (F).

1 There is a bus on fire in Regent Street.
2 Traffic isn't moving in Regent Street.
3 Some people are singing in Oxford Street.
4 These people are standing next to the cars.
5 The police are talking to the lion.
6 A car is on the wrong side of the road in East London.

4 Is traffic bad in your town?

GRAMMAR: present continuous

Use the present continuous to talk about events happening now or around now.

Form: *be* + verb + *ing*
*Traffic **is** not **moving**.*
*Someone **is driving** on the wrong side of the road.*
*What **are** they **doing**?*

> SEE LANGUAGE REFERENCE PAGE 90

1 Look at tapescript 2.27 on page 144. <u>Underline</u> examples of the present continuous.

2 Make questions and answers with the present continuous.

| What / they / do? | They / move / a car to the side of the road. |
| *What are they doing?* | *They are moving a car to the side of the road.* |

1 What / the people / do? — The people / stand / in the street.
2 Where / they / go? — They / go / to the city centre.
3 Who / the police / talk to? — They / talk to / the demonstrators.
4 What / the lion / do? — It / sit / in the road.
5 What / the car / do? — It / drive / on the wrong side of the road.
6 What / the woman / do? — She / talk / on her mobile phone.

3 Think of four people you know. What are they doing now? Make sentences about them. Use the verbs and phrases in the box to help you.

> watch TV   work   sleep   sit in traffic
> have breakfast/lunch/dinner   study
> talk on the phone   do the housework

4 Work in pairs. Write the names of the people in exercise 3 on a different piece of paper. Ask questions about the people on your partner's paper.

What's Michael doing?
He's working.

VOCABULARY: action verbs

1 Write the missing letters in the infinitive verbs.

s_ng   dr_ve   k_ss   sl_ _ p
w_lk   r_n   sm_k_

2 Make sentences about what people are doing in the pictures. Use the verbs in exercise 1 in the present continuous.

SPEAKING

1 Work in pairs. Read the instructions for the In Traffic Game.

In Traffic Game

- Work in groups of four or five. You are all in one car, in a traffic jam.
- Your teacher will give you a piece of paper with an action on it.
- Do the action. Don't say a word.
- The other students ask questions about the action.
- *Are you dancing?* Answer *Yes, we are* or *No, we aren't.*
- Take turns.

2 Play the game.

DID YOU KNOW?

1 Read the text about traffic in London.

LONDON'S TRAFFIC LAW

London had the worst traffic in the UK and was one of the worst cities in Europe. Drivers spent 50% of their time in traffic jams, and pollution was terrible. In 2003, the mayor of London made a new law to help reduce traffic. It costs £8 (€10) a day to drive in central London. More people use public transport and bicycles now in London because of this law. Traffic is bad, but not too bad now.

2 Work in pairs. Discuss these questions.

- What do you think of the congestion charge in London?
- Is it a good idea?
- Is there something similar in your country?

8c | Follow that car!

READING & LISTENING

1 Look at the pictures. What is the television show *Tracy Dick* about?

2 🔘 **2.28** Read and listen to the show. Number the pictures 1–5 in the correct order. There is one extra picture.

TRACY DICK, P.I. MOTORBIKE DETECTIVE

Tracy:	Mrs Lunan, it's Tracy Dick here.
Mrs Lunan:	Yes?
Tracy:	You asked me to call you. I'm outside your husband's office now.
Mrs Lunan:	Oh, thank you. He doesn't leave work before six o'clock. And it's now only half past five.
Tracy:	Well, Mrs Lunan, your husband is leaving work now.

Mrs Lunan:	What's he doing?
Tracy:	He's taking a taxi.
Mrs Lunan:	But my husband hardly ever takes taxis! He says they're too expensive! He usually goes by bus.
Tracy:	Do you want me to follow him?
Mrs Lunan:	Yes, yes! Follow that car!

Tracy:	Mrs Lunan? I'm in the centre of the city.
Mrs Lunan:	Where's my husband?
Tracy:	Mr Lunan is paying the taxi driver … He's getting out of the taxi.
Mrs Lunan:	Where is he exactly?
Tracy:	He's in front of a restaurant, the Green Leaf.
Mrs Lunan:	He always goes to that restaurant. We went there together in the past …

Tracy:	He's not going in the restaurant. He's going into a flower shop.
Mrs Lunan:	What?! He never buys flowers!
Tracy:	I'm parking my motorbike now.
Mrs Lunan:	Phone me back, please.

Mrs Lunan:	Hello?
Tracy:	I'm in the restaurant. Mr Lunan is at another table.
Mrs Lunan:	What is he doing now?
Tracy:	He's looking for something … his mobile phone.
Mrs Lunan:	Yes?
Tracy:	He's making a phone call.
Mrs Lunan:	Can you hear? Who's he phoning? This is terrible!

3 Read the story again. Choose the correct words to complete the sentences.

1 Mr Lunan usually leaves work
   a) at six o'clock.
   b) at half past five.

2 He hardly ever
   a) goes by bus.
   b) takes a taxi.

3 Tracy Dick follows
   a) the taxi.
   b) the motorbike.

4 Mrs Lunan
   a) knows the Green Leaf Restaurant.
   b) doesn't know the Green Leaf Restaurant.

5 Mr Lunan
   a) has some flowers.
   b) doesn't have any flowers.

6 Mr Lunan
   a) is making a phone call.
   b) is getting a phone call.

7 Tracy Dick
   a) is sitting with Mr Lunan.
   b) is sitting near Mr Lunan.

4 Work in pairs. What is happening? Who is Mr Lunan phoning? Tell your partner.

5 2.29 Listen to the end of the story. Were you right?

VOCABULARY: collocations (transport)

1 Choose the correct word.

1 Can you *ride / drive* a motorbike?
2 Can you *ride / drive* a car?
3 How often do you *take / ride* a taxi?
4 Do you *take / drive* the train to work?

2 2.30 Listen to the recording and check your answers.

3 Work in pairs. Ask and answer the questions in exercise 1.

GRAMMAR: present simple vs present continuous

Use the present simple to say what we usually do.
   *He **goes** to work by bus **every day**.*

Use the present continuous to say what we are doing now.
   *He's **taking** a taxi **now**.*

> SEE LANGUAGE REFERENCE PAGE 90

1 Decide if these sentences are present simple (PS) or present continuous (PC). Write PS or PC in the space.

1 Your husband is leaving work now.   ____
2 What is he doing?   ____
3 He's taking a taxi.   ____
4 He usually goes by bus.   ____
5 He's not going in the restaurant.   ____
6 He never buys flowers!   ____

2 Complete the conversation. Put the words in brackets into the present simple or the present continuous.

Pete: So, what (1)___ you (2)____? (*do*)
Tracy: I'm a private detective.
Pete: That's interesting. (3)___ you (4)___ (*work*) now?
Tracy: Yes, I am. At the moment I (5)_____ (*follow*) a man.
Pete: How exciting! Is he in this bar?
Tracy: Yes, he is. Right now he (6)____ (*talk*) to another woman.
Pete: Would you like a glass of wine?
Tracy: No, thank you. I never (7)___ (*drink*) at work.
Pete: So … who asked you to follow this man?
Tracy: His wife. She (8)___ (*wait*) for me to call her now.
Pete: Is she? When you finish, why don't you come with me?
Tracy: I don't think so, Mr Hunt. You see, at the moment I (9)____ (*work*) for your wife.

3 2.31 Listen to the recording to check your answers. Work in pairs. Read the dialogue with your partner.

SPEAKING

1 Work in pairs, A and B.

A: Turn to page 137.
B: Turn to page 133.

8D | Let's take the bus

SPEAKING

1 Look at the picture.
Describe what is happening.

LISTENING

1 🔊 **2.32** Rob, Meg and Delilah need to cross London. Listen to their conversation. Where are they going? How many different kinds of transport do they take?

2 🔊 **2.32** Listen again. Complete the sentences with a word from the box.

> a man   by bus   the police station
> the Royal Albert Hall   a taxi   the wrong train
> an umbrella   the directions

1
1 Valerie is taking Herb and Hannah to _____.
2 The concert is at _____.

2
3 Diana asks _____ for help.
4 They don't understand _____.

3
5 They went on _____.
6 Rob wants to go _____.

4
7 Delilah didn't take _____.
8 Delilah calls _____.

FUNCTIONAL LANGUAGE: suggestions

> **Suggestions**
> *Why don't we/you take a taxi?*
>
> *Let's*
> | *take the underground.*
> *We/You can/could*
>
> **Responses**
> *That's a good idea.*
> *OK.*
>
> *No.*
> *I don't think that's a good idea.*

> ❯ SEE LANGUAGE REFERENCE PAGE 90

1 Rearrange the words to make suggestions.

1 go   the   concert   to   we   could .
2 the   underground   we   can   take .
3 the   man   ask   over   let's   there .
4 a   nice   taxi   see   London   could   we .
5 now   take   we   that   taxi   don't   why ?
6 the   street   go   up   let's .

PRONUNCIATION: intonation 2

1 🔘 **2.33** Listen to these two suggestions said in different ways. Which way is friendlier? <u>Underline</u> 1 or 2.

 a We can take the underground. *1 / 2*
 b Let's take a bus. *1 / 2*

2 🔘 **2.33** Listen again and repeat.

3 🔘 **2.34** Listen to these suggestions. Put a tick (✓) if they are friendly and a cross (✗) if they are not.

1 Why don't we wait for the bus?
2 We can go on foot.
3 We could take a taxi.
4 Let's go by train.

4 Work in pairs. You want to get to the other side of your town quickly. Make suggestions with the pictures. Respond to the suggestions.

VOCABULARY: *take*

1 We can use the verb *take* in different ways in English. Look at the examples in the box.

> 1 *take* + transport: *We can take a bus.*
> 2 *take* + things: *I didn't take an umbrella.*
> 3 *It* + *take* + time: *It takes 40 minutes (to get to the Royal Albert Hall).*
>
> *take a photograph*
>
>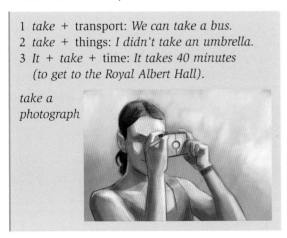

2 Look at tapescript 2.32 on page 144 and <u>underline</u> all the examples of *take* + noun(s).

3 Complete Rob's diary with words from the box.

> a photograph   a sandwich   twenty minutes
> a taxi   her camera

> *In the end, we took (1)_____. Delilah was happy of course. She took (2)_____ of us in the car. It took us (3)_____ to get to the Royal Albert Hall, and I was right, it cost a lot of money. When we got there, I wanted to take (4)_____ into the hall. The man at the door said I couldn't. No eating in the concert, he said. And he said Delilah couldn't take (5)_____ in. I don't understand this country. First the problem with the bags at the airport, and now this! Tomorrow is the bus tour. I hope it doesn't rain!*

4 Work in pairs. Think of the last long journey you were on. Ask and answer these questions and describe your journey.

* What form of transport did you take?
* Did you take a lot with you?
* How long did it take for you to get there?
* Did you take any photos?
* What did you take photos of?

SPEAKING

1 Work in two groups, Group A and Group B.
 Imagine there is no English class next week. What would you like to do?

 A: Think of a suggestion for something to do. Use the ideas in the box to help you. When you are ready, make your suggestions to students in group B.

> go to the cinema   go to a restaurant
> go to a museum
> **go shopping**   other – (your idea)

 B: When a student from group A makes a suggestion, ask him/her questions. Use the questions below to help you.

 Is it expensive?
 Where is it?
 How do we get there?

GRAMMAR

Verb + -ing

After the verbs *love, like, hate, don't mind* we use the verb + -*ing*.

☺ ☺	*I love*	
☺	*I like*	
☺	*I don't mind* +	*flying.*
☹	*I don't like*	
☹ ☹	*I hate*	

Spelling
The -*ing* form can sometimes change the spelling of the verb.

Most infinitives =   + -*ing*

  fly – flying   talk – talking   go – going

Infinitives that end in 'e' = **e** + -*ing*

  arrive – arriving   hate – hating

Infinitives that end in vowel + consonant = double consonant + -*ing*

  sit – sitting   run – running

Present continuous

Use the present continuous to talk about events happening now or around now.

To form the present continuous, we use the auxiliary verb *be* in the present with the -*ing* form of the main verb.

Affirmative				
Full form		Contraction		
I am You are He/She/It is We are They are	working.	I'm You're He's/She's/It's We're They're	working.	

Negative					
Full form			Contraction		
I am You are He/She/It is We are They are	not	working.	I'm not You aren't He/She/It isn't We aren't They aren't	working.	

Question	
Am I Are you Is he/she/it Are we Are they	working?

Present simple vs present continuous

Use the present simple to say what we usually do.

  *He **leaves** work at six o'clock.*

With these expressions we usually use the present simple:

  every day/month/year/afternoon …
  once a week/month/year …
  always/sometimes/hardly ever/often …

Use the present continuous to say what we are doing now.

  *He's **leaving** work at 5:30 today.*

With these expressions we usually use the present continuous:

  at the moment
  now
  right now
  today

Remember: with questions and negatives in the present simple, use the auxiliary verb *do/does*. See page 30.

FUNCTIONAL LANGUAGE

Suggestions

Why don't we/you + verb?
Let's + verb.
We/You can/could + verb.

Responses

That's a good idea.
OK.
No.
I don't think that's a good idea.

WORD LIST

Transport

airport *n C* ***	/'eəpɔːt/
bicycle *n C*	/'baɪsɪkl/
boat *n C* ***	/bəʊt/
bus *n C* ***	/bʌs/
bus stop *n C*	/'bʌs stɒp/
car *n C* ***	/kɑː/
car park *n C*	/'kɑː pɑːk/
drive *v* ***	/draɪv/
motorbike *n C*	/'məʊtəbaɪk/
on foot	/ɒn 'fʊt/
plane *n C* ***	/pleɪn/
port *n C* **	/pɔːt/
ride *v* **	/raɪd/
station *n C* ***	/'steɪʃn/
train *n C* ***	/treɪn/
underground *n U*	/'ʌndəɡraʊnd/

Action verbs

kiss *v* *	/kɪs/
run *v* ***	/rʌn/
sing *v* ***	/sɪŋ/
sleep *v* **	/sliːp/
smoke *v* **	/sməʊk/
walk *v* ***	/wɔːk/

Other words & phrases

accident *n C* ***	/'æksɪdənt/
adult *n C* ***	/'ædʌlt/
alone *adj* **	/ə'ləʊn/
common *adj* ***	/'kɒmn/
course *n C* ***	/kɔːs/
exactly *adv* ***	/ɪɡ'zæktli/
fear *n U* ***	/fɪə/
flight *n C* ***	/flaɪt/
follow *v* ***	/'fɒləʊ/
hand *n C* ***	/hænd/
law *n C* ***	/lɔː/
phobia *n C*	/'fəʊbiə/
photograph *n C* ***	/'fəʊtəɡrɑːf/
pilot *n C* *	/'paɪlət/
police station *n C*	/pə'liːs steɪʃn/
safe *adj* ***	/seɪf/
security *n C* ***	/sɪ'kjʊərɪti/
stranger *n C* *	/'streɪndʒə/
survive *v* ***	/sə'vaɪv/
take *v* ***	/teɪk/

Teste 9A,b,c,d Friday

SPEAKING

1 What do you notice about a person when you meet them for the first time? Put the following in order from 1 to 5 (1=very important 5=not important).

eyes ☐   face ☐   clothes ☐   voice ☐   body ☐

2 Work in pairs. Compare your lists. Do you notice the same things when you meet someone for the first time?

VOCABULARY: clothes

1 Match the pictures A–M with the words in the box.

> shoes   trainers   jacket   dress   jeans
> jumper   shirt   skirt   tie   trousers
> T-shirt   boots   sock

2 🔘 2.35 Listen and check your answers. Say the words.

3 Complete the sentences so that they are true for you.

1 I never wear …
2 I only wear … at home.
3 I sometimes wear …
4 Right now I am wearing …
5 … is wearing …

READING

www.agoodimpression.com

www.agoodimpression.com

Every personal or business relationship starts with a first impression. Psychologists say that when you meet someone for the first time; they make an impression on you in less than thirty seconds.

We evaluate another person using three Vs: visual (how you look, your clothes), vocal (your voice) and verbal (what you say). When you meet someone for the first time, your body language and your clothes make 93% of the first impression. Only 7% are the words you say.

There is an expression in English: You never get a second chance to make a first impression. But what makes a good impression on you? Send us your emails.

For me, eye contact. You should look at the other person when you meet them. I don't trust a person if he or she doesn't make eye contact.
David Hill, USA

You should wear clean and neat clothes. A dirty shirt makes a very bad impression, and so do dirty shoes.
Emma Lowry, UK

1 Read the webpage. What is it about?

2 Read the text again and answer the questions.

1 What are the three Vs?
2 Which Vs are more important?
3 Who writes about body language?
4 Who writes about clothes?
5 Who writes about men and women?

3 Work in pairs. Put a tick (✓) next to the sentences in the web page you agree with.

Your physical appearance and body language say a lot about you. Sit up straight. Your body should say 'I am a friendly and confident person'.
Gill Launders, Australia

In Canada, you should shake a person's hand, man or woman. You shouldn't kiss them for the first meeting. It's also a good idea to use the other person's first name quickly. It's more friendly.
Michael Dobbs, Canada

I think you shouldn't wear a very short skirt for a first meeting, or an interview. It can give the wrong first impression. For a man, I think a shirt and tie make a good impression at an interview.
Jennifer Dawson, USA

You should smile when you meet someone for the first time. A smile is the best introduction. It's friendly. A smile is universal.
Peter Cranford, USA

PRONUNCIATION: final -e

1 🔊 2.36 Listen to the pronunciation of these words and read the rule.

/eɪ/ make	/aɪ/ rice	/eɪ/ ate	/əʊ/ phone

In English, we don't pronounce the letter -e at the end of words.

2 How do you pronounce the underlined letters in these words?

smile   clothes   face   time   smoke   take   fine
phrase   arrive   wine   cake   nice

3 🔊 2.37 Listen to the recording to check your answers. Say the words.

GRAMMAR: should/shouldn't

We use *should/shouldn't* + verb to give advice about something.

You **should wear** clean and neat clothes.
You **shouldn't wear** a very short skirt for an important meeting or interview.

▶ SEE LANGUAGE REFERENCE PAGE 100

1 Make new sentences using the information in brackets.

1 You should wear formal clothes. (not)
You shouldn't wear formal clothes.
2 You shouldn't talk loudly. (they)
3 I should listen to the other person. (?)
4 They should do something. (he; ?)
5 I should wear smart clothes. (she; not)
6 I should ask the teacher. (you; not)
7 We shouldn't talk in English. (you; should)

2 Tim is meeting his girlfriend Judy's parents. He wants to make a good impression. Match Tim's questions to Judy's answers.

1 What should I wear?
2 What time should I arrive?
3 Should I bring a bottle of wine?
4 Should I buy a gift?
5 What should I talk about with them?

a About seven o'clock. We eat at half past seven. Don't be late!
b Your white shirt and the blue tie.
c Don't worry, they're nice people! But you shouldn't talk about politics or religion.
d It's not necessary, but my mother loves plants.
e No, you shouldn't. My parents don't drink.

SPEAKING

1 Imagine someone wants to make a good impression on your parents. What are your answers to the questions in Grammar exercise 2? Is there anything else he/she should know?

2 Work in pairs. Tell your partner how to make a good impression.

If you want to make a good impression on my parents, you should …

9B | Body moving

SPEAKING & READING

1 Work in pairs. Ask and answer the questions.

> ### HEALTH — ARE YOU SITTING COMFORTABLY?
>
> - Are you sitting comfortably?
> - Do you spend a lot of your day sitting down?
> - Do you work in an office?
> - Do you work in front of a computer?
> - Do you play computer games?
> - Are you in a classroom for many hours a day?
> - Do you travel on long plane journeys frequently?
> - Do you spend a long time in a car, or on a bus every day?
>
> *If you answered 'yes' to more than two of these questions, then read on …*

2 The text in exercise 1 comes from a magazine article. What do you think the rest of the article is about?

1 Working in an office and going on holiday
2 A history of chairs
3 Problems and advice for people who sit for a long time

3 Read the rest of the article below and find out.

4 Read the article again and put the phrases below in the right place.

a Take breaks often   c Move your body
b Drink water   d Sit correctly

5 Which of the things in exercise 4 do you do when you are sitting for a long time?

It is not normal for the human body to sit for a long time. Sitting for a long time is new in human history. Now, sitting for many hours every day is common. It is also dangerous for your health.

5 You can hurt your back, your arms, your neck and your wrists if you sit for a long time every day. People who work in offices often have health problems because they sit too long in front of a computer. People who travel many hours on planes **10** often say they feel bad at the end of a long trip. Experts say you should do the following if you don't want any problems:

(1) _Sit correctly_
Keep your back straight and **15** your feet on the floor. You should have a good, comfortable chair.

(2) _Take breaks often_
Don't sit for more than thirty **20** minutes. Stand up and walk around. Several studies showed that people who take frequent 'microbreaks' do more work in the day.

25 (3) _Drink water_
Water cleans your body and keeps you healthy. It's good for you and gives you energy. Don't drink lots of coffee or tea.

30 (4) _Move your body_
Stretching is a simple and quick way of doing some exercise while you are sitting down. Stretch your arms, your hands **35** and your shoulders. Don't stretch a lot if it hurts.

VOCABULARY: body

1 Find and underline seven words in the article on page 94 connected to the body.

2 Match the body parts with the words in the box.

> leg foot/feet knee chest back hand
> arm wrist shoulder elbow neck head
> stomach eyes fingers

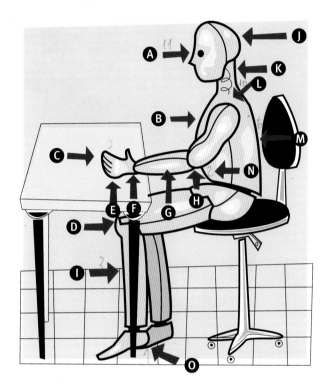

3 🔘 **2.38** Listen and tick (✓) the words you hear. Say the body parts.

4 Play Simon Says. Your teacher will explain the rules.

GRAMMAR: imperatives

> We use the imperative to give orders. The imperative form of the verb is the same as the infinitive.
> **Drink** water.
> **Sit** straight.
>
> We use *don't* + verb to make negative imperatives.
> **Don't sit** for a long time.
> **Don't** move.

> ⟩ SEE LANGUAGE REFERENCE PAGE 100

1 Underline all the examples of verbs in the imperative in the article.

2 Make a sentence for each picture. Use the verbs and phrases in the box in the imperative.

> take photos smoke speak walk
> turn right drive slowly

SPEAKING

1 🔘 **2.39** Look at the picture and listen to the instructions for a 'microbreak' exercise.

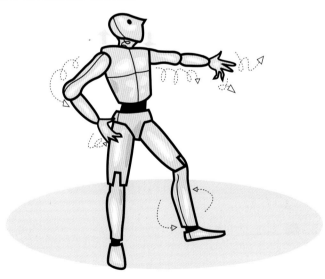

2 🔘 **2.39** Listen again and follow the instructions.

3 Work in pairs, A and B.
A: Look at page 133.
B: Look at page 135.

9c | Never forget a face

SPEAKING

1 Work in pairs. Read the sentences. Are they true for you?

1 I can remember what we learnt in our last English class.
2 I can remember the teacher's first name and last name.
3 I can remember the names of all the people in the class.
4 I never forget a face.

2 Change the sentences in exercise 1 so that they are true for you.

VOCABULARY: face

1 Match the words to the parts of the picture.

> nose   chin   eye   ear   hair
> mouth   cheek   tooth

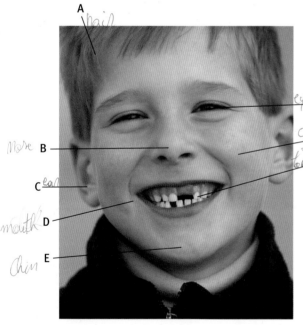

2 🔘 2.40 Listen and touch the parts of the face you hear. Say the words.

LISTENING

1 Work in pairs. Look at pictures A and B. Describe the pictures with your partner. Do you see anything strange?

2 🔘 2.41 Listen to the interview from a television interview about memory and the human face. What is wrong with the pictures in exercise 1?

3 🔘 2.41 Listen again and answer the questions.

1 Who doesn't have a very good memory: the woman or the man?
2 Which is the more important for memory: the top of the face or the bottom of the face?
3 What is strange about picture A?
4 Whose face is in picture B?
5 Whose hair is in picture B?
6 What do famous people do?

4 Look at tapescript 2.41 on page 145 to check your answers.

PRONUNCIATION: /h/

1 🔘 **2.42** Listen to the words in the box. Tick (✓) the words that begin with a /h/ sound.

> house   hot   hospital   what   whose   hair
> happy   have   his   has   hamburgers   who
> her   hour

2 Complete the sentences with words from exercise 1.

1 Helen and Harry work in a hospital.
2 They have lunch together every day.
3 He has hamburgers and she has hot soup.
4 Helen's happy with Harry.
5 But Helen has a problem.
6 She hardly ever remembers his name.

3 🔘 **2.43** Listen to the recording to check your answers.

4 🔘 **2.43** Listen again and repeat.

GRAMMAR: *whose* & possessive pronouns

> We use *whose* to ask about possession.
> **Whose** face is that? It's <u>George Washington's face</u>.
>
> We can replace the underlined words with a possessive pronoun.
> Whose face is that? It's **his**.
> My memory isn't very good. How is <u>your memory</u>?
> My memory isn't very good. How is **yours**?

> ❯ SEE LANGUAGE REFERENCE PAGE 100

1 Rewrite the sentences using possessive pronouns.

1 It's his face.   *It's his.*   5 Is this our room?
2 They're her children.   6 It isn't their flat.
3 It's my money.   7 Where's your book?
4 Here's your coffee.   8 That's his cat.

2 <u>Underline</u> the correct word.

1 Whose face is that? It's *her's / hers*. It's the Mona Lisa's.
2 I can remember his name but I can't remember *their / theirs*.
3 She always forgets *her / hers* glasses.
4 *Who's / Whose* in the picture?
5 *Who's / Whose* face is in the picture?
6 I brought my old photos today. Where are *yours / your*?

SPEAKING

1 Work in pairs. You are going to test your memory. Look at the pictures for one minute. Turn to page 134.

DID YOU KNOW?

1 Read the information about coins.

Faces on coins

The design of coins and money can say a lot about that country's culture and history. Countries often put an animal, a symbol or a person's head on their money. Many English-speaking countries have the Queen of England's head on their coins (Australia, Belize, Bermuda, Canada, Fiji, Great Britain and New Zealand are some examples). The United States has pictures of different presidents' heads on their coins.

2 Work in pairs. Discuss these questions.

● Whose face is on the money of your country?
● Do you have other symbols or animals on your money?

9D | Not feeling well

VOCABULARY: health problems

1 Match the pictures to the sentences.

b 1 I've got a headache.
c 2 I'm ill.
d 3 My back hurts.
A 4 I've got a cold.

A
B
C
D

2 Complete the sentences with the words in the box.

tired   stomach   sick   toothache   head
stomach ache   arm

I'm I feel	ill. (1) _tired_. (2) _sick_.	
My	back (3) _stomch_ (4) _____ (5) _____	hurts.
I've got I have	a headache. a cold. (6) _toothache_ (7) _stomach_ ache	

What are these in your language?

3 Work in pairs. Discuss these questions.

• Are you ill often?
• When was the last time you had a cold?
• How often do you go to the doctor?
• When was the last time you went to the doctor?

LISTENING

1 🔘 **2.44** Listen to the conversations. Tick (✔) the phrases you hear.

1	Are you alright?	Anything else?
2	I don't like it.	I don't feel well.
3	I'm fine.	Is there a doctor here?
4	How's your stomach.	You're welcome.
5	Are you OK?	I've got a headache.

2 🔘 **2.44** Listen again and put the events in the correct order.

4 Hannah calls a doctor.
5 The doctor gives Valerie some aspirin.
1 Valerie feels sick.
6 Herb feels ill.
3 Valerie goes to the toilet.
2 Valerie sits down and puts on Dave's jacket.

3 Match the words in A to the words in B to make phrases.

A		B
1 d Was it something		a too much wine?
2 e Take off		b a minute.
3 a Did she drink		c two aspirin.
4 c Take		d you ate last night?
5 b Wait		e that jacket.

aqui

FUNCTIONAL LANGUAGE: asking/saying how you feel

> **Asking how you feel**
> *How are you?* (*como vc está?*)
>
> *Are you*   *alright?*
>   *OK?*
>
> *What's*   *the matter?*
>   *wrong?*
>
> **Saying how you feel**
> *I'm fine, thanks.*
> *I'm very well, thanks.*
>
> *I don't feel (very) well.*
> *I feel sick/ill/tired.*
> *I've got a …*
>
> ❯ SEE LANGUAGE REFERENCE PAGE 101

1 Look at tapescript 2.44 on page 145. Find examples of the phrases in the box.

2 Work in pairs. Ask and answer how you feel. Use the pictures.

How are you?   *I don't feel well.*

3 Complete the dialogues using the words in the box.

1

> well   got   are   matter

A: Hi, how (1) *are* you?
B: Oh, I don't feel very (2) *well*.
A: What's the (3) *matter*?
B: I've (4) *got* a headache.
A: You should lie down.

2

> fine   wrong   home   I'm

A: Are you alright? What's (1) *wrong*?
B: I'm (2) *fine*, thanks. I'm a little tired.
A: Do you want to go (3) *home*?
B: No, (4) *I'm* fine. Really.

3

> fine   cold   head

A: Can I go out now?
B: No, you can't. You've got a (1) *cold*.
B: I feel (2) *fine*. My (3) *head* doesn't hurt now.
A: You should stay in bed.

4 🔊 **2.45** Listen to the recording to check your answers. Practise the dialogues.

Roleplay

5 Work in pairs, A and B.

Roleplay 1

A: You feel ill. You have got a headache and you feel very sick. You are very tired. You don't think you can go to work. Phone your work and explain.

B: You are A's boss. When A phones you, listen to what he/she says and respond.

Roleplay 2

A: You are B's father/mother. You think B is ill. You think he/she shouldn't go out tonight. Listen to what B says and respond.

B: You are A's son/daughter. You are often tired because you go out too much! You want to go out tonight, but you don't feel well. Ask permission to go out.

GRAMMAR

should/shouldn't

Should is a modal auxiliary verb. This means:

- it goes with the infinitive without *to*.
- it has the same form for all subjects.
- the negative is with *not* (*n't*).
- to make a question, put *should* before the subject and the infinitive after the subject.

We use *should* to give advice.

> You **should** say hello when you meet someone for the first time.

Affirmative	I/You/He/She/It/We/They	should	wear a tie.
Negative	I/You/He/She/It/We/They	shouldn't	wear a tie.
Question	Should	I/you/he/she/it/we/they	wear a tie?
Short answer	Yes,	I/you/he/she/it/we/they	should.
	No,	I/you/he/she/it/we/they	shouldn't.

Do not use *to* after *should*.

> You should arrive early.   Not ~~You should to arrive early.~~

Imperative

The imperative form of the verb is the same as the infinitive without *to*.
Use the imperative to give orders and instructions.

> **Drink** *water.*   **Sit** *straight.*

Use *don't* + verb to make negative imperatives.

> **Don't sit** *for a long time.*   **Don't move.**

You can also use imperatives to give directions (see Unit 3D page 39).

Whose & possessives

Use the question word *whose* to ask about possession. We can use *whose* with or without a noun.

> **Whose** *money is that?*   **Whose** *is that money?*

Use possessive pronouns to avoid repeating the noun.

Possessive adjective	Possessive pronoun
It's my book.	It's mine.
It's your book.	It's yours.
It's his book.	It's his.
It's her book.	It's hers.
It's our book.	It's ours.
It's their book.	It's theirs.

Do not use possessive pronouns with a noun.

> It's mine.   Not ~~It's mine book.~~

have got

Have got means the same as *have*. It is common in spoken British English.

Use *have got*:

- to talk about possession.
  I've got a car.
- to talk about relationships.
  I've got two brothers and sisters.
- to talk about states.
  I've got a headache.

Affirmative		
I/You/We/They	have got 've got	a headache.
He/She/It	has got 's got	

Negative		
I/You/We/They	haven't got	a headache.
He/She/It	hasn't got	

Question			
Have	you/I/we/they	got	a headache?
Has	he/she/it		

Short answer		
Yes,	you/I/we/they	have.
	he/she/it	has.
No,	you/I/we/they	haven't.
	he/she/it	hasn't.

The past of *have got* is *had*.

FUNCTIONAL LANGUAGE
Asking how you feel

How are you?   Are you alright?   Are you OK?

What's the matter?   What's wrong?

Saying how you feel

I'm fine, thanks.   I'm very well, thanks.

I don't feel (very) well.
I feel + adj
I've got a + noun

WORD LIST
Clothes

boot *n C* **	/buːt/
dress *n C* **	/dres/
jacket *n C* **	/ˈdʒækɪt/
jeans *n C* **	/dʒiːnz/
jumper *n C*	/ˈdʒʌmpə/
shirt *n C* ***	/ʃɜːt/
shoe *n C* ***	/ʃuː/
skirt *n C* **	/skɜːt/
tie *n C* *	/taɪ/
trainers *n C*	/ˈtreɪnəz/
trousers *n C* **	/ˈtraʊzəz/
T-shirt *n C*	/ˈtiːʃɜːt/

Body

arm *n C* ***	/ɑːm/
back *n C* ***	/bæk/
chest *n C* ***	/tʃest/
elbow *n C* **	/ˈelbəʊ/
finger *n C* ***	/ˈfɪŋɡə/
foot (plural feet) *n C* ***	/fʊt, fiːt/
hand *n C* ***	/hænd/
head *n C* ***	/hed/
knee *n C* ***	/niː/
leg *n C* ***	/leɡ/
neck *n C* ***	/nek/
shoulder *n C* ***	/ˈʃəʊldə/
stomach *n C* **	/ˈstʌmək/
wrist *n C*	/rɪst/

Face

cheek *n C* **	/tʃiːk/
chin *n C* **	/tʃɪn/
ear *n C* ***	/ɪə/
eye *n C* ***	/aɪ/
hair *n U* ***	/heə/
mouth *n C* ***	/maʊθ/
nose *n C* ***	/nəʊz/
tooth (plural teeth) *n C* ***	/tuːθ/ /tiːθ/

Health problems

cold *n C* ***	/kəʊld/
headache *n C* *	/ˈhedeɪk/
hurt *v* ***	/hɜːt/
ill *adj* ***	/ɪl/
stomach ache *n C/U*	/ˈstʌməkeɪk/
tired *adj* ***	/ˈtaɪəd/
toothache *n U*	/ˈtuːθeɪk/

10A | It's illegal

VOCABULARY: places in a city

1 Complete the sentences with a word from the box.

> shop   library   bank
> town hall   stadium

1 A _town hall_ is the building that has all the offices of the town government.
2 A _bank_ is a place where you can keep money or change money.
3 A _shop_ is a place where you buy things.
4 A _stadium_ is a place where there are sports events, like football matches.
5 A _library_ is a place where you can look at books, CDs and films.

2 Make similar sentences for these places.

> school   hotel   hospital   disco

A school is a place where …

3 Look at these signs. In which places in exercise 1 or exercise 2 do you see these signs?

READING

1 Read a magazine article about different laws and choose the best title for the article.

1 Important laws for visitors to American cities
2 School laws in American cities
3 Strange laws in American cities

Several years ago, two American students started a collection of interesting American laws and put them on the internet. It was part of a high school project. They now have several hundred different bizarre* laws from different parts of the United States on their webpage.

Here are some examples:

* If you want to go swimming in Destin, Florida, you must get dressed in your hotel room and not in your car.

* You mustn't take a pig to the beach in Miami Beach, Florida.

* You must not look into car windows on the street in Milford, Massachusetts.

* You mustn't ride a bicycle in a swimming pool in the town of Baldwin Park, California.

* In Cathedral City, California it's illegal to take a dog to school.

* In the state of Virginia, you must wear shoes while you are driving.

* A law in Walnut, California says that a man must not wear women's clothes.

* In Toledo, Ohio it's against the law to throw a snake at another person.

* You must not shout or sing in public at night in the town of Topeka, Kansas.

* In the majority of American cities, you needn't have a permit to buy or carry a gun.

> **Glossary**
> bizarre *adj* strange

2 Read the article again. Which city, cities or state have:

- a law about swimming? *California, Florida*
- a law about transport? *Virginia*
- a law about clothes?
- a law about animals? *Virginia*

3 Work in pairs. Discuss these questions.

- Which law do you think is the most interesting?
- Do you have any strange laws in your town or country?

GRAMMAR: *must/mustn't/needn't*

Use *must/mustn't* to talk about obligation.
In affirmative sentences, *must* means 'this is necessary'.
  You **must** wear shoes while you are driving.
In negative sentences, *mustn't* means 'don't do this'.
  You **mustn't** sleep on the road.
In negative sentences, *needn't* means 'this isn't necessary'.
  You **needn't** have a permit to buy a gun.

▶ SEE LANGUAGE REFERENCE PAGE 110

1 Rewrite the sentences using the words in brackets.

1 They must drive slowly. (you).
  You must drive slowly.
2 You needn't wear a tie. (must)
3 You must have a permit to buy a dog. (needn't)
4 You must go now. (he; not)
5 I mustn't call the police. (you; must)
6 The teacher must prepare the lesson. (students; needn't)

2 Complete the sentences with *must* or *mustn't* and a verb.

A library

have	~~speak~~	bring

1 You *mustn't speak* loudly.
2 You *must have* a library card to take out books.
3 You *must bring* the books back to the library.

A bus

buy	pay	smoke

4 You _____ for a ticket.
5 You _____ the ticket from the driver.
6 You *mustn't smoke* in the bus.

SPEAKING

1 Work in pairs. You are going to make some classroom laws. Look at the phrases in the box. Are they for the teacher, the students or the teacher and the students?

come to class late
explain again if the students don't understand
do the homework every day
speak in English all the time
speak quickly
turn off mobile phones in class
correct the homework
use the book in every lesson

2 Now make sentences with the phrases. Use *must*, *mustn't* or *needn't*. Add at least one more sentence of your own.

3 Work with another pair. Read your classroom laws. Do you agree? Decide on the five most important classroom laws.

DID YOU KNOW?

1 Read the article about smoking.

Ireland was the second country in Europe (after Norway) to pass a law against smoking in all public places. You mustn't smoke now in any offices, banks, restaurants and pubs in Ireland.
If you want to smoke a cigarette, you must go outside. In the year after the new law, more than 7,000 Irish people quit smoking. Today, nine out of ten people in Ireland say that the anti-smoking laws are a good thing.

No Smoking
It is illegal to smoke in these premises

Proprietor: Airzone Ltd
Please notify complaints to: Manager on Duty

Maximum Fine €3000 – Public Health (Tobacco) Acts

2 Work in pairs. Discuss these questions.

- Are there anti-smoking laws where you live?
- Where mustn't you smoke in your city or town?
- Do you think these laws are a good idea?

10B | Life in the capital

SPEAKING

1 Work in pairs. Answer the questions.

Were you born in the capital of your country?

Yes   No

Do you live there now?   *Where were you born?*
Do you live in the same place?

Yes   No

Do you like living there?   *Would you like to live in the capital?*
Why or why not?   *Why or why not?*

VOCABULARY: adjectives

1 Read the questionnaire. Check the meaning of any words you don't understand in a dictionary.

SEVEN QUESTIONS ABOUT: ROME

		Yes	No
1	Are the people *friendly*?	✓	
2	Is it an *expensive* place?	✓	
3	Is it *dangerous* to walk on the streets at night?	✓	
4	Can you visit *interesting* things in your city?	✓	
5	Is it very *noisy*?	✓	
6	Are there any *beautiful* or *historical* buildings?	✓	
7	Is the air *polluted*?	✓	

2 🔊 **2.46** Listen to Giovanni talk about life in Rome. Tick (✓) the answers yes or no in exercise 1.

3 Match the words to their opposites in exercise 1.

safe   boring   quiet   ugly   clean
unfriendly   cheap   modern

4 🔊 **2.47** Listen to the recording to check your answers. Say the words.

5 Work in pairs. Choose a city, town or village that you know well. Interview your partner about his/her city.

LISTENING

1 Look at the pictures of different capital cities. How many can you recognize?

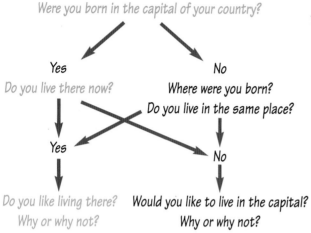

1
2
3
4
5
6

2 🔊 2.48 Listen to Nick and Sofia talking about life in different capital cities around the world. What capital cities do they talk about?

3 🔊 2.48 Listen again and decide if the sentences are true (T) or false (F).

1 Sofia lives in the capital.
2 Sofia lives with her family.
3 You can see bigger families in Alicante.
4 Nick lives in the capital.
5 Nick's city is very clean and quiet.
6 Nick thinks that people have the wrong opinion about the capital.

GRAMMAR: comparatives

Use comparatives to compare people and things with other people and things.

Alicante **is smaller than** Madrid.
Life in small cities **is more romantic**, and **calmer, than** life in the capital.
Mexico City **is more modern than** other cities in Mexico.

▶ SEE LANGUAGE REFERENCE PAGE 110

1 Make the comparative form of the adjective.

cold   bad   small   interesting   big
cosmopolitan   friendly   good   happy
dangerous   safe   polluted

2 Complete the text. Put the adjectives in brackets into the comparative form.

Many people think that Toronto is the capital of Canada. Actually, Ottawa is the capital. Ottawa is (1) _Smaller_ (small) than Toronto. It's also (2) _Colder_ (cold) in winter. Lots of people say that Toronto is (3) _more interesting_ (interesting), because it's (4) _bigger_ (big) and (5) _more cosmopolitan_ (cosmopolitan). I think that Ottawa has more historical buildings than Toronto. Canadians also say that people from other cities are (6) _friendlier_ (friendly) than Torontonians. Traffic in Toronto is (7) _worse_ (bad) than traffic in Ottawa. There are too many cars. Toronto and Ottawa are both safe cities. They are (8) _safer_ (safe) than many other North American cities.

3 Look at the statistics for two cities in the state of New York. Make sentences and put the adjectives in brackets into the comparative form.

	New York, NY	White Plains, NY
1 Became a city in	1626	1683
2 Population	8,008,278	52,105
3 Cost of living	$193.4	$172.7
4 Air quality (100=excellent)	15	21
5 Violent crimes/year	1,063.1	380
6 Distance to Washington DC	373.1 km	406.8 km

1 (old)   New York City is older than White Plains.
2 (big)   White Plains is bigger than New York City
3 (cheap)   White Plains is cheaper than New York
4 (polluted) White Plains is more polluted than New York City
5 (safe)   White Plains is safer than New York City
6 (close to capital)

PRONUNCIATION: word stress 4

1 🔊 2.49 Listen to these words and count the syllables.

             1   2
1 f r i e n d l y   frien / dly
2 c o l d
3 p o l l u t e d
4 e x p e n s i v e
5 n o i s y
6 c l e a n
7 b e a u t i f u l

2 Mark the stress in each word and say the words.
☐
frien / dly

3 🔊 2.49 Listen again to check your answers.

SPEAKING

1 Work in groups of three, A, B and C.
A: Turn to page 133.
B: Turn to page 138.
C: Turn to page 135.

2 Is life better in the capital or outside the capital in your country? Why?

10c | Best of the best

SPEAKING

1 Work in pairs. Imagine some friends are coming to visit your town or city. They only have time to see three things. What three things should they see? Make a list.

2 Compare your list with another pair. Who has the more interesting list?

READING

1 Work in pairs. What do you know about the city of Cape Town? Make some notes with a partner.

2 Read the extract from a guide book for Cape Town. Match the photographs A–C to the correct paragraphs.

BEST OF THE BEST – CAPE TOWN

Cape Town is one of South Africa's most beautiful cities. Cape Town is famous for its beaches, mountains and wine. There are lots of things to do and see during your visit. We have collected here a small
5 *sample of the best Cape Town has to offer.*

1 The most exciting thing to do
Cape Town sits next to the beautiful Table Mountain. Table Mountain is 1,086 metres high and is the most famous mountain in South Africa. If you visit Cape Town, you must take a cable car up to the top of the
10 mountain. (1) C_____.You can also go walking around the top of the mountain, which is 3km long.

2 The most frightening activity
The ocean near Cape Town is famous for sharks. On special adventure tours you can go diving with a great white shark.
15 (2) _____A_____.This is an experience that you will never forget!

3 The best shopping
For many reasons the Victoria and Albert Waterfront is the best and most popular shopping centre in the city. You can find cheap jewellery, good books and quality clothes at the shopping centre. If you want
20 African paintings and souvenirs, go shopping at the Green Point Market on Sundays. (3) _____B_____. There are hundreds of little shops at the market, and some have better prices than others.

4 The most expensive place to stay
The Cape Grace is a five-star hotel next to the sea in Cape Town. At
25 Cape Grace you can go swimming in the pool, relax in the spa or read in the library. (4) _____. The hotel bar has more than 420 different kinds of whisky!

5 The most historical place
If you want to go sightseeing, you must go to Robben Island.
30 Robben Island was one of South Africa's worst prisons during apartheid. (5) _____. Nelson Mandela, former president of South Africa, spent 27 years in prison on Robben Island.

6 The wildest night out
Cape Town is home to the biggest nightclub in South Africa, the Dockside. (6) _____. The giant building has a
35 dancefloor for 5,000 people.

3 Put the sentences a–f back in the gaps 1–6 of the article.

a A special cage protects you from the most dangerous animal in the *e* world.

b The 360° views are incredible. *1*

c It is now a national memorial and museum. *3*

d This is the best place to go dancing and have a good time. *6*

e The 122 rooms have beautiful furniture, satellite television, internet connection and lots of space.

f Some advice: you should always compare prices before you buy. *2*

4 Work in pairs. Imagine you have a free trip to Cape Town but you can only see three things. Which of the places in the brochure would you like to visit most? Decide which three places are the best to go to.

VOCABULARY: *go + verb + -ing*

1 Match column A to column B to make sentences about things you can do in Cape Town. All the expressions are in the brochure.

A	B
1 You can **go walking**	a *4* at the Dockside nightclub.
2 You can **go sightseeing**	b *2* on Robben Island.
3 You can **go diving**	c *5* at the Green Point Market on Sundays.
4 You can **go dancing**	d *6* with sharks in Gansbaai, Cape Town.
5 You can **go shopping** for souvenirs	e *1* at some of the beaches around Cape Town.
6 You can **go swimming**	f *3* on the top of Table Mountain.

2 Work in pairs. Discuss these questions.

• Which of the words in bold can you do in your city?
• Where can you do them?

GRAMMAR: superlatives

We use superlatives to compare people and things with ALL THE OTHER people and things in that group.

*Table Mountain is **the most famous** landmark in South Africa.*
*The V&A Waterfront is **the most popular** shopping centre.*

> SEE LANGUAGE REFERENCE PAGE 110

1 Look at the text. Underline all the superlatives.

2 2.50 Listen and make the superlative.

A safe city.   *The safest city.*

3 Simona and Nicky are visiting Cape Town. Complete the sentences and put the adjectives in brackets into the superlative form. Where are they in each conversation?

1 S: What about this souvenir for my brother?
 N: I don't know. It's _____ souvenir in the shop! (expensive)

2 S: Look at this place! I think it's the _____ club in town. (big)
 N: It's also very expensive, and I don't like dancing. Let's go to a different place.

3 S: Why don't you want to go?
 N: Because it's _____ thing in the guide book! It's also _____. (crazy, dangerous)

4 S: The guidebook says this is _____ part of Cape Town.
 N: Wow. You can see everything from up here. (high)

5 S: Who is Nelson Mandela?
 N: He's _____ person in modern South African history! (important)

SPEAKING

1 Make questions with the phrases below. Use the superlative. Make two more questions of your own.

1 good place to go shopping for clothes?
 What's the best place to go shopping for clothes?
2 interesting monument?
3 dangerous part of the city?
4 nice park?
5 bad time of year to visit the city?
6 important festivals in the city?

2 Work in pairs, A and B.

A: Choose a city that you know.
B: Ask the questions in 1 about A's city. Swap roles.

3 Work with a different partner. Repeat the same activity.

SPEAKING

1 Work in pairs. Discuss these questions.

- Do you have any souvenirs from other cities/countries at home? What are they? Where are they from?
- When you visit another city/country, do you buy souvenirs? Who do you buy them for? What do you buy?
- What do people buy as souvenirs from your city/country?

VOCABULARY: size & colours

1 Complete the descriptions of the souvenirs with a word from the box.

brown   blue   red   white   silver   black

1 It's a light _blue_ T-shirt.
2 It's a tiny _silver_ keyring.
3 It's a small _black_ taxi.
4 It's a large _white_ and _red_ football shirt.
5 It's a big _brown_ teddy bear.

Language note

Remember: colour words are adjectives – they come BEFORE the noun.

~~A taxi black.~~   *A black taxi.*

2 Use the words in the box to describe things in the gift shop.

	SIZE	SHADE	COLOUR	NOUN
It's a They're	small big	light dark	black white yellow silver gold red blue green brown	T-shirt. towels. pen. teddy bear. taxi. football shirt. mug.

LISTENING

1 🔘 2.51 Listen to Rob and Meg in the gift shop. What do they buy? How much does it cost?

2 🔘 2.51 Listen again and answer the questions.

1 How many mugs does Meg buy?
2 How much are the pens?
3 How many pens does Meg buy?
4 What is the book about?
5 How many bags does Meg want?

FUNCTIONAL LANGUAGE: in a shop

1 Complete the dialogues with the phrases in the box.

1

> You're welcome. I can't see a price.
> can I help you?

Shop assistant: Hello, (1) _Can I help you?_
Customer: Yes please. How much is this book?
(2) _I can't see a price_
Shop assistant: Just a minute. It's £7.95.
Customer: Thank you.
Shop assistant: (3) _You're Welcome_

2

> No, I'm sorry we don't. OK, thanks.
> Do you have any keyrings?

Customer: (4)_____
Shop assistant: Yes, we do. There are silver ones and these black ones.
Customer: Do you have any with the cathedral on it?
Shop assistant: (5)_____
Customer: (6)_____

3

> How much are they?
> The book and these postcards then, please.
> Anything else?

Shop assistant: (7)_____
Customer: Yes, I'd like some postcards please.
Shop assistant: They're over here.
Customer: (8)_____
Shop assistant: They're four for a pound.
Customer: Fine. (9)_____

4

> Would you like a bag for that? Bye. Here you are.

Shop assistant: That's £8.95.
Customer: (10)_____ Ten pounds.
Shop assistant: Here's your change. (11)_____
Customer: No thanks, that's alright. Goodbye.
Shop assistant: (12)_____

2 🔘 2.52 Listen and check your answers. Choose one dialogue and practise it in pairs.

PRONUNCIATION: word linking 2

1 🔘 2.53 Listen to these sentences. Notice how some of the words are joined together.

Can‿I help you?
How much‿is it?
Just‿a minute.
Anything‿else?
They're‿over there.
Would‿you like‿a bag?
Here you‿are.

2 Practise saying the sentences in exercise 1 quickly.

SPEAKING

1 Work in groups of three, A, B and C. Choose a city.

A and B: You are tourists. You would like to buy souvenirs from the city (decide what souvenirs you want). Buy some souvenirs.

C: You are the shop assistant. Help the tourists.

> *Useful language*
>
> *Can I help you?*   *How much is/are …?*
> *I'm sorry, we don't have any.*   *Here you are.*
> *Yes, I'd like … / Do you have …?*   *Anything else?*

GRAMMAR

Must/mustn't/needn't

Must is a modal auxiliary verb. This means:

- it goes with the infinitive without *to*.
- it has the same form for all subjects.
- the negative is with *not* (*n't*).
- to make a question, put *must* before the subject and the infinitive after the subject.

Must, mustn't, needn't		
I You	must	
He/She/It We They	mustn't must not needn't	wear shoes in this place.

We use *must* to talk about obligations.

Must has two possible negatives.

> *Mustn't* (*must not*) means *don't do this*.
> *Needn't* (*need not*) means *this isn't necessary*.

You can make questions with *must*, but this is not very common.

> **Must** *I bring a pen to the exam?*

We can also say *don't/doesn't need to* = *needn't*.

Comparatives

Use the comparative form of the adjective to compare two people or things.

> *The capital is* **more expensive than** *my town.*

Use *than*, not *that*, to compare the two things we are comparing.

> *The city is bigger than the town.*
> Not ~~*The city is bigger that the town.*~~

For most short adjectives (one syllable), add *-er*.

old	older
small	smaller

If the adjective ends in consonant + vowel + consonant, double the consonant + *-er*.

big	bigger

Longer adjectives (more than one syllable), add *more* + adjective.

expensive	more expensive
dangerous	more dangerous

Adjectives that end in *-y*, drop the *-y* and add *-ier*.

noisy	noisier

Good and *bad* have irregular comparative forms.

good	better
bad	worse

Superlatives

Use the superlative form of the adjective to compare more than two people and things.

> *It's* **the most dangerous** *part of the city.*
> *It's* **the highest** *mountain.*

With superlatives, use the article *the*.

> *He is the best player.*
> Not ~~*He is best player.*~~

For most short adjectives (one syllable), add *-est*.

short	the shortest
cheap	the cheapest
nice	the nicest

If the adjective ends in consonant + vowel + consonant, double the consonant and add *-est*.

big	the biggest
hot	the hottest

Longer adjectives (more than one syllable), add *the most* + adjective.

expensive	the most expensive
popular	the most popular

Adjectives that end in *-y*, drop the *-y* and add *-iest*.

happy	the happiest
funny	the funniest

Good and *bad* have irregular superlative forms.

good	the best
bad	the worst

FUNCTIONAL LANGUAGE

In a shop

Can I help you?
That's + price
Would you like a bag for that?

Here you are.
How much is/are ...?
Do you have any + noun?
I'd like + noun

WORD LIST

Places in a city

bank *n C* ***	/bæŋk/
disco *n C*	/ˈdɪskəʊ/
hospital *n C* ***	/ˈhɒspɪtl/
hotel *n C* ***	/həʊˈtel/
library *n C* ***	/ˈlaɪbrəri/
nightclub *n C*	/ˈnaɪtklʌb/
school *n C* ***	/skuːl/
shop *n C* ***	/ʃɒp/
shopping centre *n C*	/ˈʃɒpɪŋsentə/
stadium *n C*	/ˈsteɪdiəm/
town hall *n C*	/taʊn ˈhɔːl/

Describing a town/city

beautiful *adj* ***	/ˈbjuːtɪfl/
boring *adj* **	/ˈbɔːrɪŋ/
cheap *adj* ***	/tʃiːp/
cosmopolitan *adj*	/kɒzməˈpɒlɪtn/
dangerous *adj* ***	/ˈdeɪndʒərəs/
expensive *adj* ***	/ɪkˈspensɪv/
friendly *adj* **	/ˈfrendli/
historical *adj* **	/hɪsˈtɒrɪkl/
interesting *adj* ***	/ˈɪntrəstɪŋ/
modern *adj* ***	/ˈmɒdən/
noisy *adj* *	/ˈnɔɪzɪ/
polluted *adj*	/pəˈluːtɪd/
quiet *adj* ***	/ˈkwaɪjət/
safe *adj* ***	/seɪf/
ugly *adj* *	/ˈʌgli/
unfriendly *adj*	/ʌnˈfrendli/

go + -ing

go dancing	/gəʊ ˈdɑːnsɪŋ/
go diving	/gəʊ ˈdaɪvɪŋ/
go sightseeing	/gəʊ ˈsaɪtsiːɪŋ/
go shopping	/gəʊ ˈʃɒpɪŋ/
go swimming	/gəʊ ˈswɪmɪŋ/
go walking	/gəʊ ˈwɔːkɪŋ/

Size & colours

big *adj* ***	/bɪg/
dark *adj* ***	/dɑːk/
gold *adj*	/gəʊld/
large *adj* ***	/lɑːdʒ/
light *adj* ***	/laɪt/
silver *adj*	/ˈsɪlvə/
small *adj* ***	/smɔːl/
tiny *adj* **	/ˈtaɪni/

Other words & phrases

apartheid *n U*	/əˈpɑːtheɪt/
at least	
bizarre *adj*	/bɪˈzaː/
carry *v* ***	/ˈkæri/
dancefloor	
get dressed	
gun *n C* ***	/gʌn/
illegal *adj* **	/ɪˈliːgəl/
jewellery *n U* **	/ˈdʒuːəlri/
keyring *n C*	
lose *v* ***	/luːz/
offer *v* ***	/ˈɒfə/
permit *n C*	/ˈpəmɪt/
pig *n C* *	/pɪg/
quality *n C* ***	/ˈkwɒləti/
shark *n C*	/ʃɑːk/
shout *v* ***	/ʃaʊt/
skill *n C* ***	/skɪl/
snake *n C*	/sneɪk/
spa *n C*	/spɑː/
strange *adj* ***	/streɪndʒ/
teddy bear *n C*	/ˈtedi beə/
throw *v* ***	/θrəʊ/
towel *n C* *	/ˈtaʊəl/

11A | Working behind the scenes

VOCABULARY & SPEAKING: jobs

1 Complete the sentences.

> a doctor   a security guard
> an accountant   an actor
> a secretary   a waiter

What do you do?

1 I'm _____.

6 I'm _____.

2 I'm _____.

5 I'm _____.

4 I'm _____.

3 I'm _____.

2 🔘 **2.54** Listen to the recording to check your answers.

3 🔘 **2.55** Listen and <u>underline</u> the correct words.

1 I work *for / to* a big company.
2 I'm in charge *for / of* other people.
3 I work *in / to* a restaurant.
4 I work *in / at* home.
5 I work *with / to* the public.
6 I often work *on / in* a computer.

4 Work in pairs. Discuss these questions.

- What do you do?
- Do you like your work?
- Do you know people who do the jobs in exercise 1?
  Which job would you like to do?

PRONUNCIATION: /w/ /v/ & /b/

1 🔘 **2.56** Listen and say the words.

/w/	/v/	/b/
waiter	vet	builder
Will	Victoria	Bob
Washington	Vincent	Barbara
Wendy	vegetables	Brighton
working	vocabulary	bread
whisky	Vienna	beer

2 🔘 **2.57** Listen and read the text.

Will is a waiter. He lives in Washington. He likes working and whisky.

3 Make similar texts with other words from the box.

_____ is a _____. He/She lives in _____.

He/She likes _____ and _____.

LISTENING

1 Read the description of the television documentary show *Behind the Scenes*.

BEHIND THE SCENES

Every week, *Behind the Scenes* visits a big organization and talks to the people who do the invisible jobs, the work behind the scenes. This week, we visit a _____ in England and talk to a _____ and an _____.

2 🔘 2.58 Listen to the show and complete the description in exercise 1.

3 🔘 2.58 Listen again. Underline the correct words to complete the sentences.

1 Janet works with *two men / a man and a woman*.
2 Janet got the job *eleven / two* years ago.
3 Janet's father *likes / doesn't like* her job.
4 Michael works with *three people / two people* in the accounts department.
5 Michael got his job *ten years ago / last year*.
6 Michael thinks his job *is boring / isn't boring*.

4 Work in pairs. Discuss these questions.

• Do you know anybody who works in a hospital?
• What is his/her job?
• Does he/she work behind the scenes?

GRAMMAR: question review

Why, when, where, who, what and *how* are all question words.
We can combine *how* and *what* with other words to begin questions.
How + many/much/often/old …
What + time

Remember the word order with questions: (auxiliary) + subject + verb.

▶ SEE LANGUAGE REFERENCE PAGE 120

1 Look at the interviewer's questions from *Behind the Scenes*. Correct the mistakes in the questions.

1 What you do?
2 When did start you here?
3 What do other people thinks of your job?
4 You like your job?
5 Where you work in the hospital?
6 Why you do like your job?

2 Look at tapescript 2.58 on page 145 to check your answers.

3 Complete the questions about work with a question word from the box.

what	what	when	who	how many	why	where

1 _____ are you from?
2 _____ did you study at school?
3 _____ do you work with?
4 _____ did you start work today?
5 _____ did you do today at work?
6 _____ do you like your job?
7 _____ days do you work every week?

4 Work in pairs. Ask and answer the questions in exercise 3.

SPEAKING

1 Play Guess the job. Work in pairs, A and B.

A: Choose a job.
B: Ask questions and guess the job. Use the questions from grammar exercise 3 to help you.

2 Swap roles and repeat the activity.

DID YOU KNOW?

1 Read the text about the National Health Service.

The NHS (National Health Service) is a public health care service in Britain. It's free for all British people. In Britain, 11% of nurses are men, and 89% are women. 35% of new nurses and 25% of new doctors every year come from other countries. In a report in 2004, 75% of NHS workers said that it was difficult work, but they liked their jobs.

2 Work in pairs. Discuss these questions.

• Are hospitals in your country public or private?
• Are nurses usually women in your country?
• Do you know someone who works in another country? What do they do?

11B | The future of work

SPEAKING

1 Read the sentences and (circle) *I agree*/*I disagree*/*I don't know*.

1 It is normal to change jobs many times.
  I agree.   I disagree.   I don't know.

2 It is easy to get a job in my country.
  I agree.   I disagree.   I don't know.

3 Many people work at home in my country.
  I agree.   I disagree.   I don't know.

4 You must know how to use a computer to get a job.
  I agree.   I disagree.   I don't know.

2 Work in pairs. Compare your answers. Explain why you agree or disagree.

READING

1 Read the text. What is *Futurework*?

1 A book about the future of work in Britain.
2 A webpage about the best jobs in the future in Britain.
3 A magazine article about work and life in Britain.

2 Read the text again and decide if the sentences are true (T) or false (F).

1 *Futurework* is about the future of work around the world.
2 Lancaster wrote *Futurework* quickly.
3 Lancaster thinks that people will change jobs often.
4 Mobile phones will create more stress in the future.
5 Lancaster thinks that working at home is a good thing.
6 There are more old people in Britain now than in the past.
7 It will be important to know other languages to get a good job.

3 Work in pairs. Look at the predictions about work. Do you think these are true for your country? Discuss with your partner.

---

the future won't wait … will you?

In *Futurework*, author **Lee Lancaster** describes the world of work for the rest of the 21st century. Lancaster makes these predictions several years after investigation into jobs in Britain and around the world. Chapters include:

How many jobs? You won't have a permanent job for life in the future. People will change jobs many times during their lives. Part-time jobs will be more common than full-time jobs.

Work/life balance? With mobile phones, laptop computers, email and the internet it will be difficult to separate your job and your personal life. People will be more stressed.

Office in the living room? Working from home will be more popular in the future. That is good news and bad news. If your job is at home, where will you go for a day off?

A life of service? Britain's population is getting older, and the economy is changing. This means that more people will be employed in the service sector: shops, hospitals, centres for old people, hotels and restaurants.

Languages and jobs? How many languages do you speak? Yes, English will be a very important language in the future of work, but it won't be the only language. Many people in Britain only speak English at the moment. People who speak two or more languages will have better opportunities.

Other important skills for future jobs? Computers, the internet and communication skills. You need to know these important things if you want a good, well-paid job in the future.

'If you want to know what the future is, you must read Lancaster's work!'
Daily Sun Times

'Lancaster explains clearly and completely what the dangers of future work will be, and how we can prepare for them.'
Publisher's Circle

See also the website www.futurework.com

VOCABULARY: describing work

1 Find the opposites of these words in the text.

> part-time   badly-paid   temporary
> unemployed

2 Complete the sentences with a word from exercise 1.

1 There is a _____ job at the school. They are looking for a person to work from February to July.
2 She has a _____ job in the bank. She only works Tuesdays and Thursdays.
3 He hates his job. It's dirty, dangerous and _____. He never has any extra money.
4 I'm _____ at the moment. I can't find a job.

3 Work in pairs. Discuss these questions.

* What jobs are well-paid in your country? What jobs are badly-paid?
* Are many people in your country unemployed?
* Do students often have part-time jobs in your country?

GRAMMAR: predictions (*will*)

> Use *will* to talk about predictions in the future.
> Use *will* when we are certain something will happen in the future.
> The negative of *will* is *will not* (won't).
> *Part-time jobs* **will** *be more common than full-time jobs.*
> *You* **won't** *have a permanent job for life in the future.*
> *Where* **will** *you go for a day off?*

> ◗ SEE LANGUAGE REFERENCE PAGE 120

1 Complete the sentences with *will/will not* + the verb in brackets. Use contractions.

1 Public transport, like buses, _____ (*not use*) petrol. They _____ (*work*) on electricity.
2 A computer _____ (*control*) everything in your house: lights, fridge, television ...
3 Every car _____ (*have*) a computer with satellite technology.
4 There _____ (*be*) more problems with bad meat and people _____ (*be*) ill.
5 People _____ (*not cook*), they _____ (*buy*) prepared food.
6 People _____ (*not live*) in tall buildings, they _____ (*live*) underground.

2 Match the sentences in exercise 1 to the other books about life in the future in the box below.

> Futurelive   Futuredrive   Futureeat

3 ◉ 2.59 What is your future? Listen to the words and make sentences with *I'll* or *I won't.*

1 be rich   *I'll be rich.* or *I won't be rich.*

4 ◉ 2.59 Work in pairs. Listen to the recording again. Now make questions and answers.

1 be rich   *Will you be rich? Yes, I will. / No, I won't.*

SPEAKING

1 Do the My Future Working Life quiz.

My Future Working Life

In 10 years ...

1 I'll have (a) a good job (b) an OK job (c) no job.
2 I'll work (a) many hours (b) part-time (c) not many hours.
3 Work will be (a) the most important part (b) very important (c) not important in my life.
4 I'll work (a) close to home (b) far from home (c) at home.
5 (a) Some people (b) Lots of people (c) Nobody will work for me.
6 I'll be (a) happy (b) satisfied (c) unhappy with my job.
7 In my work (a) I'll travel to other countries (b) I'll travel inside my country (c) I won't travel.
8 I'll go to work (a) in the company limousine (b) in my own car (c) by bus.

2 Work in pairs. Tell your partner about your future working life. Who will have a better future?

SPEAKING & READING

1 Work in pairs. Complete the sentences.

1 If you want to be happy at work, you should …
2 If you want to live a long time, you shouldn't …
3 If you want to be happy when you're 60 years old, you should …

2 Compare with another pair in the class.

3 Read the magazine article '16 things to do before you're 60 years old'. Match the photos A–C with the correct paragraph.

16 *things to do before you're 60 years old*

Are you living your life as best as you can? Are you working to live, or living for your work? We have collected a list of 16 things that usually make people happier and healthier. It's time to take a look at your life critically. Which of these things do you do? Which are you going to do?

1 Take a break
Take a break from work to do something different: go back to school, try a different job or travel to a different country. Make plans now.

2 Say 'no'
It's difficult to say 'no' when someone asks you to do a job. If you say 'yes' to things that are impossible for you, then you will be unhappy, and more stressed.

3 Exercise
If you do more exercise, you feel better and look better.

4 Learn from your mistakes
When you make a mistake, see this as a chance to learn something new. Don't make the same mistake again and again.

5 Make things simple
People often have too many things. If you don't use it, or love it, then you don't need it!

6 Do some volunteer work
Help others and it helps you. Research shows that helping other people who need you makes you happier and live longer.

7 See the positive side
One American study showed that optimists live 7.5 years longer than pessimists. Happy people make friends more easily too.

8 Make a difference in society
If you can vote, then you should.

9 Sleep well
We sleep more than 30% of our lives. Experts say you should have a good bed and sleep between seven and eight hours every night.

10 Save money
It's never too late to save money, and it needn't be a lot. Start early!

11 Eat well
A healthy diet, with lots of fruit and vegetables, protects you from health problems.

12 Quit
If you smoke, today is the best day to stop. Your body notices the difference in 24 hours.

13 Check your teeth
Many people hate the dentist, but if you don't go you will regret it later. Make an appointment with the dentist twice a year for a healthy smile.

14 Laugh more
According to an American doctor, if you laugh more, you will be healthier. A good laugh is good exercise.

15 Drink water
Because water makes you healthier, more beautiful and more relaxed.

16 Don't worry!
Don't feel bad about all the things you can't do – enjoy what you can do!

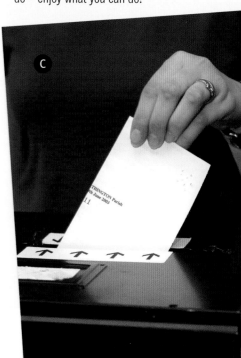

4 Read the article again. Which paragraphs talk about:

1 food and drink ___ ___   6 money ___
2 exercise ___   7 your teeth ___
3 feelings ___ ___   8 sleep ___
4 cigarettes ___   9 politics ___
5 school ___   10 work ___ ___ ___

5 Match the highlighted words to the definitions.

1 _____ work for no money
2 _____ to stop and relax for a short time
3 _____ to feel bad about something you did
4 _____ to stop doing something
5 _____ opportunity
6 _____ to put money in the bank for the future

6 Read the article again. Put a tick (✓) next to the things that you already do, or did in the past.

7 Work in pairs. Compare your lists. Which are the same?

VOCABULARY: collocations *make* & *do*

1 Find all the examples of *make* and *do* used as a main verb in the text. Underline them and the words that come after them.

2 Make sentences that are true for you using the words in the box.

I never I always I sometimes I usually	do make	my homework every night. friends easily. a good job when I'm motivated. mistakes in English. coffee in the morning. plans for the future.

LISTENING

1 🔘 **2.60** Five people talk about '16 things to do before you're 60'. Put a tick (✓) next to points in the article you hear.

2 🔘 **2.60** Listen again and match the sentences to the people - David, Sandra, Will, Ali, and Jarvis.

1 He's a student.
2 She's going to go to a gym next year.
3 Her husband is a pessimist.
4 He's going to live in France.
5 He plays football.

GRAMMAR: *going to*

> We use *be* + *going to* + infinitive to talk about plans in the future.
>
> Affirmative   *She's **going to go** to the gym next year.*
> Negative   *I'm **not going to stop** smoking.*
> Question   *What **are you going to do**?*

> ⟩ SEE LANGUAGE REFERENCE PAGE 120

1 Rearrange the words to make sentences.

1 to a is going buy David good bed .
2 going water drink she is to more .
3 in live country Will is not another going to .
4 stop smoking going to I'm .

2 Complete the reporter's questions to Jarvis about the trip he is going to make.

1 Where / go? *Where are you going to go?*
  To China.
2 Who / go with? _____
  My best friend, Charlie.
3 When / make this trip? _____
  In two years, when I finish my studies.
4 How / get there? _____
  By plane.
5 What / do? _____
  We're going to ride around the country on motorbikes.

3 Think of a trip you are going to make in the future. Make notes about the trip.

4 Work in pairs. Interview your partner about the trip. Use the questions in exercise 2.

PRONUNCIATION: /tə/

1 🔘 **2.61** Listen to the pronunciation of the word *to* in these sentences.

1 I'm going to drink more water.
2 I'm going to stop smoking.
3 What are you going to do?
4 Who are you going to go with?

2 Practise saying the sentences.

SPEAKING

1 Look at the list of '16 things to do before you're 60'. Make sentences about things you are going to do in the future and things you aren't going to do in the future

2 Work in pairs. Compare your lists. Are there other things you are going to do?

11D | Love and work

READING & SPEAKING

1 Look at the pictures and the heading of the webpage below. What is the webpage about?

2 Read the comments about 'Love and Work' on an internet discussion board. Which people think it's good and which people think it's bad?

Love and work.org

Love and work – a good idea?

1 My boss asked me out. It was terrible. I said no. I lost my job two weeks ago.

2 I met my wife at work. We were in the same office. We got married ten years ago. We are married now, and we still work together. It's great.

3 I think it's awful. I never go out with the people I work with. It's not professional.

4 I'm a teacher and my husband is a teacher. We get along very well, but we can't work at the same school. He has his work and I have mine. It's better that way.

5 I went out with a colleague for three months. Then we broke up. We don't talk now, but we still work together. I hate the situation, because everybody at work is talking about us.

6 I met my ex-husband when I was his secretary. We had a relationship and got married. Now we are divorced, and guess what? He's in a relationship with his new secretary!

---

3 Work in pairs. Discuss these questions.

* Is it good or bad to have a romantic relationship with a person you work with?
* Why or why not?

VOCABULARY: phrasal verbs

> **Language note**
>
> A phrasal verb is a combination of two or three words that you use like a verb. *Go out, take off, get up* are phrasal verbs.

1 Underline these phrasal verbs in the text.

> ask out   go out   break up   get along

2 Match the phrasal verbs from exercise 1 with the definitions.

1 to have a romantic relationship with
2 if people _____, they like each other and are friendly to each other
3 to end a romantic relationship
4 to invite someone to go somewhere because you want to start a romantic relationship with them

3 Complete the sentences with a verb from the box.

> ask   go   get   break

1 Older men ___ **out with** younger women.
   Younger men ___ **out with** older women.
2 The man ___ the woman **out**.
   The woman ___ the man **out**.
3 People ___ **up** by phone.
   People ___ **up** face to face.
4 People who like the same things ___ **along** well.
   People who like different things ___ **along** well.

4 Which of the sentences in exercise 3 is more common in your country?

LISTENING

1 🔘 **2.62** Listen to three conversations between the people in the pictures. Who invites who?

A

B

C

2 🔘 **2.62** Listen again and decide if the sentences are true (T) or false (F).

1
1 The tour finishes tomorrow.
2 The hotel manager doesn't want to have dinner with Valerie.

2
3 Dave invites Valerie for a drink.
4 Valerie doesn't want to have a drink with Dave.

3
5 Dave is a police officer.
6 Sam invites Dave to the police station.

FUNCTIONAL LANGUAGE: invitations

Invitations		
	go to the theatre	
Would you like to	*have dinner*	*(with me/us)?*
	come	

Responses

Yes,	*I'd love to.*
	that would be nice.

	I'm working/going shopping.
No,	*thanks/sorry. I can't.*
	I'm busy.

> SEE LANGUAGE REFERENCE PAGE 121

1 Correct the mistakes in the sentences.

1 Would you like have dinner with me tomorrow night?
2 No, I'm sorry. I busy.
3 Would you like to have a drink me?
4 Yes, I love to.
5 Do you like to come with us now to the police station?

2 Look at tapescript 2.62 on page 146 to check your answers.

SPEAKING

1 🔘 **2.63** Read and listen to the dialogue.

A: Hello.
B: Hi. How are you?
A: Fine, thanks.
   What are you doing?
B: Oh, nothing much.
A: Would you like to have a cup of tea with me?
B: Oh, yes. That would be nice.
A: I know a very good café near here.
B: Good. Let's go.

2 Work in pairs. Practise the dialogue.

3 Work in pairs. Choose one of the roles in the box. Prepare a similar dialogue.

The President of the United States and the president of your country.
Two students after class
Two famous film stars (you decide who)
Other (you decide the roles)

11 | Language reference

GRAMMAR

Question review

When, where, what, how, who and *why* are all question words. We use them to begin a question.

Remember these rules about questions in English.
We make questions with the verb *be* by putting the verb in front of the subject.

verb	subject	
Are	*you*	*a doctor?*
Where were	*you*	*yesterday?*

We make questions in the present simple and past simple with an auxiliary verb (*do/does/did*) and the infinitive. We put the auxiliary verb before the subject and we put the infinitive after the subject.

auxiliary	subject	infinitive	
Do	*you*	*work*	*at night?*
When did	*you*	*finish*	*today?*

Other verb forms (present continuous, *can*, *should*) already have an auxiliary verb and a main verb. We put the auxiliary verb before the subject and we put the infinitive after the subject.

auxiliary	subject	infinitive	
Can	*you*	*speak*	*English?*
What should	*he*	*do?*	

Will / won't

We use *will* to talk about predictions in the future.

Will is a modal auxiliary verb. This means:

- it goes with the infinitive without *to*.
- it has the same form for all subjects.
- the negative is with *not* (*n't*).
- to make a question, put *will* before the subject and the infinitive after the subject.

Affirmative & negative

I You He/She/It We They	will 'll / won't	have a job in ten years.

Question & short answer

Will	I you he she it we they	have a job in ten years?	Yes, No,	I you he she it we they	will. won't.

Going to future

Use *be* + *going to* + verb to talk about plans for the future.

She's going to go to the gym next year.

Affirmative

Full form			Contraction		
I am You are He/She/It is We are They are	going to	vote in the next election.	I'm You're He's/She's/It's We're They're	going to	do exercise.

Negative

Full form				Contraction		
I am You are He/She/It is We are They are	not	going to	learn another language.	I'm not You aren't He/She/It isn't We aren't They aren't	going to	learn another language.

Question & short answer

Am I Are you Is he/she/it Are we Are they	going to	visit England?	Yes, I am. No, I'm not. Yes, he/she/it is. No, he/she/it isn't. Yes, you/they/we are. No, you/they/we aren't.

120

FUNCTIONAL LANGUAGE

Invitations

Would you like to + verb (*with me/us*)?

Responses

Yes, I'd love to.
That would be nice.
No, thanks.
Sorry, I can't.
Sorry/Thanks, but I'm busy.

WORD LIST

Jobs

accountant *n C*	/əˈkaʊntənt/
actor *n C* ***	/ˈæktə/
builder *n C*	/ˈbɪldə/
doctor *n C* ***	/ˈdɒktə/
nurse *n C* **	/nɜːs/
secretary *n C* *	/ˈsekrətri/
security guard *n C*	
vet *n C*	/vet/
waiter *n C*	/ˈweɪtə/

Describing work

badly-paid *adj*	/ˈbædli peɪd/
employed *adj*	/ɪmˈplɔɪd/
full-time *adj*	/ˈfʊltaɪm/
part-time *adj*	/ˈpɑːtaɪm/
permanent *adj* **	/ˈpɜːmənənt/
temporary *adj* ***	/ˈtempərəri/
unemployed *adj* *	/ˌʌnɪmˈplɔɪd/
well-paid *adj*	

Collocations with *make* & *do*

do a good job
do homework
make a friend
make a mistake
make coffee
make plans

Phrasal verbs

ask out *v*
break up *v*
get along *v*
get up *v*
go out *v*

Other words & phrases

chance *n C* ***	/tʃɑːns/
chapter *n C* ***	/ˈtʃæptə/
invisible *adj*	/ɪnˈvɪz(ə)bl/
opportunity *n C* ***	/ˌɒpəˈtjuːnɪti/
public *adj* ***	/ˈpʌblɪk/
quit *v* *	/kwɪt/
regret *v* **	/rɪˈgret/
save (money) *v* ***	/seɪv/
volunteer work	

12A | Lifetime achievements

SPEAKING & VOCABULARY: music

1 Put the words into two groups.

> singer   rock   pop   musician   songwriter
> jazz   R&B   band   rap   folk   classical

People who make music	Kinds of music

2 What are these words in your language? Which ones are similar?

3 🔘 2.64 Listen to different kinds of music. What kind of music is each one? Do you like it?

4 Work in pairs. Discuss these questions.

- What kind of music do you listen to?
- Can you sing or play a musical instrument?
- Do you like going to concerts? What kind?

READING

1 You are going to read an article about the Grammy Awards. Look at the photos on the page. What do you think the Grammy Awards are?

2 Read the article. Look at the pictures A–D. Which person is not in the article?

3 Read the biographies again and answer the questions.

1 How many Lifetime Achievement Awards does the Grammy Foundation give every year?
2 Name two songs by Bob Dylan and two by Aretha Franklin.
3 Where are the Rolling Stones from?
4 Where have the Rolling Stones given concerts?
5 What is Aretha Franklin's other name?
6 Which musician has also won an Oscar?

4 Work in pairs. Discuss the questions.

- Do you know any of these singers or groups?
- What do you think of them?
- Do you like their music?

The Grammy Awards, or Grammys, started in 1959 and are held every year in New York or Los Angeles. They celebrate the best in the music business. Every year the Grammy Foundation gives a Lifetime
5 Achievement Award to individuals or groups who have made an important contribution to the music business. Here are some winners from the past.

The Rolling Stones
Rock and roll band from Britain.
Received the Grammy Lifetime Achievement Award in 1986.
10 They are the longest and most successful rock and roll band in history. They haven't stopped making music for more than 40 years. They have made over 35 albums and have had more than 50 top ten songs. They have given concerts on
15 every continent.

GRAMMAR: present perfect 1 – affirmative

> Use the present perfect to talk about general events or experiences in the past. When we use the present perfect, we don't talk about a specific time in the past.
>
> The present perfect uses *have/has* + past participle.
> He **has written** more than 450 songs.
> She **has won** 17 Grammys.

> SEE LANGUAGE REFERENCE PAGE 130

1 Underline all the examples of the present perfect affirmative in the article.

2 Make the past participles of these verbs.

make say write stop change give sing have win

3 Complete the text about another Grammy Award winner. Put the words in brackets into the present perfect.

Joni Mitchell
Born in 1943, Canada.
Received the Grammy Lifetime Achievement Award in 2002.
Joni Mitchell is one of the most important woman singers and songwriters of the twentieth century. She (1)_____ (make) 21 albums. The musicians Prince, Seal and Annie Lennox (of the Eurythmics) (2)_____ (say) that she was an influence on their music. Joni Mitchell (3)_____ (write) poetry and is famous for her work as a painter. She (4)_____ (win) many awards for her work.

Bob Dylan
Born in 1941, Minnesota, USA.
Received the Grammy Lifetime Achievement Award in 1991.
People have said that Bob Dylan is the greatest songwriter
20 ever. He has written more than 450 songs, including the hits 'Blowin' in the Wind', and 'Mr Tambourine Man'. He has won many Grammys and an Oscar for his work. Bob Dylan is also famous because he has changed musical styles many times.

25 *Aretha Franklin*
Born in 1942, Tennessee, USA.
Received the Grammy Lifetime Achievement Award in 1994.
Aretha Franklin is also called the 'Queen of Soul'. She has made more than 20 albums and has sung some of the most
30 famous R&B songs in history, including 'Respect', 'You Make Me Feel Like a Natural Woman' and 'I Never Loved a Man (The Way I Love You)'.

PRONUNCIATION: contractions

1 2.65 Listen to these contractions.

I have won an award.	I've won an award.
He has not won an award.	He hasn't won an award.
They have won an award.	They've won an award.

2 Say the sentences below with contractions.

1 We have not won an award.
2 He has written a song.
3 She has not changed musical style.
4 You have not won.
5 It has not been easy.
6 I have not said the truth.

3 2.66 Listen to the recording to check your answers. Say the sentences.

SPEAKING

1 2.67 Read and listen to a person talking about her favourite singer.

I think Robbie Williams should get a Lifetime Achievement Award. He has made some great CDs. He's written lots of songs. He's given concerts all round the world. He's been number one in many countries, and he has written a book. I think he's a great singer.

2 Work in pairs. Which musician or group from your country should get a Lifetime Achievement Award for their work? Why? Prepare your reasons. Look at exercise 1 for an example.

3 Work with another pair. Explain who should get the Lifetime Achievement Award.

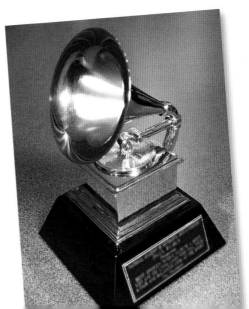

12B | A public life

SPEAKING

1 Work in pairs, A and B.

A: Choose one of the photos. Describe it to your partner.
B: Guess the picture. Swap roles and repeat.

2 Have you been in one of these situations? How did you feel?

I was on television. I didn't like it. I was very nervous.

I spoke at a friend's wedding. It was great.

LISTENING

1 in 4 Americans have been on television, study says

Number 1 dream: to be on television say young people

Psychologists say 'we are obsessed with public lives'

1 Look at the headlines. Do you think these statements are true for your country?

2 🔘 **2.68** Listen to someone doing a survey in Britain. Tick (✓) the words you hear.

television	camera	radio	game show	newspaper
a letter	the morning news		the evening news	

3 🔘 **2.68** Listen to the recording again and complete the table.

✓ Yes   ✗ No   ? doesn't say

	Speaker 1	Speaker 2	Speaker 3
been on TV	✗		
spoken on radio	✗		
written to newspaper	?		

GRAMMAR: present perfect 2 – questions & negative

Use the present perfect to ask about experiences in the past.
In questions in the present perfect, we can use *ever*. *Ever* usually means 'in your life'.

*Have you **ever** been on television?   Yes, I have.*
*Have you **ever** written to a newspaper?   No, I haven't.*

We can use *never* in negatives. *Never* = not ever.
*I've **never** been on television.*

*Have you **ever** been in the newspaper?   No, **never**.*

> SEE LANGUAGE REFERENCE PAGE 130

1 Complete the past participles. Then match them to the infinitives in the box.

be	write	have	hear	call	speak	see

1 b _ _ n   4 h_d   7 h_ _rd
2 sp_k_n   5 s _ _ n
3 c_ll_d   6 wr_tt_n

2 Complete the dialogue. Put the words in brackets into the present perfect.

Journalist: (1)_____ (*you ever be*) on television?
Martin: No, I haven't.
Journalist: (2)_____ (*you ever speak*) on the radio?
Martin: What do you mean?
Journalist: Well, (3)_____ (*you called*) a radio station?
Martin: Yes, I have.
Journalist: (4)_____ (*you ever have*) your photo in the newspaper?
Martin: Yes, I have. I (5)_____ (*write*) several letters to the newspaper. One time my photo was next to my letter. (6)_____ (*you hear*) of the *Daily Star*?
Journalist: No, I haven't. I (7)_____ (*never hear*) of it. I work for the *Weekly Times*.
Martin: I (8)_____ (*never see*) your newspaper.

3 🔘 **2.69** Work in pairs. Listen to the recording to check your answers. Practise the dialogue with a partner.

Pronunciation: irregular past participles

1 🔘 **2.70** Listen to the past participles.

/əʊ/	/ɪ/	/ʌ/	/eɪ/	/e/
known	given	won	made	read
spoken	driven	done	paid	met

2 Put the words in the correct column in exercise 1.

> broken   slept   come   written   taken

3 🔘 **2.71** Listen to the recording to check your answers. Say the words.

Speaking

1 Read the A Public Life questionnaire. Make the questions.

A Public Life
— Are you a **public** person or a **private** person?

Have you ever ...

be on television?	When?
speak in public?	Where?
call a radio programme?	When?
have your photo in the newspaper?	When?
write a letter to the newspaper?	When?
receive an award in public?	When?
sing in public?	When? What song?

2 Work in pairs. Ask and answer the questions from exercise 1. Answer *Yes, I have* or *No, I haven't*. If your partner answers *Yes, I have,* ask the next question (*Where? When?* etc).

A: *Have you ever been on television?*
B: *No, I haven't.*
A: *Have you ever spoken in public?*
B: *Yes, I have.*
A: *Where?*
B: *At school.*

3 Tell the rest of the class about the people you interviewed. Who has the most public life in the class?

Did you know?

1 Read the information about *Time* magazine.

The American magazine *Time* has a special issue every year called Person of the Year. *Time* chooses the Person of the Year as the individual or group of individuals who have had the biggest effect on the year's news. They have had very public lives.

Some of the people of the year for *Time* magazine have been:

Mohandas Gandhi, Indian leader (1930)
Adolf Hitler, German leader (1938)
Elizabeth II, Queen of England (1952)
Martin Luther King, American Civil Rights leader (1963)
Jeff Bezos, founder of Amazon (1999)

2 Work in pairs. Discuss these questions.

- Do you know the magazine *Time*? Is there a similar news magazine in your country?
- Think of some people who are on television or in the news a lot at the moment. Why are they in the news? Do they have a very public life?

12c | English in your life

SPEAKING

1 Work in pairs. When you are learning English, what is important? Read the sentences and choose three that are very important and three that aren't very important.

1 A good relationship with other people in the class.
2 A small class (not many students)
3 A comfortable classroom, with good chairs and desks for the students
4 Interesting lessons
5 A CD player and television in the classroom
6 A good teacher
7 A computer with internet for every student
8 Lots of homework

2 Compare your answers with another pair. What other things are important when you are learning English?

READING

1 Read the text. What kind of text is it?

- An advertisement brochure for a language school
- A newspaper article about a language school
- A story about people at a language school

2 Read the text again and answer the questions.

1 Who didn't feel relaxed when she came to the school?
2 Who likes speaking in class?
3 Who is going to take an important exam?
4 Who didn't learn English when he was younger?
5 Who says there aren't many students in the class?
6 Who comes to the school because it isn't expensive?
7 Who thought that English was difficult, but liked it?
8 Who makes a prediction about English in his country?

3 Work in pairs. Are you similar to one of these students? Discuss with a partner.

WHY LEARN ENGLISH WITH US? BECAUSE WE'RE THE BEST.

If you don't believe us, read what our students say.

I came to your school because I wanted to learn English. I thought English was difficult and boring work, only grammar, lots of vocabulary to memorise, etc. But then I saw that here you can also learn English with films, or songs. We also had computer classes on the internet. I didn't know any English when I started at your school, but one year later I knew a lot of English.
Doris

I have been at the International School of English for two years. I'm studying now for an important exam. I like this school because there are not many students in the class and the teacher gives us a lot of personal attention.
Kanda

I'm a student at your school. I speak a lot of English, but I don't practise outside of class, so I come here to the conversation classes. I'm learning lots of English expressions. The teachers at your school have helped me a lot. The classes are good, and they are cheaper than other schools. That's why I'm with the International School.
Monica

I haven't studied English before. When I was a child, we didn't study English at school. Now all the children in my country are learning English when they are very young. I'm studying English because I need it for my work. In the future, everybody in my country will speak English.
Constantine

When I had my first lesson at the International School of English, I was very nervous because I could not speak English very well. But I liked studying English because all the teachers were very friendly, and they always made students relax so we could understand the lessons. I'm going to come back next year.
Renata

If you want
English for school.   English for work.   English for fun.

Come to
International School of English.   **English ... in your life.**

GRAMMAR: verb forms (review)

SEE LANGUAGE REFERENCE PAGE 130

1 Find examples of the following verb forms in the text.

1 two different future verb forms
2 a present continuous
3 a present simple
4 a present simple in the negative
5 a past simple in the negative
6 an irregular past simple verb form
7 a regular past simple verb form
8 a present perfect

2 Complete the English in Your Life questionnaire. Put the words in brackets into the correct form of the verb.

ENGLISH IN YOUR LIFE

1 Why *are you learning* (you learn) English now?
2 How often _____ (you have) English classes?
3 How often _____ (you do) English homework?
4 Who _____ (be) your first English teacher?
5 When _____ (you start) studying English?
6 _____ (you ever see) a film in English?
7 _____ (you ever speak) on the phone in English?
8 _____ (you study) English next year?
9 _____ (you visit) an English-speaking country in the future?

3 Work in pairs. Ask and answer the questions in exercise 2.

SPEAKING

1 🔊 2.72 Listen to someone give a one-minute presentation in English. Tick (✓) the topic they are talking about.

Foods I like and don't like
Where I live
The capital city of my country
A typical day
A person that should win an award
A favourite thing
Learning a language

2 You are going to prepare a one-minute presentation in English. Choose a topic.

3 Prepare your presentation. Make notes of what you want to say in English.

4 Work in small groups. One person presents his/her topic.

• You must talk about your topic for one minute.
• You must talk only in English.
• You can look at your notes, but you mustn't read them.
• If you are not talking, you must listen to the speaker and think of one question to ask him/her after the presentation. Use the question words and phrases to help you.

Why?   When?
What happened next?
Where?
What did you think?
How often...?
How much/many...?

5 The others in the group ask the speaker one question. Answer the questions. Swap roles.

12D | The end

All good things must come to an end.

Every end is a new beginning.

SPEAKING

1 Translate the proverbs above into your own language. Are there any similar expressions in your language? What are they in English?

2 Work in pairs. Ask and answer these questions.

- How do you feel at the end of an exam?
- How do you feel at the end of the school year?
- How do you feel at the end of the weekend?
- How do you feel at the end of a holiday?

LISTENING

1 🔘 **2.73** It's the end of the Explore London tour. Listen to the recording. Match the five conversations 1–5 to the sentences a–e below.

a Hannah invites Sam. ____
b Valerie explains what happened with Dave. ____
c Rob and Meg ask how to get to the train station. ____
d Delilah asks permission to do something. ____
e Valerie says goodbye to the group. ____

2 🔘 **2.73** Listen to the recording again and answer the questions.

Conversation 1
1 Where was the Curtises' money?
2 What is Sam's job?

Conversation 2
3 Where is Brian going to take people?
4 What does Valerie want the people to write on the piece of paper?

Conversation 3
5 What does Delilah want to do?

Conversation 4
6 Does Rob want to take a taxi to the station?
7 How are Rob and Meg going to get to the station?

Conversation 5
8 Where does Mrs Curtis invite Sam?
9 Where is Sam going to work next month?

FUNCTIONAL LANGUAGE: thanking

Thanking	Responses
Thank you.	*You're w_ _ _ _ _ _.*
Thank you v_ _ _ much.	*Don't mention it.*
Thanks a l_ _.	*That's alr_ _ _ _.*
That's very kind of you.	

1 Look at tapescript 2.73 on page 146. Find all the examples of thanking and the responses. Complete the functional language box above.

2 Choose the correct response.

1 We've bought you a little gift.
 a) Oh, thank you.   b) You're welcome.

2 Thank you very much for dinner.
 a) You're welcome.   b) You're alright.

3 Here, you can have my pen.
 a) You're welcome.   b) Thanks.

4 Thank you very much for everything you've done.
 a) Sorry.   b) Don't mention it.

5 Excuse me. You left your wallet in the shop.
 a) Thank you very much.   b) Not at all.

3 🔘 **2.74** Listen to the recording to check your answers. Practise the dialogues.

4 Work in pairs. Prepare two similar dialogues and practise them with your partner.

SPEAKING

1 Work in groups of three or four. Turn to page 139. Read the instructions and play the travel game on page 129.

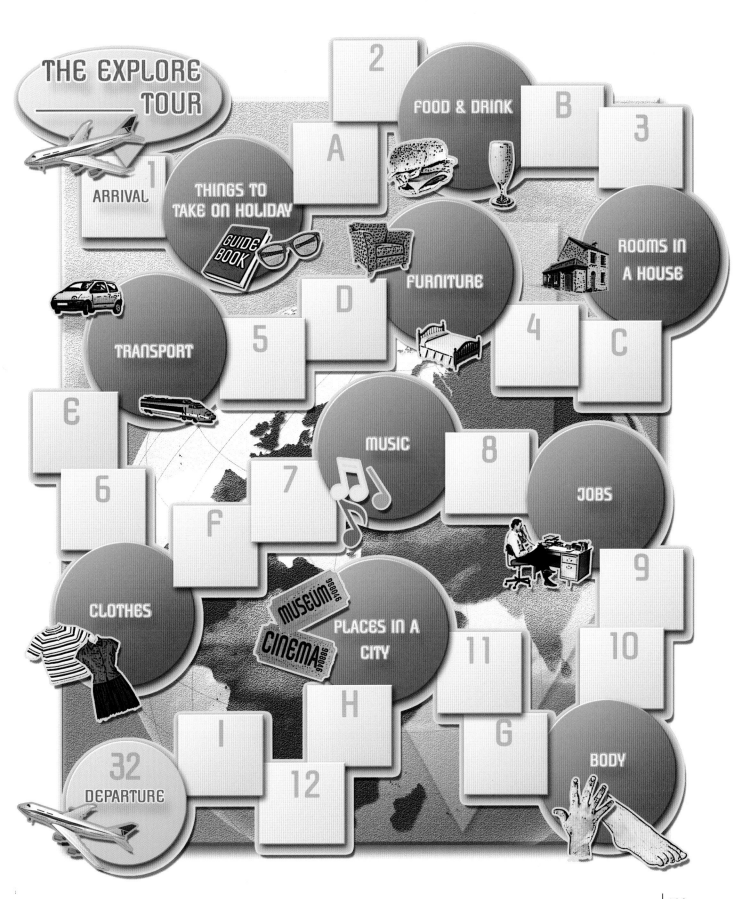

THE EXPLORE _____ TOUR

1 ARRIVAL

THINGS TO TAKE ON HOLIDAY

2

FOOD & DRINK

B

3

A

ROOMS IN A HOUSE

FURNITURE

TRANSPORT

D

5

4

C

E

MUSIC

8

JOBS

6

7

F

9

CLOTHES

PLACES IN A CITY

11

10

I

H

G

BODY

32 DEPARTURE

12

Grammar

Present perfect

Use the present perfect to talk about events that happened in the past when we don't say a specific time.

The present perfect is formed with the auxiliary *have/has* + past participle.

> He **has won** an award.
> They **have made** 35 albums.

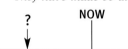

He's been to London.

There are two kinds of past participle in English:

- regular (ends in –ed) *visited, received, opened*
- irregular (different form) *spoken, eaten, met*

See page 159 for a list of irregular past participles.

Affirmative

Full form			Contraction	
I have You have He has She has It has We have They have	been to London.		I've You've He's She's It's We've They've	been to London.

Negative

I haven't You haven't He hasn't She hasn't It hasn't We haven't They haven't	(ever)	won an award.

In the negative, we can use *not* + *ever*.

> I **haven't ever won** an award.

We can also use *never* to make a negative sentence. *Never* = *not ever*.

> I **have never won** an award.
> I **have never heard** him speak.

Use the present perfect to ask about experiences in the past. We can use *ever* in questions. *Ever* usually means 'in your life'.

Question

Have I Have you Has he Has she Have we Have they	(ever)	spoken in public?

Short answer

Yes,	I have. you have. he/she/it has. we have. they have.
No,	I haven't. you haven't. he/she/it hasn't. we haven't. they haven't.

Verb forms review

Tense	Affirmative	Negative	Question	Short answer	Use
Present simple	I live in Spain.	He doesn't work here.	Do you like chocolate?	Yes, I do. No, they don't.	routines habits facts
Past simple	They took the bus.	We didn't go to class.	Did you study for the exam?	Yes, he did. No, I didn't.	events in the past
Present continuous	He is working at home.	I'm not working at the moment.	Are they playing football?	Yes, they are. No, he isn't.	actions happening now
Future (going to)	We are going to see a film.	He isn't going to have a holiday.	Are you going to stop?	Yes, I am. No, they aren't.	future plans
Future (will)	He will get married.	They won't have a job.	Will I work at home?	Yes, you will. No, we won't.	future predictions
Present perfect	They've sung in many countries.	She hasn't won a Grammy Award.	Have you ever spoken in public?	Yes, I have. No, I haven't.	experiences unspecified past

FUNCTIONAL LANGUAGE

Thanking

Thank you.
Thank you very much.
Thanks a lot.

That's very kind of you.

Responses

You're welcome.
Don't mention it.
That's alright.

WORD LIST

Music

band *n C* ***	/bænd/
classical (music) *n U*	/ˈklæsɪkl/
folk (music) *n U*	/fəʊk/
jazz *n U*	/dʒæz/
musician *n C* *	/mjuˈzɪʃn/
pop (music) *n U* *	/pɒp/
R&B *n U*	/ˌɑː(r)nˈbiː/
rap *n U*	/ræp/
rock (music) *n U* ***	/rɒk/
singer *n C*	/ˈsɪŋə/
song *n C* ***	/sɒŋ/
songwriter *n C*	/ˈsɒŋraɪtə/

Media

camera *n C* ***	/ˈkæm(ə)rə/
game show *n C*	/ˈɡeɪm ʃəʊ/
journalist *n C* **	/ˈdʒɜːnəlɪst/
newspaper *n C* ***	/ˈnjuːspeɪpə/
radio *n C* ***	/ˈreɪdiəʊ/
the (morning/evening) news *n U* ***	/ðə ˈnjuːz/

Other words & phrases

achievement *n C* **	/əˈtʃiːvmənt/
award *n C* **	/əˈwɔːd/
beginning *n C* ***	/bɪˈɡɪnɪŋ/
brochure *n C*	/ˈbrəʊʃə/
choose *v* ***	/tʃuːz/
lifetime *n C*	/ˈlaɪftaɪm/
memorize *v*	/ˈmeməraɪz/

Communication activities

2D Speaking exercise 1 page 29

Student A

Describe your pictures to your partner. Decide if the pictures are the same or different.

In my picture 1, Elvis is young. He's thin and has short hair.

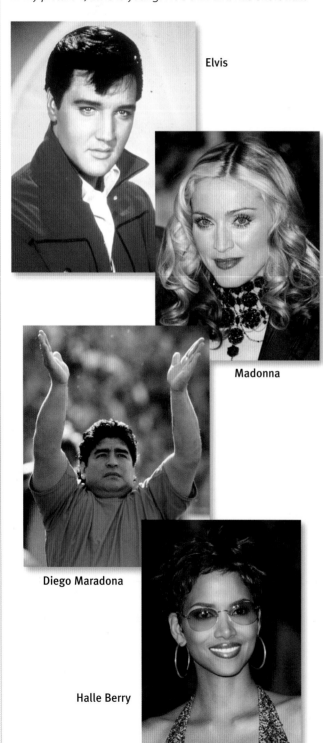

Elvis

Madonna

Diego Maradona

Halle Berry

3C Speaking exercise 1 page 37

Student A

Look at the picture of the room. Ask your partner questions. Find six differences in your pictures.

Ask questions.
Are there any ...?
How many ... are there?
Is there a ...?

5D Functional language exercise 3 page 59

Student A

You are a guest at the Stratford Central Hotel. You are at reception. You want:

* to connect your laptop computer to the internet in your room
* to leave your passport and money at reception
* to change rooms (you want a room with a view)
* to pay the bill with your Visa card

Ask your partner.

4A Speaking exercise 1 page 43

Student A

Interview your partner. Ask questions about these activities.

What time / get up? *What time do you get up?*
have breakfast? *Do you have breakfast?*
What time / go to work or classes?
get the bus or train?
have coffee?
What time / have lunch?
have a nap?
What time / get home?

Answer your partner's questions. Ask: *What about you?*

10B Speaking exercise 1 page 105

Student A

You have a new job. You can live in the capital city or a smaller city. Discuss your choice with students B and C.

At the end of the roleplay, choose which city you would like to live in.

9B Speaking exercise 3 page 95

Student A

Teach your partner how to do this exercise.

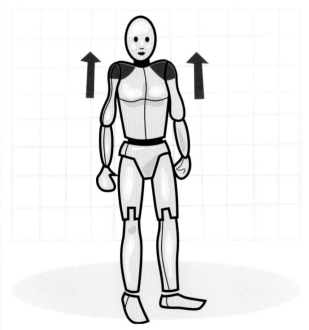

Hold: five seconds   Repeat: three times (x 3)

Do you know any other exercises like this? What are they? Tell your partner.

7B Speaking exercise 1 page 75

Student A

Look at the photo. Find six differences with your partner's photo. Ask questions.

Do you have any rice? How much rice do you have?

8C Speaking exercise 1 page 87

Student B

Listen to what Phil usually does. Answer your partner's questions about what Phil is doing today.

Phil's having cake for breakfast.

Today
(have) cake for breakfast
(take) a taxi
(go) to the cinema
(eat) in a restaurant
(go) to a birthday party

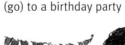

Tell your partner what Sarah does every Saturday. Find out what Sarah is doing today.

Sarah wakes up early on Saturday. What is she doing today?

Every Saturday
(wake up) late
(have) breakfast
(do) the shopping
(go) for a walk in the park
(watch) TV in the afternoon
Guess why Sarah is doing different things.

5A Grammar exercise 2 page 53

Student A

Read the example and then use the pictures to interview your partner.

swim
cook
drive
play tennis

Can you play football?   *Yes, I can. /No, I can't.*
How well?   *Very well.*

> ### Useful language
>
> *Very well.* 😊 😊
> *Quite well.* 😐
> *Not very well.* 🙁

8A Grammar exercise 4 page 83

Student A

Read the example and use the pictures to interview your partner.

Do you like doing the dishes?
Yes, I do. I love it. /No, I don't. I hate it.

2C Vocabulary exercise 2 page 27

Student A

Look at Emily's family tree.
Ask questions about the people.
Who is Ian?
He's Emily's grandfather.

Answer B's questions.
Who is Liz?
She's Emily's grandmother.

7B Speaking exercise 1 page 75

Student B

Look at the photo. Find six differences with your partner's photo. Ask questions.

Do you have any eggs? How many eggs do you have?

9C Speaking exercise 1 page 97

Ask questions about the objects and their owners.

Whose dog is this?   *It's theirs.*
Whose sunglasses are these?   *They're his.*

Who has the better memory?

Ian (_____) = Liz (grandmother)

Laura (aunt) = Roger (_____)   Jack (father) = Doris (_____)

Nathan (_____) = *Emily*   Andy (_____)

Robbie (son)   Kylie (_____)

2D Speaking exercise 1 page 29
Student B

Describe your pictures to your partner. Decide if the pictures are the same or different.

In my picture 1, Elvis is middle-aged. He's fat and has long hair.

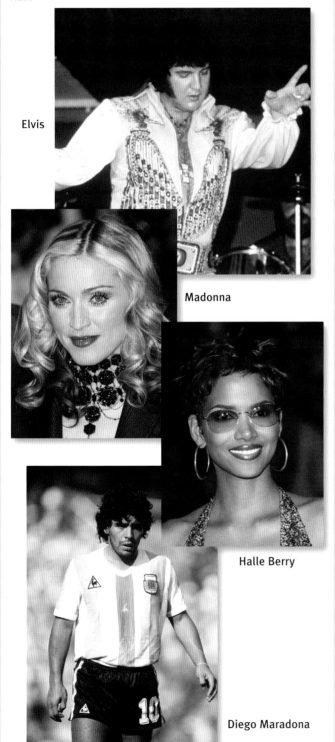

Elvis

Madonna

Halle Berry

Diego Maradona

6B Vocabulary & speaking exercise 4 page 64
Student B

Interview your partner about books and reading. Ask these questions.

Do you read a lot?
What was the last book you read? What was it about?
How many books do you read every year?
Who are the most famous authors from your country?

9B Speaking exercise 3 page 95
Student B

Teach your partner how to do this exercise.

Hold: five seconds.   Repeat: twice (x 2)

Do you know any other exercises like this? What are they? Tell your partner.

10B Speaking exercise 1 page 105
Student C

Student A has a new job. He/She can live in the capital city or a smaller city. You think Student A should live in a smaller city, not the capital. Here are some reasons why you think the smaller city is a better choice:
- it's safer in a smaller city
- traffic in the capital is worse
- people in the smaller cities are friendlier

Think of other reasons.

I think you should choose …. because …

2c Vocabulary exercise 2 page 27
Student B

Look at Emily's family tree.
Ask questions about the people.
Who is Liz?
She's Emily's grandmother.

Answer A's questions.
Who is Ian?
He's Emily's grandfather.

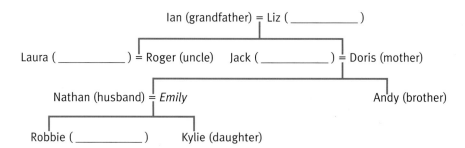

Ian (grandfather) = Liz (_____)

Laura (_____) = Roger (uncle)   Jack (_____) = Doris (mother)

Nathan (husband) = *Emily*   Andy (brother)

Robbie (_____)   Kylie (daughter)

3c Speaking exercise 1 page 37
Student B

Look at the picture of the room. Ask your partner questions. Find six differences in your pictures.

Ask questions.
Are there any ...?
How many ... are there?
Is there a ...?

4A Speaking exercise 1 page 43
Student B

Answer your partner's questions. Ask: *What about you?*
Interview your partner. Ask questions about these activities.

What time / wake up?   *What time do you wake up?*
have a shower in the morning?   *Do you have a shower in the morning?*
What time / get to work or classes?
have a break?
have meetings?
What time / go home?
What time / have dinner?
What time / go to sleep?

5A Grammar exercise 2 page 53
Student B

Read the example and then use the pictures to interview your partner.

play chess   type   draw   sing

Can you play football?   *Yes, I can. /No, I can't.*
How well?   *Very well.*

> ### Useful language
>
> *Very well.* ☺ ☺
> *Quite well.* 😐
> *Not very well.* 😞

8A Grammar exercise 4 page 83
Student B

Read the example and use the pictures to interview your partner.

Do you like doing the dishes?
Yes, I do. I love it. /No, I don't. I hate it.

8c Speaking exercise 1 page 87

Student A

Tell your partner what Phil usually does. Find out what Phil is doing today.

Phil usually takes the bus. What is he doing today?

Usually
(have) bread and coffee for breakfast
(take) the bus
(go) to work
(eat) at home
(go) to English class in the evening

Guess why Phil is doing different things.

Listen to what Sarah usually does. Answer your partner's questions about what Sarah is doing today.

Sarah's waking up early.

Today
(wake up) early
(not have) breakfast
(go) to the hairdresser
(take) a limousine
(go) to the church

BASICS 1 Numbers 1 – 10 page 6

Student A

Look at the numbers on the page. Say a number to your partner.

Student B

Listen to your partner. Point to the number your partner says.

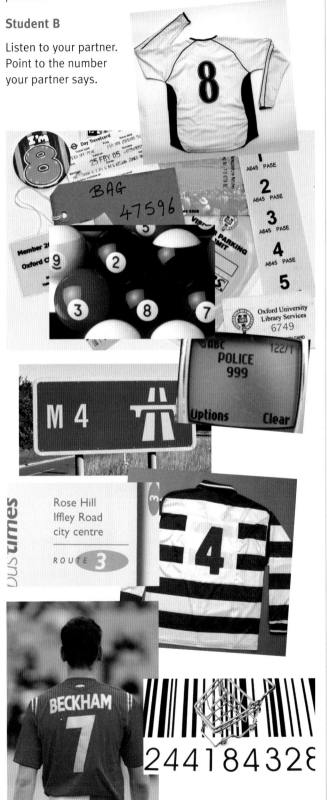

5D Functional language exercise 3 page 59

Student B

You are the receptionist at the Stratford Central Hotel. Here is information to help you with A's questions:

- the internet connection doesn't work at the moment
- there is a safe at reception for guests. It is £3 a day.
- there are no rooms with a view available this week
- the hotel accepts all credit cards

10B Speaking exercise 1 page 105

Student B

Student A has a new job. He/She can live in the capital city or a smaller city. You think student A should live in the capital city. Here are some reasons why you think the capital city is a better choice:

- the nightlife is more exciting
- the shops are better (there are more shops, and better quality)
- the people in the capital are more interesting

Think of other reasons.

I think you should choose …. because …

6B Vocabulary & speaking exercise 4 page 64

Student A

Interview your partner about the cinema. Ask these questions.

Do you often go to the cinema? How often do you go?
How often do you watch videos/DVDs?
What film would you like to see at the moment?
Who are your favourite actors/actresses?

INSTRUCTIONS

- Play the game in groups of three or four. You will need a dice and some counters.
- In the game, you are all on a tour. Decide what country you are touring and write it next to the plane.
- Place your counters on the square marked ARRIVAL (square 1).
- The first player to throw a six starts the game.
- The first player throws the dice and moves their counter according to the number on the dice.
- When a player lands on a letter square, they must talk about the subject for 30 seconds. Look at the 'Talk about' subjects on this page.
- When a player lands on a number square, they must roleplay the situation with other people in the group. Look at the roleplays on this page.
- When a player lands on a red circle, they must say as many English words in that category as they can in 30 seconds.
- The game continues until the first player reaches the circle marked DEPARTURE.

MINI ROLEPLAYS

1 You meet other tourists. Introduce yourself.
2 You are at a party. Offer the others food or drink.
3 Spell your first and last name for the hotel receptionist.
4 Give directions to the men's/women's toilets.
5 Phone the others in the group. Tell them that the museum visit is cancelled.
6 Ask permission to take a photograph.
7 Order something to eat.
8 You have the afternoon free. Make suggestions.
9 The bus is moving too quickly and you don't feel well. Tell the others.
10 Buy some souvenirs.
11 Thank the others for a nice tour.
12 Say goodbye.

TALK ABOUT

a Talk about a friend or someone from your family.
b Talk about an ugly/beautiful/interesting building that you know.
c Talk about an important public holiday in your country.
d Talk about the weather in the country you are visiting.
e Talk about an actor/director/singer you like.
f Talk about things to see in the country you are visiting.
g Talk about the last time you went on a plane/train/boat.
h Talk about the most interesting/ugliest/most expensive souvenir you have.
i Talk about your job or school.

Tapescripts

Introductions 1 exercise 3
 1.6

1   C = computer A = astronaut
C: Hello.
A: Hi.
C: What's your name?
A: My name's John.
C: Nice to meet you, John.
A: Nice to meet you.

2   SC = ship's captain C = castaway
SC: Hello.
C: Hello.
SC: What's your name?
C: My name's Robinson.
SC: Nice to meet you.
C: Nice to meet you.

BASICS 2 Days of the week exercise 3
1.16

1
A: What day is it today?
B: It's Monday.
A: I thought so.

2
A: When is English class?
B: It's on Thursday this week.
A: OK.

3
A: Do you want to go out this Saturday?
B: *This* Saturday?
A: Yes.

4
A: So, what did you do last Saturday?
B: Nothing much. And you?
A: No. Nothing.

5
A: Hello, class. What day is it today?
B: It's Friday!
A: Yes, Friday.

1A Vocabulary exercise 3   1.24

M: Hello.
A: Hi. My name's Alyssa.
M: Yes. I know. I'm Margaret.
A: Nice to meet you.
M: You're new, so I'll explain. This is our desk.
A: Great.
M: This is your computer.
A: Yes.
M: And this is my computer. Don't touch.
A: OK. I understand.
M: This is my phone. You don't have a phone.
A: And this?
M: Your paper. This is my paper. And this is my cup. And that's it.
A: OK. Thank you.

1B Vocabulary exercise 4   1.25

Russian, British, Chinese, Greek
Brazilian, Polish, Japanese, French
German, Turkish
Italian, Irish

1B Listening exercises 2 & 3   1.26

R = receptionist M = Mark
R: Good afternoon. Language Link.
M: Hi. I would like to register for Language Link, please.
R: Of course. What's your name?
M: My name's Mark.
R: What's your last name?
M: Richards.
R: How do you spell that?
M: R-I-C-H-A-R-D-S.
R: Thank you. Are you a language teacher?

M: No, I'm not.
R: Are you a language student?
M: Yes, I am.
R: What is your language of study?
M: I'm a German student.
R: German …. OK. We have lots of German students for you on Language Link.
M: Great.
R: How old are you?
M: Um, I'm 26 years old.
R: Twenty … six. Good. Where are you from?
M: I'm from Sydney.
R: Are you Australian?
M: Yes, I am.
R: I love Australia. Nicole Kidman is my favourite actress.
M: Where are you from?
R: Me? I'm from London. OK, what's your email address?
M: Mark at mail dot com.
R: Thank you.

1C Listening exercise 2   1.28

1   It's an umbrella.
2   It's a mobile phone.
3   They're keys.
4   It's an alarm clock.
5   It's a bottle of water.
6   They're pens.
7   It's a camera.
8   They're glasses.
9   It's a newspaper.
10 It's a book.

1C Listening exercise 1   1.29

M = man W = woman
1
M: What's this?
W: It's my book. My private book.
M: OK. OK. Relax.

2
M: Wait a minute, is that a camera?
M 2: Err…yes. Just one photo please Mr Pott.
M: No cameras! No cameras!

3
M: Excuse me.
W: Yes?
M: I think these are your keys.
W: Yes, they are! Thank you.
M: You're welcome.

4
W: Is that the alarm clock, James?
Man: No, that's my mobile phone.
Hello?
Man: Hello, Mister Pond.

5
W: Are those your glasses?
M: Huh? What? Where?
W: Oh, David! Those are your glasses.
M: Oh nooooo.

1D Listening exercises 1 & 2   1.31

1 R = Rob M = Meg Re = receptionist
Re: Good afternoon.
R: Good afternoon. We have a reservation.
Re: What's your name?
R: Rob and Meg Sherman.
Re: How do you spell that?
R: S H E R M A N
Re: Sherman, yes. Are you with the tour?
M: Yes we are.
Re: Room 34. These are your keys.
M/R: Thank you.

2 He = Herb Ha = Hannah Wr = waiter
He: Is this the bar?
Ha: Yes, sweetheart, I think it is. Look … BAR.

He: It's very English!
Ha: I know!
Wr: Good afternoon. Would you like a drink?
He: Yes, please. A beer.
Ha: Tea, please.
He: Well, darling. We're here. We're in London. Listen to that. That's London.
Ha: Wonderful.
Wr: Tea?
Ha: Here.
He: Beer over here. Thanks.
Wr: You're welcome.

3 S = Sam V = Valerie Re = receptionist
Re: And these are your keys, Mr Moore.
S: Thank you.
V: Hello, are you Sam Moore?
S: Yes, I am.
V: Hi. My name's Valerie. I'm the tour guide for your tour.
S: Oh, hello. Nice to meet you.
V: Nice to meet you. Would you like a drink? Our welcome party is in the bar.
S: No, thank you. I'm tired, and I'll just go to my room.
V: Really? OK then. See you tomorrow.
S: Thank you again. Goodbye.

4 S = Sam Vo = voice
S: Hello?
Vo: Hello, Sam. Where are you?
S: In the hotel.
Vo: Are you in the bar?
S: No, I'm not. I'm in my room.
Vo: Is he in the hotel now?
S: No, he isn't. Not at the moment.
Vo: Stay in contact.
S: Alright.

5 He = Herb Curtis Ha = Hannah Curtis
   V = Valerie R = Rob M = Meg
V: Hello! My name's Valerie.
He: Well, hi Valerie! I'm Herb Curtis. This is my wife, Hannah.
V: Nice to meet you.
Ha: Nice to meet you.
V: This is Rob, and Meg. They're on your tour.
R: Hello.
He: Where are you from Rob?
R: We're Australian.
Ha: Australia! Wow!
He: Hannah and I are from Dallas, Texas.
Ha: That's in the United States of America.

6 V = Valerie R = Rob M = Meg
V: Would you like a drink, Rob?
R: Yes, please, coffee.
V: Meg? Would you like a drink?
M: Yes, please. A mineral water, please.

2A Listening exercises 1 & 2   1.36

My name's David MacKinnon, that's M-A-C-K-I-N-N-O-N. I'm from Scotland but now I live in Istanbul. My life is very different here. I live in a flat, not a house. I only eat Turkish food now. I still read English newspapers, and I have the BBC on the internet in my flat. Oh yeah, I go to football matches here in Istanbul. That's different, because in Scotland I don't like football! I work at a university. I'm an English teacher. I speak Turkish, because I have a Turkish girlfriend! I really like it here, it's great.

2B Listening exercises 2 & 3   1.37

I = interviewer
P = Dr Palmer
I: What about women? Do women talk about sports?
P: No, no, they don't. Not like men. Women friends are more personal. They talk more

about personal things. They talk about their feelings.

I: What other things are different?
P: Well, women listen to their friends a lot more.
I: Really?
P: Yes. That's why women know more about their friends.
I: Do men know a lot about their friends?
P: No, they don't. Ask a man what he knows about his friends and he can say 'My friend likes this music, and this sport, and this football team, and this kind of woman ...' but after that, not much.
I: Very interesting. What about you, Doctor? Do you have a lot of friends?
P: No, I don't. I have one or two friends.
I: Do you play sports with your friends?
P: No, no, I don't. I'm seventy years old. But we talk about movies, and politics ...
I: Thank you, Dr Palmer.
P: You're welcome.

2B Grammar exercise 2 1.38

I = Interviewer T = Tom J = Jane

I: Do you have a lot of friends?
T: No, I don't. Not really. I have one good friend at the sports club, Tony.
I: The article says men do activities together. Do you play sports with your friends?
T: Yes, I do. Tony and I play tennis. Sometimes we watch the football together, but that's always at the sports club.
I: Do you talk about personal things, feelings, with your friends?
T: No, I don't. We don't talk a lot. If we do, we talk about sports.
I: Do you have women friends?
T: No, I don't. My wife wouldn't like it I think, if I had women friends.

I: Do you have a lot of friends?
J: Yes, I do. I have a lot of friends, yes.
I: Do you talk about personal things?
J: Yes, we do. We talk about problems, love life, things like that.
I: Do you do things together?
J: Yes, we do. Of course. But not typical things like shopping if that's what you mean. We go out for a drink, or to a disco.
I: Do you have men friends?
J: Yes, I do! A lot of my friends are men friends. They talk about all their problems to me.

2D Listening exercises 2 & 3 1.44

V = Valerie B = Brian D = David

B: Hello?
V: Hi, Brian? It's Valerie. Are you at the airport?
B: Yes, I am.
V: I'm sorry I'm not there. Is the plane from New Zealand there?
B: Yes, it is. Who's on the plane?
V: You have to meet two women, Delilah Williams and Patti Owen.
B: Fine. Delilah and Patti. What do they look like?
V: Hold on, I have their photos here. OK, Delilah is short and pretty. She has long dark hair.
B: How old is she?
V: Around 30.
B: OK. And Patti?
V: Patti's also around 30 years old. They're friends. Patti's tall. She has fair hair.
B: Hello? Hello?
V: Hello?
B: Hi, it's Brian again. Sorry about that, my mobile phone. OK, Patti and Delilah. Who else?
V: There's also Dave.
B: Dave?
V: Yes, Dave Matthews. He's on the plane from Canada.
B: OK, what does he look like?
V: He's around 25. He's a little fat, he has dark

hair. Oh, he has glasses.
B: OK. Wait a minute. I think I see Dave now.
V: Great. Call me when you meet everyone.
B: Sure. Bye. Excuse me. Are you Dave Matthews?
D: Yes, I am. Hi!

3B Listening exercises 2 & 3 1.47

O = official V = visitor

V: What is the name of the house?
O: There are at least four names for the house at 1600 Pennsylvania Avenue, including the President's Palace, the President's House and the Executive Mansion. But this famous building's common name is the White House.
V: Where is it?
O: The White House is in the centre of Washington, DC, the capital of the United States of America.
V: Who lives there?
O: The President of the United States and his family officially live in the White House. But there are hundreds of people who work there, and there are thousands of visitors every day.
V: How old is it?
O: The White House was built in 1800. It's now more than 200 years old.
V: How many rooms are there?
O: There are 132 rooms in the White House. There are 16 family bedrooms, 3 kitchens and 32 bathrooms. There are also 6 floors, 7 staircases, 3 elevators, 147 windows and 412 doors. There is a games room, a mini golf course, a tennis court, two swimming pools, a bowling alley and even a small cinema.
V: Are there public visits?
O: Yes, there are. Public visits are available for groups of 10 people or more from Tuesday to Saturday, from 7:30 am to 12:30 pm. Please note that there aren't any public telephones or public bathrooms on the tour of the White House.

3B Vocabulary exercise 2 1.49

M = man W = woman

1
M: So, come in, come in.
W: Wow. So this is your new flat.
M: Yeah. Look, this is the hall. These are my pictures, here and here.
W: Mmmm.
2
M: The bedroom.
W: Nice and big.
M: Yes. Look out the window. You can see the park...
W: Ooohh.
3
W: What's this room?
M: It's the dining room. I don't go in here really, there's only me.
4
W: Is this living room?
M: Yes, I'm here a lot of the time.
W: I like your TV.
M: Thanks.
5
M: Would you like a drink?
W: Umm, yes please. What do you have?
M: Come into the kitchen. Let's see.
6
W: Where's the bathroom?
M: Next to you. Right there.
W: I see.
7
W: Look at this balcony. You have a nice flat.
M: Thanks, it's not exactly the White House, but it's home.

3C Vocabulary exercise 4 1.51

L = landlord S = Shelly C = Claudia

L: OK, this is the flat. Bedroom here ... and here. The beds are a little old.
S/C: Oh.
L: Here's the living room. You have a window, a sofa and a TV. The TV's Japanese. It's in good condition. It's my mother's TV.
S: That TV isn't new.
L: The kitchen. I know it's dirty, but look – the cooker works perfectly, and the fridge too. Look, oh ... a sandwich. What's that doing there?
C: Yuk.
L: Anyway, it's 50 pounds per week. Do you want it or not?
C: Ummm.
S: Yes, we do, thank you.

3D Listening exercises 3 & 4 1.55

I = information desk V = Valerie D = Dave
S = Sam W = woman

I: Can I help you?
V: Yes. Where is the café?
I: It's on the second floor. Go up the stairs and turn right.
V: Is there a lift?
I: Yes, there is. It's behind you.
V: Oh, yes. Thank you.

D: Excuse me. Where are the toilets?
I: Sorry?
D: The men's toilets.
I: The toilets? They're over there. They're on the left, next to the lift.
D: Where?
I: Look, the brown doors.
D: Great.

S: Is there a public telephone here?
I: Yes there is. It's next to the stairs. It's on the right.
S: Thank you.
I: You need a card.
S: What?
I: You need a card. It doesn't accept coins.

W: Is there a baby changing room?
I: Sorry?
W: A baby changing room. I need to change the baby.
I: Yes, go down these stairs here. Then turn left and go along the hall. It's next to the women's toilets.
W: Thank you. Shhhhh.

3D Functional language exercise 2 1.56

1 Where is the café?
2 It's on the second floor. Go up the stairs and turn right.
3 Where are the men's toilets?
4 They're over there. They're on the left, next to the lift.
5 It's next to the stairs. It's on the right.
6 Go down these stairs here. Then turn left and go along the hall.

4A Functional language exercise 2 1.57

W = Will M = man Wo = woman

1
W: Excuse me, what time is it please?
M: It's five past twelve.
W: Thanks.
2
Wo: Excuse me, hello? What's the time, please?
W: I'm sorry, I don't know. I don't have a watch.
Wo: Oh, OK.

3
W: What time is your class?
M: It's at eight thirty pm.
W: That's late.

4
W: I'm tired. What's the time?
Wo: It's half past one.
W: Half past one? Time for bed!

4B Listening exercises 1 & 2 1.62

1 This day is on May 15th. We don't have this day in Britain, but I live in Mexico and it's great. That's because I'm a teacher. All the teachers take the day off and have a nice lunch together. On the next day my students give me things: a bottle of wine, a book. I love it.

2 May Day. I don't work on this day, nobody works. It's a day to celebrate workers. My friends and I play a big game of football in the park. We have a drink together after the game too, of course. I go to the May Fair with my family.

3 While everybody is at a party or a restaurant or disco, I spend December 31st in my taxi. It's a very busy night, but I get a lot of money. There are lots of taxi drivers on the streets, and they all have customers. I get home early in the morning on January 1st and I go to bed. In the afternoon, my family and I go to a good restaurant for lunch.

4 This is a very important day, I think. It is a day for us to remember some of the important things that have happened for women in the past. It's on March 8th, which is in winter for me. It's not an official bank holiday, so I go to work. But I go on the Women's Day march every year, and then have a hot cup of tea with friends and talk.

4C Listening exercises 1, 2 & 3
 1.64

H = host R = Ralph T = Tom A = Anne

H: Hello, and welcome to our morning phone in. A survey in the newspaper, the *Daily Post*, says that 75% of British men never do the housework. That's the topic for our phone in today. Is that true for you? Please ring 0800 607607. Are you a man who does the housework? Who does the housework in your house? We have several callers on the line. Let's go to the first one. What's your name?
R: Ralph.
H: Where are you from, Ralph?
R: I'm from Scotland.
H: How often do you do the housework, Ralph?
R: I sometimes do the shopping.
H: What does 'sometimes' mean for you, Ralph?
R: Well, every Saturday.
H: Alright, that's normal. What other housework do you do?
R: Nothing.
H: Nothing?
R: My mother always does all the housework.
H: Lucky you. Do you want to say something to your mother on the radio?
R: Yeah, thanks, Mum!
H: That's nice. OK, who's the next caller?
T: Tom, from Liverpool.
H: Good morning, Tom. How are you?
T: Fine, thanks.
H: That's good. Here's our question of the day: how often do you do the housework?
T: Every day.
H: That's interesting. What housework do you do?
T: I make the bed every morning.
H: Excellent, Tom!
T: And I wash the clothes.
H: Great.
T: Thank you very much.
H: Next caller. Who is this?
A: I'm Anne, from Liverpool. I'm Tom's wife.
H: Hello, Anne. You have a very nice husband.
A: But it isn't true. Tom hardly ever does the

housework. I do it!
H: Oh dear.
A: He never makes the bed. And the clothes? Ha! He washes them once a year.
H: What does he do?
A: He works in an office. He's always on the phone to silly radio shows!
H: Thank you very much for your call.

4D Listening exercises 1 & 2 1.70

V = Valerie D = Dave S = Sam A = Angie
W = woman M = man

1
V: Anyway, so this is my first job.
D: Really?
D: I'm sorry, that's my phone. Just a minute … Hello?
A: Dave, it's Angie.
D: Oh, hi. How did you get this number?
A: Oh Dave … where are you? Why did you go?
D: Now's not a good time. Can I call you back?
A: No, I want to talk now!
D: Sorry, that was my girlfriend. Well, ex-girlfriend.
V: I understand.

2
W: Hello?
S: Hello, I'd like to speak to Mr Green, please.
W: Sorry, he isn't here at the moment.
S: Where is he?
W: He's at the airport. Who's calling, please?
S: It's Sam Moore.
W: Would you like to leave a message?
S: Yes. Please tell him to call me.

3
V: Hello?
M: Is Simon there, please?
V: Sorry, you have the wrong number.
M: Oh, sorry. Goodbye.
V: Bye.

4D Listening exercises 3 1.71

Sh = Sharon R = Rob He = Herb
TA = travel agent

1
Sh: Hello, National History Society. Can I help you?
R: Sharon, hi. It's Rob.
Sh: Hello, Rob. How's the tour?
R: Fine, fine. The museum was very interesting. Are there any messages for me?
Sh: Yes, a woman called. Colleen Kerr.
R: OK. Meg, give me a pen. How do you spell that?
Sh: C-O-L-L-E-E-N Kerr K-E-R-R.
R: Yes. And what's her phone number?
Sh: 0865 455 901.
R: 0865 455 901. OK. Thanks, Sharon.
Sh: No problem. Bye.
R: Goodbye.

2
He: Come on, pick up the phone.
TA: Hello, Basic Airways?
He: Hello, I'd like to confirm a flight, please.
TA: Of course. Where to?
He: It's to Dallas, Texas.
TA: Flight number?
He: Just a minute … here it is – BAW 288.
TA: Date?
He: June 20th.
TA: And your name?
He: Herb Curtis.
TA: Just a minute, please.
He: OK.
TA: Mr Curtis?
He: Yes?
TA: Your flight is confirmed. Flight BAW 288 to Dallas on Thursday June 20th at 8:45 am. Terminal 2.
He: Thank you very much.
TA: Thank you for calling. Have a nice day.

5A Speaking exercise 1 1.75

1 W = woman M = man
W: Travellers from Europe go to desk A, travellers from outside Europe go to desk B.
M: Excuse me, can you repeat that, please?
W: Yes, if you are from Europe, go to desk A.

2 W = woman M = man
W: So, today in class we're going to do some vocabulary, vocabulary of tourism. You know tourism? Hotels, airports, visits to other countries … tourism. Open your books on page 80.
M: Excuse me, can you speak more slowly please?
W: Of course. I'm sorry. Open your books on page 80 please.

5B Listening exercises 1 & 2 1.77

L = Lara T = Tom
L: Our holiday in Canada was lovely. It was a cross Canada trip. This is a photo of our train. We were on the train for ten days. The scenery in Canada is beautiful. This photo … oh, where was this one, Tom?
T: This photo was in Halifax. I remember it. Too bad about the weather. It wasn't very good.
L: That's right, it wasn't. It was rainy all the time there. The houses were lovely though, and the people were very nice.
T: Look at this one. This was amazing.
L: Yeah, yeah. Where was this? Was it in Quebec?
T: No it wasn't. It was Montreal. We were there for two days. This city has great jazz concerts.
L: Who was this musician?
T: I don't know. I can't remember his name. He was good though.
T: I remember this photo.
L: This is Toronto. You can see the CN Tower there. The shops weren't open that day. So we were in the park … doing nothing. I wasn't very happy.
T: No, you weren't. You were miserable.
L: It was cold!
T: Alright. Next photo?
L: Hmm.
L: I love this hotel.
T: This was in a big natural park. The park is called Banff. It was a perfect place to go skiing. Unfortunately, I can't ski. But Lara's right, the hotel was very good.
L: There was a Jacuzzi in our room!
T: Yep, good hotel. How many days were we in this park?
L: Three days, I think.

5C Reading & listening exercise 4
 1.79

W = Walter T = Thelma
Wo = woman
Wo: Good morning, tickets and passports, please.
W: Here you are, tickets and … oh, wait a minute, where did you put the passports?
T: The passports? That was your job.
W: Was it?
T: Yes, it was. Do you have them?
W: Wait a minute.
T: Did you look in the black bag?
W: Yes, I did. Oh no …
T: Oh, Walter!

5D Listening exercise 1 1.82

V = Valerie He = Herb Ha = Hannah
Ha: Oh Herb, is this our hotel?
He: I think so, dear. Isn't it beautiful?
Ha: Yes. What does the book say?
He: "A happy, friendly 18th-century guest house, with gardens and barbeque …" This is good, darling.

Ha: So English! I love it.
V: Is this your first time in an English bed and breakfast?
Ha: Yes, it is. We don't have things like this in Texas. Did Shakespeare live here?
V: Umm, this guest house is only 200 years old, so no, I don't think so.
He: Too bad. Maybe he lived close to here.

5D Listening exercises 2 & 3 💿 1.83

V = Valerie He = Herb Ha = Hannah
O = owner

1
Ha: Darling, look. A dog.
O: Oi! Excuse me! You can't go there!
Ha: I'm sorry. I was only looking. What's his name?
O: Rex.
Ha: Can I touch him?
O: I'm afraid you can't. He's very dangerous.

2
O: Hello.
He: Hi. Excuse me, but could I use your phone? My mobile phone doesn't work here.
O: I'm afraid we don't have a phone for the public.
He: What do you mean, no phone? What about that phone?
O: Sorry, it's private.
V: Hi, is there a problem?
He: Yes, my phone doesn't work. He says this phone is not for guests. May I use your phone, please?
V: Of course. Here you are.
He: Thank you.

3
He: I'd like to pay the bill. Can I pay by credit card?
O: Of course. Visa? Mastercard?
He: American Express.
O: Oh no, I'm sorry, but we don't take American Express.
He: Fine. Visa then.

4
He: Oh, one more thing. Our bus leaves at a quarter past four. Is it OK to leave our bags here, please?
O: Certainly. It's £2 an hour.
He: But it's only for fifteen minutes!
O: I'm sorry, it's £2 minimum to keep bags.
He: I can't believe this.
Ha: Herb, what's wrong?
He: Happy, friendly hotel? I don't think so.

6B Listening exercise 1 💿 2.1

J = Jim S = Steph M = Mike

J: Hello everybody and welcome to a new episode of *Actor! Author!* My name's Jim and today we have two new contestants: Mike from London.
M: Hello, Jim.
J: And Steph, from Birmingham.
S: Hi!
J: Now remember the rules. Each person takes a turn and chooses a category: Actor or Author. I give you four clues about the person, and you guess who it is. OK?
M/S: Yes.

6B Listening exercises 2 & 3 💿 2.2

J = Jim S = Steph M = Mike

J: Mike, we'll start with you. When was the last time you saw a film?
M: Well, Jim, I saw *Gladiator* last night.
J: Great film. Now, what category would you like?
M: Actor.
J: Alright, here we go. He was born in Manhattan in 1952. He fell off a horse 12 years ago and was paralysed. His most famous movies were *Superman*, *Superman II* and

Superman III. He died in 2004.
M: Christopher Reeve!
J: Yes!
J: OK Steph, now it's your turn. What category would you like?
S: Author, please.
J: Do you read a lot, Steph?
S: Yes, I do.
J: What was the last book you read?
S: Umm. I finished a book two weeks ago, but I can't remember the name. I'm a bit nervous.
J: That's all right. Right then, here we go. He is American. His books are translated into more than 40 languages. He wrote a very famous thriller. The book is set in Paris, it starts in the Louvre Museum. The main character is an art professor called Robert Langdon. It's about symbols in the art of a famous Italian painter, Leonardo da Vinci.
S: Oh, wait … I read that book last year. Oh no ….
J: Almost time …
S: David … Dan …
J: Yes?
S: Dan Brown.
J: Well done!
J: Back to you Mike. What category would you like?
M: Author this time, please.
J: She's from England and she taught English in Portugal more than ten years ago. She is now very, very rich. Her books are also movies. She wrote about a boy called Harry Potter. There are more than six books in the series.
M: I know *Harry Potter*, but the author …?
J: Time, Mike.
M: I don't know!
J: Steph?
S: JK Rowling!
J: Co-rrect!
J: Right, Steph you can win this. What category would you like?
S: Actor.
J: OK, this time it's an *actress*.
S: That's fine.
J: She was born in 1967. She's from Australia. She won an Oscar for the film, *The Hours*. She was married to Tom Cruise and made several films with him.
S: Nicole Kidman! Nicole Kidman!
J: Co-rrect! Steph, you're the winner.

6C Pronunciation exercise 2 💿 2.7

1 M = man W = woman
M: Come here, I want to tell you something.
W: What is it?
M: I love you.

2 M = man W = woman W2 = woman 2
W: What's that?
W2: Where?
W: I think there's a man at the window.

3 W = woman C = child
W: Now listen to me, because I don't want to repeat this.
C: OK.

4 M = man W = woman
M: Did you remember my book?
W: No, I didn't.
M: Doh!

6D Listening exercises 1 & 2 💿 2.9

V = Valerie He = Herb Ha = Hannah
D = Dave S = Sam Vo = voice

V: So, what did you do yesterday?
D: I went to a football match.
V: Oh really? What did you think of it?
D: It was OK.
V: I love football. Chelsea are my favourite team.
D: Oh.
V: What? You don't like football?
D: I'm not crazy about it.

V: Why did you go then?
D: I don't know. I went shopping yesterday, too. That was good.

He: Wasn't that awful?
Ha: Sorry?
He: It was awful.
Ha: I liked it.
He: I'm sorry, did we see the same movie? It was terrible. The actors were bad, the music was bad, everything was bad. I can't say a good word about that film.

Vo: So, where is he now?
S: He's at the hotel. I have my eye on him.
Vo: How's London? Do you like the tour?
S: It's alright. I went shopping yesterday.
Vo: Shopping?
S: Well, he went shopping, so I went shopping!
Vo: What do you think of the shopping in London?
S: I can't stand it. I hate shopping in general.
Vo: Poor you. Did you buy anything?
S: No, I didn't. Look. I'll call you back, OK?
Vo: Fine then. Buy me a souvenir, will you? A lovely little London bus.

7A Listening exercises 2 & 3 💿 2.11

D = Daniel Barber M = Martha Jones
A = Alex Willis

D: Good evening. I'm speaking to Martha Jones, famous for the Two Fs diet: Fruit and Fish. Martha, tell me about your diet.
M: Sure. It's simple. On our diet you can only eat fruit and fish. For example, have some fruit for breakfast. Don't eat any bread or drink any coffee in the morning. For lunch, eat fish and some tomatoes.
D: Tomatoes?
M: Yes, tomatoes are a fruit.
D: OK. What can I drink?
M: Water and fruit juice. You can't drink any wine, or beer or anything like that.
D: And what does this diet do for me?
M: You can see results very fast. Two or three kilos in a week. You feel good, too. Fish and fruit are a very good combination.
D: Thank you.

D: Our second diet is a Low C diet – that's C for carbohydrates. I asked Alex Willis about this diet. Alex, what can I eat on the Low C diet?
A: First, let me say it's a variation of the No C diet. So, eat lots of meat, chicken and fish.
D: Meat and chicken and fish?
A: Well, not at the same time. Eggs are good, too.
D: So, if I have eggs for breakfast, with some bread …
A: No, no, no, no, no! Bread, no.
D: No bread?
A: Bread is a carbohydrate. Don't eat any bread or pasta. And don't eat any fruit either. This is the key to this diet.
D: What about vegetables?
A: You can eat some lettuce for example, but don't eat any potatoes or carrots.
D: And what does this diet do for me?
A: Amazing results, fast! Many famous people follow this diet and it works, I guarantee you. Here, look at our list of celebrities …
D: Thank you.

D: Our third diet was the Soup diet. I couldn't speak to a representative of the Soup diet, but this is what their website says: 'In our amazing Soup diet, you can eat anything you want, but it has to be in soup form. This is because the human body digests soups very easily'. They have a list of soups you can buy from their website: fish soup, pasta soup and my favourite, banana and chocolate soup. Their website says that you can lose five kilos in a week with their diet.

7C Speaking & vocabulary exercise 2 2.16

A: What's this?
B: Sushi.
A: Sushi?
B: Yes, it's Japanese. It's raw fish. It's cold.

A: Would you like any salt with your chips?
B: No, thanks. These chips are very salty already.
A: Oh, I always put extra salt on.

B: How's your curry?
B: Excellent. It's very spicy. Can you give me some water, please?

A: Oh no. I can't stand spinach.
B: You can't?
A: No, not cooked spinach anyway. Horrible.

A: Brownies à la mode.
B: What does brownies 'à la mode' mean?
A: Well, the brownies are like a nice hot chocolate cake, and then you add a spoonful of cold ice cream. That's à la mode.
B: It looks very sweet to me.
A: I know.

7C Listening exercises 2 & 3 2.17

1 M = man W = woman
W: I'm not a fussy eater. But my brother is. He's a very fussy eater. It's terrible. He only eats hamburgers, and he drinks lots of cola.
M: How old is your brother?
W: He's twenty-six years old! That's why it's terrible!

2 M = man W = woman
M: This red wine is very good.
W: I don't know. I think it's too young.
M: What year is it?
W: Just a minute. 2004. Yes, definitely too young.
M: I think it's good.

3 M = man W = woman
W: How can you eat that?
M: What?
W: That cake!
M: Do you want some?
W: Good Lord, no. It's too sweet.
M: You're too fussy. Relax a little.

4 M = man W = woman
W: And so we didn't eat it. Is there a fussy eater in your family?
M: Oh, yes. We invited my daughter and her boyfriend for dinner. It was awful. My wife made a delicious steak, and my daughter's boyfriend didn't eat anything. He said it was too salty. He was on a special diet. He's a swimmer and he can only eat rice.
W: What did you do?
M: My wife made him a very big plate of rice.

7D Listening exercises 1 & 2 2.21

He = Herb Ha = Hannah Wr = Waiter
Wr: Can I help you?
He: Table for two, please.
Wr: Smoking or non smoking?
He: Non smoking, please.
Wr: This way, please.

Wr: Anything to drink?
He: Yes, a beer, please.
Ha: And a mineral water for me, please.
Wr: Sparkling or still?
Ha: Sparkling, please.
He: Could we have the menu too, please?
Wr: Of course.

Wr: Here you are. A beer and a sparkling mineral water.
He/Ha: Thank you.
Wr: Are you ready to order?
He: Yes, we are. Hannah?
Ha: Can I have the mushroom risotto?
Wr: Yes.

He: And can I have the Mexican spicy pizza?
Wr: Thank you.

He: Well, that was delicious! Not too spicy.
Ha: I loved my risotto.
He: Waiter!
Wr: Yes?
He: Can we have the bill, please?
Wr: Would you like a dessert? Coffee?
He: No, thanks. You?
Ha: No coffee for me, thank you. Just the bill.
Wr: Of course. Here you are.

7D Listening exercise 3 2.22

He = Herb Ha = Hannah
Wr = Waiter
He: Can I pay by credit card?
Wr: Of course.
He: Fine … wait a minute. I don't have my money here. Hannah, do you have my wallet?
Ha: I don't think so, Herb. No, I don't. I can pay with my credit card. Oh no.
He: What is it?
Ha: My money isn't here!
He: What do you mean?
Ha: I think someone took our money, Herb.
He: I can't believe this.
Ha: Oh no …

7D Pronunciation exercises 1 & 3 2.23

1 Can I help you?
2 Are you ready to order?
3 Could we have the menu, please?
4 I'd like a pizza, please.
5 Would you like a drink?
6 Can I have the bill?

8B Listening exercises 2 & 3 2.27

K = Kate J = John
K: Yes, that was Aretha Franklin, another classic tune. Coming up we have lots more music and news, but first here's the traffic news. And it's a busy day out on the roads, isn't it, John?
J: Yes, it is, Kate. Good morning. We have an accident in Regent Street. There's a bus on fire. Everybody is OK, but traffic is moving very slowly.
A large group of people are standing in the middle of Oxford Street. I can't hear them, but I think they are standing in front of the cars and singing! So, traffic isn't moving. The police are talking to them at the moment.
K: Can you tell us anything about the incident on Euston Road?
J: Yes, Kate. There's a lion – yes, I said a lion – on Euston Road. I'm looking at the camera now. A lot of cars are moving slowly around it. It's sitting in the middle of the road and looking at the cars …
K: Where did it come from! Do you have any more news?
J: Well, the police say that they think it escaped from the zoo. I'm waiting for more information on that. We have a report coming in now from East London. There's a big traffic problem. Someone is driving on the wrong side of the road.
K: It's another crazy day for drivers, then. Next traffic update at half past ten. Thanks, John.

8C Listening exercise 5 2.29

T = Tracy ML = Mrs Lunan
MRL = Mr Lunan
ML: Can you hear? Who is he phoning? This is terrible! Just a minute, it's my mobile phone. Hello?
MRL: Hello, darling.
ML: John?
MRL: Yes, it's me. I have a surprise for you.
ML: Oh John …

MRL: Do you remember the Green Leaf restaurant?
ML: Yes …
MRL: I'm waiting for you. I have a table for two.
ML: Oh John …
MRL: Darling, take a taxi.
ML: Yes, I … yes.
MRL: Come quickly, darling. I love you.
ML: I love you, too.

ML: Sorry, Ms Dick?
T: That's alright, Mrs Lunan. I heard. I'm happy everything is OK.
ML: Yes, I …
T: Don't worry. You can pay me by cheque or credit card.

8D Listening exercises 1 & 2 2.32

R = Rob M = Meg D = Delilah Ma = man
D: Hi, guys.
R/M: Hi, Hello.
D: I'm ready for the concert. Where's Valerie?
R: She's taking Herb and Hannah to the police station.
D: Really? Why? Are they alright?
R: Someone took their money and passports.
D: That's terrible.
M: So, what do we do now?
R: We could go to the concert. Just the three of us.
D: OK. Where is it?
R: At the … Royal Albert Hall.
D: I know. Let's take a taxi.
R: A taxi? No, no, no. Taxis here are too expensive. We can take the underground.
D: Where are we?
R: We're here. Camden Town.
M: Camden Town or Camden Road?
R: Camden Town. So, we can take the black line here…
D: Let's ask the man over there.
R: No, no, no. It's OK. Look, the black line to Euston, then change to the … Victoria line … wait a minute, where am I?
D: Excuse me, we're going to the Royal Albert Hall, and er …?
Ma: That's easy, love. Take the Northern Line to Euston, change at Euston onto the Victoria Line, then get off at Victoria station. Get on the District line, the green line, and go to South Kensington. It takes around 40 minutes.
D: Thank you. Did you understand that?
R/M: No.
D: Why don't we take that taxi now?
R: Wait. He said the Northern Line! Let's go on that.

M: I think we took the wrong train. This is Kings Cross.
D: What do we do now?
R: Let's go up to the street and take a bus. At least we can see London that way. And we can take photographs.
M: That's a good idea.
D: We could also see London in a nice taxi.

M: That was the third bus! I'm tired of buses.
R: We're nearly there. We can walk now. It takes 15 minutes to the concert hall.
M: I don't think that's a good idea. I don't want to walk.
D: It's raining. I didn't take an umbrella!
R: Wait … It's not far.
D: Taxi! Taxi!

9B Speaking exercises 1 & 2 2.39

Stand up. Move your fingers. At the same time you're moving your fingers, move your arms. Now move your shoulders and arms. Stop moving your arms. Move one leg and then the other leg. Sit down again.

9c Listening exercises 2 & 3 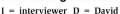 2.41

I = interviewer D = David

I: Good afternoon. In the studio with us today we have David Barker. David works for the Exploratorium museum in San Francisco and is going to talk to us about memory and the human face. Hello, David.
D: Hello.
I: Now, my memory isn't very good. How's yours?
D: It's OK.
I: There's an expression in English, 'I never forget a face'. Is that true for you?
D: Well, it depends really. I'm interested in how we remember a human face. Many experts now believe that the top part of the face is more important than the bottom part.
I: What do you mean?
D: OK. For example, look at this picture.
I: This one here, with all the boys?
D: Yes. What do you notice about it?
I: I think this is an old picture. They're young, on a sports team. That's all.
D: Interesting. Because in this picture, if you look closely, all the boys have exactly the same face.
I: Really?! Oh, yes, you're right!
D: Hair is very important for memory. In fact, hair is the most important factor, then the eyes, then the nose.
I: This is the top part of the face.
D: Yes, the bottom part of the face, the mouth and err … chin are not so important. Look at this photo.
I: It looks very funny!
D: Yes. It's a combination of two faces, but with different hair again. Whose face is it, do you think?
I: Hmmm … very difficult. Is that … is that the Mona Lisa's face?
D: Yes, it's hers.
I: Why is this difficult?
D: Because we've put Elvis' hair on her face.
I: Whose hair is it?
D: Elvis The King of Rock and Roll.
I: Oh, yes. Now I can see it.
D: Yes. So you see how the hair makes it difficult. This is why famous people wear hats when they don't want people to know who they are.
I: They also wear sunglasses.
D: Yes, that's right.

9d Listening exercises 1 & 2 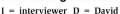 2.44

D = Dave V = Valerie Ha = Hannah
He = Herb Dr = doctor

1
D: Valerie, are you alright?
V: Hi, Dave. I don't know, I don't feel well.
D: Here, sit down. Sit down.
V: Oh, OK.
D: What's wrong?
V: I've got a headache. I feel cold. Oh, and my stomach.
D: Here, put on my jacket.
V: Thank you.

2
Ha: What's the matter, sweetie?
V: I don't feel well.
Ha: Oh, no.
V: It's alright. I'm fine, really.
Ha: Was it something you ate last night?
V: I don't know. Maybe …
Ha: Here, take off that jacket.
V: OK.

3
V: Oh, no.
He/Ha: What's wrong?

V: I think … I think I'm going to be sick.
Ha: Do you want to go to the toilet?
V: Yes, sorry.
He: What's wrong with Valerie? Did she drink too much wine?
Ha: Is there a doctor here? Somebody call a doctor!

4
V: Hello. Are you a doctor?
Dr: Yes, I am. How do you feel?
V: I feel alright now, thanks.
Dr: Good, good. Stand up. How's your stomach?
V: Not very good, but better now.
Dr: What did you eat for dinner last night?
V: I had a pizza, a Mexican spicy pizza at Bella Pizza restaurant. Was that the problem?
Dr: I'm sorry, but it probably was. Here, take two aspirin and lie down. You should sleep.
V: Thank you, doctor.

5
D: Is she alright, doctor?
Dr: She'll be fine. Did anyone else eat the Mexican spicy pizza yesterday?
He/Ha/D: No, no …
Ha: Herb, didn't you …?
He: Wait a minute. You're right. Oh …
D: Are you OK, Herb?
He: Oh, no. I don't think so. I feel sick …

10b Vocabulary exercise 2 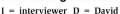 2.46

I = interviewer G = Giovanni

I: So, tell me about Rome. Are the people friendly?
G: Yes, they are. They're very friendly.
I: Is it an expensive place?
G: Yes, it is. That's the problem with life in the capital.
I: Is it dangerous to walk on the streets at night?
G: It depends where you are. In some areas yes, it can be dangerous.
I: Can you visit interesting things in your city?
G: Yes, you can. Of course! There are lots of museums, art galleries, monuments …
I: Is it very noisy?
G: Yes, it is. Very noisy. Rome is famous for noise.
I: Are there any beautiful or historical buildings?
G: Of course. It has the most beautiful buildings in Europe. The Colosseum, for example. There's also the Vatican.
I: Is the air polluted?
G: Yes, it is. Unfortunately.

10b Listening exercises 2 & 3 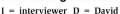 2.48

1
Sofia: Oh no, I don't live in the capital, Madrid. I live in Alicante with my husband and two sons. It's in the south of Spain, on the coast of the Mediterranean Sea. It's smaller than Madrid, but life is much better. Madrid is too big. In the summer it's too hot, and in the winter it's too cold. That's why people from Madrid come here. And there are a lot more children here – at least you see more families with two or three children. Life is more expensive in Madrid, too expensive for many big families.

2
Nick: Life in the capital city, Athens, is faster than in other cities of Greece. I was born in Athens, I live in Athens, and it's true - life is very fast! Athens is noisier and dirtier – but it has more of everything: more money, opportunities, jobs, noise, pollution, entertainment … bigger and better stadiums and sports facilities …
Many Greeks say that people in Athens aren't very friendly, they don't have time for you. This isn't true. I know lots of very friendly people here in Athens.

10d Listening exercises 1 & 2 2.51

M = Meg R = Rob SA = shop assistant

SA: Hello, can I help you?
R: No, I'm just looking, thank you.
M: Excuse me, hello?
SA: Yes?
M: Do you have any small London mugs?
SA: No, just these.
M: Can I have two of the red mugs then, please?
SA: Of course.
M: These pens are pretty. How much are they?
SA: £1.50 each.
M: Can I have five pens too, please?
SA: Yes, here you are.
M: Thank you.
R: Are we OK, now?
M: Yes, look. I've got two mugs for my parents and these pens for the children.
R: And I have a book on London football teams. Look! Only two pounds!
SA: Hello.
M: Yes, these please.
SA: The pens, two mugs and the book. That's £24.90, please.
M: Here you are. Could I have two bags, please?
SA: Bags are over there.
M: Thank you.

11a Listening exercises 2 & 3 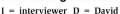 2.58

I = interviewer J = Janet M = Michael

I: Tell us about yourself.
J: OK, my name's Janet. I'm from Canada, and I work in the security office of a big hospital in London.
I: What do you do?
J: I'm a security guard. Er … most of the time I watch the security televisions. It's not a very difficult job.
I: Who do you work with?
J: I work with two other security guards in the office. They are both men.
I: When did you start here?
J: I started at this hospital two years ago.
I: Do you like your job?
J: Yes, yes, I do.
I: Why?
J: Well, I like working at night. I always like working at night. It's quiet. It's easy work. I have a nice boss.
I: What do other people think of your job?
J: I think my job is great, but my parents don't like it. My father is very traditional. He says that a security guard is a man's job. Yeah, well … what can you do?
I: Hello, what's your name?
M: Michael.
I: Where do you work in the hospital?
M: I work in the accounts department.
I: So you're an accountant?
M: Yes, I am.
I: Who do you work with?
M: There are three people in the office.
I: When did you start here?
M: I worked in London for ten years in a big company. But I didn't like it. I started at this hospital last year.
I: Do you like your job?
M: Yes, I do. Many people say 'Oh, accounts, that's boring'. But I like it.
I: Why do you like your job?
M: Because it's interesting, I like working with numbers.

11c Listening exercises 1 & 2 2.60

D = David S = Sandra W = Will
A = Ali J = Jarvis R = reporter

R: What about you, David?
D: Well, I'm already 64 years old. Next year I'm

not going to work any more. So, number 1 is good for me. I'm going to go and live in France. I'd like to practise my French more. Let's see, what else … a good bed. Yes, that makes me think. I'm going to get a good bed. The bed we have is ten years old.

R: Sandra, what things are you going to do?

S: Oh yes, I read all about the benefits of water in a magazine once. That's my resolution. I'm going to drink more water. And I'm going to tell my husband about optimists living longer than pessimists do. He always sees the bad side of everything!

R: So Will, is there anything here for you?

W: Well, I already play football and do lots of sports, so number 3 isn't a new thing for me. I'm not going to live in another country, or stop work, either.

R: Well, are you going to do anything on the list?

W: OK, OK. Ummm … Number 5. My desk, especially, which is terrible. I'm going to clean my desk.

R: Ali, what about you?

A: Every year I say I'm going to stop smoking, I'm going to stop smoking. But then I always find an excuse to start again. What else is on the list? Exercise is a good idea. Yes, I'm going to go to a gym, starting next year. And I'm going to quit smoking.

R: And what about you, Jarvis?

J: I only work here part time, I'm still at university. When I finish, in two years, I'm going to take a long break. I'm going to travel around China on a motorbike with a friend. I got the idea from a film. I'm also going to vote in the next election, but I always vote in elections because I think that's important.

11D Listening exercises 1 & 2
🔘 2.62

HM = Hotel Manager V = Valerie
S = Sam D = Dave

1

HM: So, you're the tour guide.

V: Sorry, oh yes, yes, I am.

HM: What's your name?

V: Valerie.

HM: My name's James. I'm the hotel manager. You can call me Jim.

V: Nice to meet you, Jim.

HM: So, when does the tour finish?

V: Tomorrow.

HM: Would you like to have dinner with me tomorrow night?

V: No, I'm sorry. I'm busy.

HM: Oh, well, then. Too bad.

V: Mmm.

2

D: Hi, Valerie.

V: Hello, Dave.

D: I was thinking. The tour is going to finish tomorrow. Are you busy tomorrow night?

V: Umm. I … no, I'm not. Why?

D: Would you like to have a drink with me?

V: Yes, I'd love to.

3

S: Excuse me, Dave?

D: Yes.

S: Can we speak in private for a moment?

D: What do you want to talk about? Who are these people?

S: I'm a police officer. These are my colleagues.

D: What?! Why?

V: What's the matter?

S: We want to talk to Dave about the Curtises' money, and passports. Can you open your bag, please?

D: I want a lawyer.

S: Don't worry, you can make a phone call. Would you like to come with us now to the police station?

12B Listening exercises 2 and 3
🔘 2.68

J = Journalist M1 = man 1 W = woman
M2 = man 2

1

J: Hi. Can I ask you some questions?

M1: I'm busy, but OK.

J: One survey says that one in four Americans have been on television. Have you ever been on television?

M1: No, I haven't. I've never been on television. And I don't want to be.

J: Have you ever spoken on the radio?

M1: No, never. Sorry, I'm very busy now.

J: OK, thank you.

2

J: Excuse me, have you ever been on television?

W: Yes, I have! I was on a game show once. Have you heard of *The Big Award*?

J: Yes, I have. It's on Channel 4. Did you win anything?

W: No, I was in the audience.

J: Great. One more question. Have you spoken on the radio?

W: No, I haven't.

J: Have you written a letter to a newspaper?

W: No, I haven't.

J: Thanks.

3

J: Hello.

M2: Hello.

J: I'm doing a survey. Can I ask you some questions?

M2: Sure.

J: Have you ever been on television?

M2: What do you think?

J: I'm sorry? I don't understand.

M2: I work on television. I announce the evening news. Have you seen me?

J: Oh, yes, I have! You're wearing a hat. I didn't recognize you.

M2: That's alright.

J: Well, thanks anyway.

12C Speaking exercise 1 🔘 2.72

In my country, English is an important language. It wasn't always important, but it is now. In the past, people learnt French or German at school. Now, everybody is learning English. For learning a language, I think it's important to learn new vocabulary and grammar, but it's also very important to practise speaking. For me, learning English is difficult, and I think speaking is the most difficult. I can understand English in books, and in magazines, but when I listen to English or American people I don't understand. In my classes, we practise speaking a lot. When I started the year, it was impossible. I couldn't pronounce any sentences in English. Now it's better.

12D Listening exercises 1 & 2
🔘 2.73

V = Valerie M = Meg R = Rob D = Delilah
HM = Hotel Manager Ha = Hannah S = Sam

1

M: So, Valerie, what happened in the end with Dave?

V: Well, Sam and the police came and took him to the police station.

M: Sam?

V: Yes, I didn't know, but he's a police officer. He's followed Dave from the beginning of the tour.

M: No!

V: Yes. It seems that Dave has taken money from people, usually older, richer Americans, on several different tours. This wasn't the

first time.

M: No!!

V: Yes. The police found all the Curtises' money in Dave's room, and credit cards from lots of other people.

M: That's incredible. Where's Dave now?

V: He's in jail. And I thought he was really nice.

M: You just can never tell about some people.

2

V: Well, everyone, this is the end of our tour. Brian is going to take people to the airport. He's waiting outside. I also wanted to say thank you very much. It was really, really nice to meet you. I mean that honestly! This was my first tour and I had a very nice time. There's a paper going round for you to put your email addresses on if you want to write to each other. My email address is at the top. You can write to me!

3

D: Hi there.

HM: Hello.

D: Are you the hotel manager?

HM: Yes, I am.

D: Look, I know this is a busy time …

HM: That's fine. I always have time for a beautiful young woman …

D: Thanks. Can I leave my bags here for half an hour?

HM: Of course. Of course. I can keep them in my private room.

D: No, here is fine.

HM: They will be safe here.

D: Thank you.

HM: You're welcome.

4

R: Meg?

M: Yes?

R: We're going to the train station, right?

M: Yes, that's right.

R: So, how do we get there?

M: I don't know. Why don't we take a taxi?

R: No, no, no taxis this time. Excuse me, Valerie?

V: Yes?

R: How can we get to the train station?

V: Don't worry, Brian can take you later.

R: Really? Thanks a lot!

V: Don't mention it.

5

Ha: Oh, there you are! Sam!

S: Hello, Mrs Curtis.

Ha: I never knew you were a *policeman*.

S: Well, I was undercover.

Ha: My husband and I just want to say thank you *very much* for getting our money back and catching that *bad man*.

S: That's alright. It's my job.

Ha: I know, I know. And you do a *very good* job, too.

S: Mm.

Ha: Would you like to come to our ranch in Texas next month? We'd love to see you.

S: I … Texas?

Ha: Don't worry, we can pay for everything for you. My husband has *lots* of money.

S: Thank you very much, but I can't. I'm sorry. I'm going to … Scotland.

Ha: Oh.

S: Yes, Scotland. Very important case. Maybe another time?

1 | Review

1 Match the words to the pictures.

> a computer   a chair   a phone   a bottle of water
> a clock   a newspaper

2 Complete with *his/her/their*.

1 She's the tour guide. ___ name is Valerie.
2 Sam isn't at the party. He is in ___ room.
3 They are from America. ___ names are Herb and Hannah.
4 Meg and Rob are in London. This is ___ hotel.
5 She's new. It's ___ first day at work.
6 He's famous. ___ photo is in the newspaper.

3 Make questions and answers.

Emily Pryde is a teacher in Rio de Janeiro, Brazil. She's 43 years old. She teaches English and French. She's from Dublin, Ireland.

1 / her name Emily? *Is her name Emily? Yes, it is.*
2 / Brazilian?
3 / her last name Janeiro?
4 / a language teacher?
5 / Irish?
6 / 21 years old?

4 In each of the short dialogues below, there is a word missing. Insert the missing word.

1 Julian, this Alyssa. She's new.
   Nice to meet you.
2 How you spell your name?
   A-L-Y-S-S-A.
3 Are you language teacher?
   Yes, I am.
4 Where is she from?
   She from Warsaw. She's Polish.
5 Are these your keys?
   No, aren't. My keys are here.
6 Would you like a drink?
   No, thank.

5 Complete the dialogues with the phrases in the box.

> Would you like   How are you   I'm fine
> Yes, please   No, it isn't

A: Good morning.
B: Oh, hi. (1)_____?
A: Fine, thanks. And you?
B: Oh, (2)_____.
A: There's a bar over there. (3)_____ a drink?
B: (4)_____. A coffee, please.

A: OK, two coffees.
B: Is this your coffee?
A: (5)_____. This is my coffee.

6 Work in pairs. Read the dialogue.

2 | Review

1 Read the text and complete with a word from the box.

eat	go	have	speak	live	work

---
friends

Friends.com – the place to make friends
Friend of the week

My name's Pauline. I'm from Scotland. I (1) _____ in a house in Edinburgh. I live alone, but I (2) _____ a cat. Her name is Tabby. I (3) _____ to university, and I (4) _____ in a shop on Saturdays. I (5) _____ English and a little French. My favourite food is chocolate. I (6) _____ lots of chocolate. I'm thirty years old.

---

2 Make more sentences about Pauline. Use the words.

1 play football(✓) *She plays football.*
2 smoke (✗) *She doesn't smoke.*
3 drink beer (✓)
4 speak Spanish (✗)
5 have lots of friends (✓)
6 have a boyfriend (✗)
7 go dancing (✓)
8 live with her parents (✗)

3 Complete the sentences with a word from the box.

aunt	brother	daughter	father	grandfather
mother	son	uncle	sisters	

1 He is my mother's brother. He is my _____.
2 He's my father's father. He is my _____.
3 She's my father's wife. She is my _____.
4 She's my uncle's wife. She is my _____.
5 He's my father's son. He is my _____.
6 She's my sister. She is my parents' _____.

4 Make sentences for the other three words in the box in exercise 3.

5 There is a grammatical mistake in each sentence or question. Correct the mistakes.

1 We doesn't work.
2 No, he don't.
3 Do you has lots of friends?
4 She speak French and Spanish.
5 I don't lives in London.
6 Is you married?

6 Rearrange the words to make questions.

1 you / of / lot / have / friends / a / do / ?
2 with/ you / do / your parents/ live / ?
3 different / is / how / life / your / ?
4 do / do / you / what / ?
5 name / your / what / is / ?
6 are / from / where / you / ?
7 you / with / who / live / do / ?

7 Match the questions from exercise 6 with the answers in the article.

An interview with an expat

a _____ I'm Joe Matthews and I'm 28.
b _____ I'm from Dublin in Ireland.
c _____ No, I don't. I live in Paris now.
d _____ I'm a student. I study Art at The Sorbonne University.
e _____ I speak French everyday and I drink lots of wine.
f _____ Yes, I do.
g _____ I have a flat with friends.

8 Complete the sentences with the adjectives in the box.

beautiful	fair	tall	thin	young

1 She isn't old. She's _____.
2 She isn't fat. She's _____.
3 She isn't short. She's _____.
4 She isn't ugly. She's _____.
5 Her hair isn't dark. It's _____.

3 | Review

1 Complete the sentences. Write the words in brackets as an ordinal number.

1 This is my _____ (3) visit to Britain.
2 The toilets are on the _____ (4) floor.
3 Today is the _____ (1) day of school.
4 This wall is from the _____ (5) century.
5 Hannah is Herb's _____ (2) wife.

2 Look at the picture and make questions and answers.

1 a bed? *Is there a bed? Yes, there is.*
2 how many windows? *How many windows are there? There are two windows.*
3 how many chairs?
4 a desk?
5 a computer?
6 how many lamps?
7 any plants?
8 a television?
9 any curtains?

3 In the text below there are five grammatical mistakes. Underline and correct the mistakes.

The MoMA (Museum of Modern Art) is in New York near from Madison Avenue, between Fifth and Sixth Avenue. There are lots of differents types of art in the MoMA. There is paintings, sculptures, drawings and any photographs. There is an education centre on the one floor of the museum.

4 Underline the five adjectives in the text below and match them to opposites below.

This is my home. I live in a lovely cottage in a small village near to the mountains. The village is very old. It is beautiful here and very quiet.

1 big: _____
2 ugly: _____
3 horrible: _____
4 noisy: _____
5 new: _____

5 Complete the phone conversation with *some*, *any*, *a*, *is* and *are*.

A: Good morning. Welcome to Houseswap USA. How can I help you?
B: Hi! I'd like a house for my holiday. Are there (1) _____ places in Florida?
A: Yes, there are (2) _____ houses near Miami. What kind of house do you want?
B: I'd like (3) _____ house with three bedrooms and a big garden.
A: OK, there (4) _____ three houses that match that description.
B: Do they have (5) _____ swimming pool?
A: Yes, they do.
B: Great. (6) _____ there a garage?
A: Yes, there (7) _____.

6 Complete the dialogue with phrases from the box.

The toilets. OK, go along the hall here and turn left.
No, down the stairs.
opposite the information desk.
Then go down the stairs.
Turn left …
Yes, can I help you?

Man: Excuse me!
Woman: (1) _____
Man: Yes, where are the toilets please?
Woman: (2) _____
Man: Sorry? Turn …?
Woman: (3) _____
Man: Left, OK.
Woman: (4) _____
Man: Up the stairs.
Woman: (5) _____
Man: Sorry! Down the stairs.
Woman: Yes, and the toilets are on the left (6) _____
Man: Thank you.

4 | Review

1 Will Cotton's wife works as a nurse. Look at the pictures and complete the sentences with the correct verb.

1 She ____ breakfast with Will.

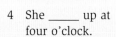

2 She ____ coffee.

3 She ____ to bed.

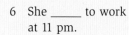

4 She ____ up at four o'clock.

5 She ____ dinner alone.

6 She ____ to work at 11 pm.

2 Work in pairs. Cover the sentences. Look at the pictures and say the sentences.

3 Complete the text about Nothing Day with the correct prepositions.

(1) ___ January 16th, I celebrate Nothing Day. This year Nothing Day is (2) ___ Tuesday, so I don't go to work of course! I wake up (3) ___ 11 o'clock (4) ___ the morning. I read a newspaper and have a big breakfast. I watch television (5) ___ the afternoon. (6) ___ 6 o'clock, I go for a walk with a friend. I read a book (7) ___ the evening and I do nothing (8) ___ night. It's a boring day, but a good day.

4 Match the dates in the box to the special days in the United States for the year 2007. There are two extra dates you do not need.

note: dates are Day/Month/Year

13/05/2007	14/06/2007	22/11/2007
12/01/2007	04/09/2007	30/03/2007
04/07/2007	~~19/02/2007~~	

1 The third Monday in February is Presidents'Day. *19/02/2007*
2 The second Sunday in May is Mother's Day.
3 July the fourth is Independence Day.
4 June the fourteenth is Flag Day.
5 The first Monday in September is Labor Day.
6 Thanksgiving Day is the fourth Thursday in November.

5 Rearrange the words to make questions and sentences.

1 dishes / do / do / how / often / the / you / ?
2 do / you / what / usually / Saturdays / on / do / ?
3 never / Saturdays / I / on / work .
4 make / always / the / morning / in / the / bed / I .
5 up / you / often / morning / get / in / do / early / the / ?
6 rubbish / I / the / out / rarely / take .
7 Saturday / the / do / on / morning / you / shopping / sometimes / do / ?

6 Choose the correct response, a or b.

1 Good morning, Explore London tours.
 a) Hello, I'm Valerie.
 b) Hello, it's Valerie.

2 Hello, I'd like to speak to Brian, please.
 a) I'm sorry, he isn't here.
 b) Please tell him to call me.

3 Hello, is that Michelle?
 a) I'm sorry, you have the wrong number.
 b) Is Michelle there please?

4 Dave can't answer the phone right now.
 a) Can I leave a message?
 b) Can I speak to Dave, please?

5 Would you like to leave a message?
 a) Yes, please. Please tell her to call me.
 b) You have the wrong number.

5 | Review

1 Make questions in the past from the prompts.

1 when / you on holiday?
2 where / you?
3 how many days/ you there?
4 who / you with?
5 what / the weather like?
6 the people nice?
7 what / the food like?
8 it a good holiday?

2 Match each answer to a question in exercise 1.

☐ a Five days.
☐ b Yes, it was a very good holiday.
☐ c I was in the south of France.
☐ d Yes, they were.
☐ e I was with my brother and his wife.
☐ f It was sunny and warm.
☐ g I was on holiday last summer.
☐ h The food was excellent.

3 Work in pairs. Think of your last holiday. Ask and answer the questions in exercise 1.

4 Complete the text with *was* or *were*.

Famous Canadians

Wayne Gretsky (1)_____ a famous hockey player in Canada in the 1980s. He (2) _____ born in 1961 in Brantford, Ontario.
The games of basketball and Trivial Pursuit (3) _____ two Canadian inventions.
The actress Pamela Anderson (4) _____ born in 1967. She (5) _____ in the television show *Baywatch* with David Hasselhof.
Pierre Elliot Trudeau (6) _____ the Prime Minister of Canada from 1968 to 1984.
Alexander Graham Bell (7) _____ born in Canada. He (8) _____ the inventor of the telephone.
The singers Avril Lavigne, Celine Dion and Shania Twain (9) _____ all born in Canada.

5 In each of the sentences below, one word is not necessary. Cross out the unnecessary word in each sentence.

1 What's your favourite weather to like?
2 The Lingo Global 29 can to translate lots of languages.
3 I can't not speak English very well.
4 The weather was lovely and was sunny.
5 Yes, I no agree. We can take lots of money.
6 I did remembered. Look! It's here.
7 Can I use your phone, please me?
8 Of course you can use.

6 Rewrite the sentences with the past tense.

1 Every night when I arrive home, I cook dinner.
   Last night when I arrived home …
2 I don't watch television.
3 I listen to music and study English for a couple of hours.
4 I use the internet to practise my English.
5 I look at English websites.
6 I don't go to bed late, around 11 o'clock.

7 Work in pairs. Which of the sentences in exercise 6 are true for you? What did you do last night?

8 Work in pairs, A and B.

A: Ask for permission using the pictures and words to help you.
B: Respond.

Swap roles and repeat.

smoke here?
pay?
use?
turn on?
use?
ask question?

6 | Review

1 In the text below there are five grammatical mistakes. <u>Underline</u> and correct the mistakes.

> *Our new baby blog*
>
> Marcos is now one week old! We goed for a walk in the park with him yesterday. He opened his eyes and looked at his mother for five minutes! It was beautiful. I not go to work last week. I stayed at home and doed the housework. My parents saw Marcos on Saturday. They was very happy. My father sayed Marcos looks exactly like me! Here is a photo of Marcos with his grandparents.

2 Complete the text. Put the verbs in brackets into the past simple.

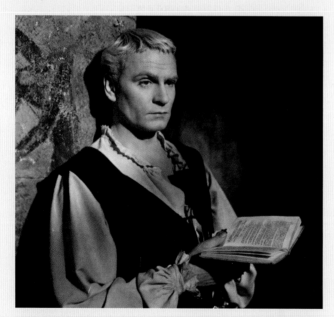

Laurence Oliver (1) _____ (*be*) born in England in 1907. He (2) _____ (*study*) acting in London, and (3) _____ (*start*) his career in 1926. He (4) _____ (*work*) in all the great Shakespeare plays when he (5) _____ (*be*) young, and (6) _____ (*make*) film versions of *Henry V*, *Hamlet* and *Richard III*. *Hamlet* (7) _____ (*win*) the Oscar for best film in 1948. In 1947, he (8) _____ (*become*) a knight and his name (9) _____ (*change*) to Sir Laurence Oliver. He (10) _____ (*be*) married three times. Laurence Olivier (11) _____ (*die*) in 1989.

3 Complete the sentences with a verb from the box. Put the verbs into the past simple. There is one verb you don't need.

write	win	die	read	make

1 John Wayne _____ in 1979. He was 72 years old.
2 The author Octavio Paz, from Mexico, _____ the Nobel Prize for Literature in 1990.
3 Frank Sinatra was a famous singer, but he also _____ more than 15 films.
4 JK Rowling _____ the first *Harry Potter* book at a time when she didn't have a job.
5 Clint Eastwood _____ an Oscar for the films *Unforgiven* and *Million Dollar Baby*.
6 Agatha Christie _____ more than eighty novels and plays. She is one of the most famous authors in the English language.
7 Peter Jackson _____ the film version of the *Lord of the Rings* in 2000. The third film, *Return of the King*, _____ many awards, including Best Picture Oscar.

4 Change the adjectives in the brackets to adverbs and put the word in the correct position in the sentence.

1 Can you read this very please? (careful)
2 He cried really and we couldn't hear him. (quiet)
3 She speaks English. (good)
4 You sing very. Can you sing again, please? (beautiful)
5 Can you speak? I can't understand you. (slow)

5 Decide if the sentence is positive (☺), negative (☹) or neutral (😐).

1 I really like Chinese food. ☺ ☹ 😐
2 I think the *Star Wars* movies are terrible. ☺ ☹ 😐
3 I'm not crazy about holidays on the beach. ☺ ☹ 😐
4 I can't stand football. ☺ ☹ 😐
5 This food is awful! ☺ ☹ 😐
6 I don't mind rainy weather. ☺ ☹ 😐
7 I love old westerns. ☺ ☹ 😐

6 Work in pairs. Change the sentences in exercise 6 so they are true for you.

7 | Review

1 Underline the word that doesn't belong.

1 bread   rice   pasta   fish
2 cheese   milk   carrots   eggs
3 tomatoes   lettuce   rice   carrots
4 eggs   oranges   apples   bananas
5 cake   chicken   chocolate ice cream

2 Tick (✓) *how much* or *how many*.

	How much …?	How many …?
apples		
chocolate		
milk		
oranges		
eggs		
sugar		
tomatoes		
juice		
chicken		

3 Make questions from the sentences. Use the chart in exercise 2 to help you.

1 We need some apples. *How many apples do you need?*
2 We have chocolate.
3 I want some milk.
4 We need oranges.
5 I have eggs.
6 We need tomatoes.

4 Read the recipe for risotto and tick the pictures of the food you need.

This is a recipe for basic risotto. It's an Italian dish. An Italian friend taught me. You need special Arborio rice, butter, an onion, some white wine, water and Parmesan cheese. Oh, and some salt and pepper too. You can put fish, vegetables or chicken in the risotto.

5 Rearrange the words to make sentences or questions.

1 you / week / rice / much / how / every / eat / do / ?
2 have / wine / I / some / please / can / ?
3 a / for / I'd / like / please / table / two .
4 is / this / excuse / too / soup / salty / me !
5 any / you / German / have / do / beer / ?
6 vegetables / raw / eat / I / don't .

6 Choose the correct phrases to complete the sentences.

1 Can I have   a) that's twenty pounds?
                       b) the menu, please?

2 Do you have   a) any salt?
                       b) the bill, please?

3 We haven't   a) the four cheese pasta.
   got any   b) mineral water.

4 Would you like a   a) smoking or non smoking table?
                       b) thank you.

5 Could we   a) look the menu, please?
                       b) have the menu, please?

7 Complete the dialogues with a word from the box. There is an extra word.

> tip   non smoking   dessert   bill   main course   menu

1 A table for two, please.
   Yes, of course. Smoking or _____?

2 What would you like for the _____?
   The steak, please.

3 What would you like for _____?
   Can I have chocolate ice cream, please?

4 How much is the _____?
   £12. That's cheap.

5 Did you leave a _____?
   Yes, I left £1 for the waiter.

8 | Review

1 Complete the sentences with a suitable word.

1 JFK International, Heathrow and Charles de Gaulle are very big a_____.
2 Ferrari, Volkswagen and Ford are different c_____.
3 Suzuki, Vespa and Honda are different m_____.
4 Paddington, Grand Central and Belloruskaya are important r_____ s_____.
5 Boeing, Airbus and Concorde are all names of p_____.

2 Complete the text with the correct form of the words in the box.

drive	stand	take	travel	wait

Everyday I (1) _____ a bus to work. I can't stand (2) _____ by bus, but I live too far away to walk and I can't (3) _____ a car. I don't like (4) _____ at the bus stop and I hate (5) _____ . I can never get a seat.

3 Choose the correct phrase to complete the dialogues.

1 a) What do you do?   I'm sitting in a restaurant.
  b) What are you doing?

2 Are you listening to me?   a) Yes, I am.
                             b) Yes, I do.

3 a) Do you often take taxis?   No, I don't.
  b) Are you often taking taxis?

4 Can you talk right now? a) No, I'm driving.
                          b) No, I drive.

5 What does she do?   a) She's a teacher.
                      b) She's talking to the students.

6 What is he doing?   a) He works.
                      b) He's working

4 Put the dialogue in the correct order.

_1_ Alan! What are you doing?
_9_ Indian.
___ No, I don't want to see a film.
___ Nothing at the moment. Why?
___ That's a good idea. Where do you want to go?
___ We could go to the cinema.
___ If you don't want to see a film, let's go out for a meal.
___ Why don't we go out?
___ Yes, that sounds nice. Italian or Indian?

5 Complete the sentences with *love* or *hate* and the correct form of a word from the box.

eat	fly	play	watch

Venus Williams (tennis star) (1) _____ horror movies. Sometimes she's frightened and wants to leave the cinema, but she still thinks they are great!

Jennifer Aniston (actress) really (2) _____ Mexican food. Her favourite is Tortilla chips with Salsa.

Dennis Bergkamp (football player – Arsenal & Holland) was on a plane to the USA and there was a storm. Now he really (3) _____ .

Dan Brown (author – *The Da Vinci Code*) (4) _____ tennis. He plays every afternoon.

6 Look at the picture and make six sentences using the present continuous.

9 | Review

1 Look at the picture and label the clothes words A (for the top part of the body), B (for the bottom part of the body) or AB (for both).

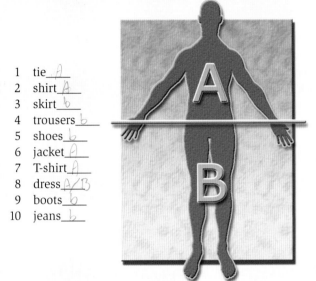

1   tie _A_
2   shirt _A_
3   skirt _b_
4   trousers _b_
5   shoes _b_
6   jacket _A_
7   T-shirt _A_
8   dress _A/B_
9   boots _b_
10 jeans _b_

2 Here is some advice for making a good impression at a job interview in Britain. Complete with *should*/*shouldn't* + a verb from the box.

smoke	wear	find out	be	answer	say

1   You _____ SAY _____ hello with confidence.
2   You _shouldn't wear_ jeans or trainers.
3   You _should find out_ information about the job and company first.
4   You _shouldn't tru_ questions truthfully.
5   You _shouldn't be_ late.
6   You _shouldn't smoke_ during the interview.

3 Work in pairs. Choose a situation from the box below. Ask your partner for advice about the clothes you *should* or *shouldn't* wear.

| a party   a job interview   a walk in the mountains |
| at the beach   going to the cinema   to school |

4 Replace the underlined words in the dialogues with possessive pronouns.

1   A: I have brown eyes. What colour are <u>your eyes</u>? *yours*
    B: <u>My eyes</u> are green. *mines*

2   A: I know her name is Laura. What's <u>his name</u>?
    B: Michael. What about the baby? Is it <u>their baby</u>? *theirs*
    A: It's <u>her son</u>, but not <u>his son</u>. *hires*

3   A: Mr Smith, please explain this money in your bag.
    B: It's not <u>my money</u>. *yours*
    A: Mr Smith, if the money isn't <u>your money</u>, whose money is it? *hers*
    B: I can't remember his name. I can only remember his face!

4   A: I have a terrible memory. Is this <u>your book</u>? *yours*
    B: No, it's not <u>my book</u>. It's <u>his book</u>.

5 In each sentence below there is a word missing. Insert the missing word.

1   What's matter? *What's the matter*
2   Thank you much.
3   I've got stomach ache. And I'm cold.
4   Here, put my jacket.
5   Are alright?
6   I don't very well.

6 Rearrange the lines in exercise 5 to make a dialogue. Practise the dialogue with a partner.

   _5_ ___ ___ ___ ___ ___

10 | Review

1 Complete the sentences.

1 A library is *a place where you can look at books and CDs.*
2 A hotel is *a place where you can sleep*
3 A bank is *a place where you can take money*
4 A town hall is *a place of gouvernement.*
5 A shop is *a place where you can*
6 A hospital is *a place where you can get*
7 A stadium is *a place where you can see sports*
8 A school is *a place where you go to learn*

2 Each of these sentences has one extra word. Cross out the extra word.

√ 1 You mustn't to take photographs in the airport.
√ 2 Children mustn't not buy cigarettes.
√ 3 You needn't to go to school after you are 16 years old.
4 You must to be 15 years old to get married.
5 You don't mustn't smoke in public buildings.
6 You must can have a licence to have a television.
7 You needn't not have a licence to buy a gun.

3 Work with a partner. Put a tick (✓) next to the laws in exercise 2 that are true for your country. Put a cross (✗) next to the laws that are not true.

4 Underline the word that has a different comparative form. Write the comparative form of the underlined word in the space.

1 nice   cheap   small   <u>interesting</u>   *more interesting*
2 easy   hot   happy   friendly   *hotter*
3 safe   polluted   dangerous   beautiful   *safer*
4 big   nice   good   cold   *better*
5 beautiful   modern   ugly   historical   *unglier*
6 cheap   clean   safe   expensive   *more expensive*

5 Look at the pictures of three different souvenirs from South Africa and decide if the sentences are true (T) or false (F).

mask $5 $150 $15

1 ✗ The keyring is bigger than the mask.
2 ✓ The keyring is the cheapest souvenir.
3 ✗ The CD is the most expensive souvenir.
4 ✓ The CD is smaller than the mask.
5 ✓ The mask is the most expensive souvenir.
6 ✓ The mask is bigger than the CD.

6 Make three other sentences about the souvenirs.

7 Read the facts about South Africa. Underline the correct form of the adjective.

1 South Africa is one of the *richest / richer* countries in Africa.
2 It is *biggest / bigger* than its neighbours Namibia, Botswana, Zimbabwe and Mozambique.
3 The weather is hot and dry, but it's *coldest / colder* at night than during the day.
4 It is the *biggest / bigger* English-speaking country in Africa.
5 South Africa is one of the *largest / larger* producers of gold and diamonds in the world.
6 South Africa has three capitals: Pretoria, Cape Town and Bloemfontein. Pretoria is *biggest / bigger* than Bloemfontein, and Cape Town is the *biggest / bigger*.

8 Put the dialogue in order.

3 Of course. What size?
2 Yes, please. Do you have any other T-shirts?
4 Medium, please.
5 Yes, we do. We have the souvenir T-shirts over here.
6 Good, can I have two, please?
1 Hello, can I help you?
7 Two medium souvenir T-shirts. That's twelve pounds.

9 Work in pairs. Practise the dialogue in exercise 9.

11 | Review

1 Complete the sentences.

1 My brother is going to work ___ a big company.
2 He's going to be in charge ___ lots of people.
3 It's going be a full-___ job.
4 He isn't going to work ___ the public.
5 It's a well-___ job.

2 Complete the questions.

1 _____ do?
I'm a shop assistant.

2 _____ work?
I work in a shoe shop.

3 _____ with?
I work with two other people. Janet is the other shop
assistant and Kerry is the manager.

4 _____ start work?
The shop opens at nine o'clock, but I get to work at
eight thirty.

5 _____ here?
I started here five years ago.

6 _____ your job?
Yes, I do. I like working with the public and I can get
cheap shoes!

3 Rearrange the words to make predictions.

In fifty years …

1 work / will / people / home /from .
2 colder / than / it / much / will / be / now .
3 and / eat / fresh / fruit / people / vegetables / won't .
4 speak / everyone / the / language / will / same .
5 will / travel / everyone / electric / cars / by .
6 in / live / people / houses / won't / underground /
   will / live / they .
7 cities / people / in / live / the / countryside /
   they / will / in / live / won't .

4 Work in pairs. Tick (✓) the predictions you agree with and
compare.

5 Here are some phrasal verbs that are in *Straightforward
Elementary*. Choose the correct preposition.

1 Take *off / on* your jacket if you feel hot.
2 Will Cotton gets *out / up* at six o'clock every morning.
3 Did you turn *off / in* the lights?
4 You look tired. Maybe you should sit *down / up*.
5 OK, everybody please stand *up / out* to do this exercise.
6 Did you take *off / out* the rubbish last night?
7 Can you turn *along / on* the radio please?

6 Work in pairs, A and B.

A Invite B to one of these places.
B Respond.

Swap roles and repeat.

7 Complete the sentences with the words in the box.

went	were	met	asked	broke	got

1 They ____ out together for six years.
2 They ____ in the same French class.
3 Chris ____ Jennifer out.
4 Jennifer got a job in a different country and
   they ____ up.
5 Chris ____ Jennifer at university.
6 They ____ along well together.

8 Put the sentences in exercise 7 in order to make a story.

___5___ ___ ___ ___ ___ ___

12 | Review

1 Complete the sentences with the present perfect of the verbs in the box.

> make be write win sing

1 We _____ in concerts around the world.
2 I _____ lots of books.
3 We _____ many CDs.
4 I _____ many sports competitions.
5 I _____ a singer for over 40 years.

2 Work in pairs. Look at the sentences in exercise 1. Think of a *living* famous person for each of the sentences.

We have sung in concerts around the world.
U2. Yes, or maybe Coldplay.

3 Make questions using the words in the box.

	had read cooked visited gone	an English-speaking country? a book in English? diving in the sea? breakfast in bed? a meal for more than eight people?
Have you ever		

4 Work in pairs. Ask the questions in exercise 3. Answer *Yes, I have* or *No, I haven't*.

5 Do the *Grammar Rules* quiz. For each definition, choose the correct verb form from the box.

> present simple present continuous past simple future (going to) future (will) present perfect

6 Each dialogue below has one mistake. Correct the mistake.

1
A: What a beautiful gift! Thank you very much.
B: You welcome.

2
A: Excuse me, I could use your phone for a minute?
B: Sure. Here you are.
A: Thank you.

3
A: Why we don't ask the teacher?
B: Yes, that's a good idea.
A: OK then.

4
A: What does the matter?
B: Nothing. I'm fine.
A: You look tired.

5
A: What do you think of the *Star Wars* films?
B: I think they great.
A: I don't like them.

7 Match the dialogues to the functions. There is one extra function.

___ suggesting   ___ asking/saying how you feel
___ talking about likes/dislikes ___ asking permission
___ thanking   ___ inviting someone

G R A M M A R   R U L E S

Part One
Rules of Form

1 There is no change to infinitive EXCEPT third person (add 's'). _____
2 The form is *to be* + verb+*ing*. _____
3 For regular verbs, add –ed to the verb. There are irregular verbs, eg *went, saw, made*. _____
4 The form is the auxiliary *will* + infinitive. _____
5 For questions and negatives the form is the auxiliary verb *do/does* + infinitive. _____
6 The form is the auxiliary verb *have* + past participle. _____
7 The form for questions and negatives is the auxiliary verb *did* + infinitive. _____
8 The form is the auxiliary to *be* + *going to* + infinitive. _____

Part Two
Rules of Use

1 We use this verb form to talk about things we usually do. _____
2 We use this verb form to talk about things that happened at an unspecific time in the past. _____
3 We use this verb form to talk about things that happened at a specific time in the past. _____
4 We use this verb form to talk about things we are doing NOW. _____
5 We use this verb form to talk about predictions in the future. _____
6 We can use this verb form to ask about people's experiences. _____
7 We use this verb form to talk about plans for the future. _____

Irregular verb list

Infinitive	Past simple	Past participle
be	was / were	been
begin	began	begun
break	broke	broken
bring	brought	brought
buy	bought	bought
can	could	been able
choose	chose	chosen
come	came	come
cost	cost	cost
do	did	done
drink	drank	drunk
drive	drove	driven
eat	ate	eaten
feel	felt	felt
fly	flew	flown
forget	forgot	forgotten
get	got	got
give	gave	given
go	went	gone
have	had	had
hear	heard	heard
hurt	hurt	hurt
keep	kept	kept
know	knew	known
learn	learned / learnt	learned / learnt
leave	left	left
lose	lost	lost
make	made	made
mean	meant	meant
meet	met	met
pay	paid	paid
put	put	put
read	read	read
ride	rode	ridden
run	ran	run
say	said	said
see	saw	seen
sell	sold	sold
shine	shine	shone
show	showed	shown
shut	shut	shut
sing	sang	sung
sit	sat	sat
sleep	slept	slept
speak	spoke	spoken
spell	spelt / spelled	spelt / spelled
stand	stood	stood
swim	swam	swum
take	took	taken
teach	taught	taught
tell	told	told
think	thought	thought
throw	threw	thrown
understand	understood	understood
wake	woke	woken
wear	wore	worn
win	won	won
write	wrote	written

Macmillan Education
Between Towns Road, Oxford OX4 3PP
A division of Macmillan Publishers Limited
Companies and representatives throughout the world
ISBN 978-1-4050-1073-3
ISBN 978-0-230-02077-1 (with CD Rom)
Text © Lindsay Clandfield 2006
Design and illustration © Macmillan Publishers Limited 2006

First published 2006

Designed by Newton Harris Design Partnership

Illustrated by Paul Collicutt pp 17, 33, 40, 89, 92, 97, 99, 134, 136, 150, 155, 157; Mark Duffin pp 6, 8, 9, 14, 15, 16, 18, 19, 20, 29, 33, 34, 39, 43, 47, 49, 50, 54, 55, 64, 66, 79, 94, 95, 102, 115, 129, 147, 149, 151, 153, 155, 156; Geoff Jones pp 36, 37, 53, 56, 84, 112, 118, 132, 133, 136, 137; Joanna Kerr pp 8, 13, 25, 28, 57, 72, 83, 85, 95, 98, 107, 133, 135; Peter Lubach pp 7, 8, 12, 24, 46, 63, 77, 102, 119, 154; Peter Richardson pp 18, 28, 29, 49, 56, 59, 69, 78, 86, 88, 98, 108, 119, 128.

Cover design by Macmillan Publishers Limited

Cover photographs by:
Top line (left to right) Zefa ©Masterfile/Roy Ooms, Peter Titmuss/Alamy, Al Rod/Corbis, Gallo Images/Getty Images (and lower half of front cover right), LWA-Stephen Welstead/Corbis, IMAGINA/Atushi Tsunoda/Alamy (and lower half of front cover left), Rex Features/Eye Ubiquitous, Stockbyte, Zefa K.H.Haenel, ©Metronap, John Powell Photographer/Alamy, Stone/Getty.
Back cover photos courtesy of (left to right): John Marshall Cheary III, ©Metronap, Stockbyte.

Author's acknowledgements
I would like to thank the following teachers for their valuable suggestions and comments: Mark McKinnon at the Universidad Autonoma de Barcelona; Lino Seraglia, Marie and Claire Murphy, Manuel Molla, Mari Carmen Stubbs, Vanessa Parody and Joaquin Gerardo from St Andrew's School, Elche; Lee Lancaster at ICL in Barcelona; Duncan Foord, Nick Rawlinson and the staff at Oxford TEFL; Nicky Hockly and Gavin Dudeney at the Consultants-E.
Thanks to Scott Thornbury for his millennium blog story and Luke Prodromou for helpful hints and encouragement. Also to Bryan Fletcher for his help with the project in its early days.
Of course, I'd like to thank Philip Kerr, Katy Wright and Sue F Jones for all their help and support during the writing of this book. I really could not have done it without you. I also owe Chris Dawson, Sergio Guerra, Beppe Olivetti, Laura Hudson, Tamas Lorincz and the rest of the team at Macmillan my gratitude for all their help.
Thanks to Adrian Tennant for his work on the Workbook and Mike Sayer on the Teacher's Book. Onwards and upwards as usual.
To all the teacher trainees whom I've worked with on the Trinity LTCL TESOL Diploma courses: your enthusiasm, insights and ideas have been motivating me while writing this book and it's been a joy to have you as my students.
Finally, I'd like to thank my wife, Sofia and my sons, Lucas and Marcos for being so supportive and understanding of all my research trips and time in the office in front of the computer.

The author and publishers would like to thank the following people for their help and contribution:
Carolina Mussons, Mari-Carmen Lafuente, Eliseo Picó Mas, Carmen Roig-Papiol and Lourdes Montoro, EOI Sta Coloma de Gramanet, Barcelona. Maggie Hawes, Tony Isaac, Tom Radman and Anita Roberts, British Council, Barcelona. Rosie Dickson and Sarah Hartley, Merit School, Barcelona. Christina Anastasiadis, Andrew Graydon, Steven McGuire, Alan Hammans, Heather Shortland and Roger Edwards, International House, Madrid. Guy Heath, British Council, Madrid. Ramón Silles, EOI Majadahonda. Javier Martinez Maestro, EOI Parla. Rosa Melgar, EOI Valdezarza. Susana Galan, The English Centre, Madrid. Yolanda Scott-Tennent Basallote, EOI Tarragona. Ceri Jones.
Marzenna Raczkowska. Yaffite Mor, Alicja Fialek and Ricky Krzyzewski, UEC-Bell School of English, Warsaw. Steve Allen, Joanna Zymelka, Marek Kazmierski, Przemek Skrzyniarz, Colin Hinde, Mireille Szepaniak, Gabriela Pawlikowska and Simon Over, English First, Warsaw. Fiona Harrison-Rees, British Council, Warsaw. Karina Davies and Katarzyna Wywial, Szkola Jezykow Obcych 'Bakalarz', Warsaw. Peter Moran and Joanna Trojanowska, International House, Krakow. Walter Nowlan, British Council, Krakow. Agnieszka Bieniek, Anna Galus, Malgorzata Paprota and Joanna Berej, U Metodystow, Lublin. Mr Paudyna, Alicja Grajek, Eliza Trojanowska and Monika Bochyn'ska, Studium Jezykow Obcych, Minsk Mazowiecki. Paola Randali. Paola Povesi. Roberta Giugni. Mirella Fantin. Rossella Salmoiraghi. Marco Nervegna and Rebecca Kirby, Linguaviva, Milan. Peter Sheekey, Oxford Group, Milan. Irina Kuznetsova, Elena Ivanova, Olga Keksheova and Yulia Mukoseeva, Tom's House, Moscow. Asya Zakirova, Tatyana Tsukanova, Natalia Brynzynyuk, Anna Karazhas, Anastasia Karazhas and Nadya Shishkina, Mr English Club, Moscow. Inna Turchin, English First Zhulebino, Moscow. Tatiana Shepelenko, Ljuba Sicheva and Tatiana Brjushkova, Higher School of Economics, Moscow.
David Willis. Susan Hutchison. Kirsten Holt. Laila Meachin. Howard Smith, Clare Dunlop, Clare Waring and Andrew Mitchell, Oxford House, London. Garth Cadden, Lefteris Panteli and Vicky McWilliam, St Giles College, London. Sarah James, Sarah Lurie, Karen Mathewman, Chris Wroth, Olivia Smith, Sue Clark, Alan Greenslade-Hibbert, King's School of English, Oxford.
Sara Fiorini, CEFETI Centro de Linguas, São Paulo. Neide Silva and Maria Helena Iema, Cultura Inglesa Pinheiros, São Paulo. José Olavo de Amorim and Amini Rassoul, Colégio Bandeirantes, São Paulo. Maria Antonieta and Sabrina Teixeira, Centro Britânico, Perdizes, São Paulo. Loreliz Kessler, Unilínguas, São Leopoldo. Marli Zim, Acele, Porto Alegre. Luciane Duarte Calcara, Britannia, Porto Alegre. Magali Mente, Lingua Lindóia, Porto Alegre. Maria Higina, Cultura Inglesa Savassi, Belo Horizonte. Eliane Peixoto, Green System, Belo Horizonte. Adriana Bozzolla Vieira, Britain English School, Belo Horizonte. Roberto Amorin, ICBEU Centro, Belo Horizonte.
Patrícia Brasileiro, Cultura Inglesa Casa Forte, Recife. Eleonor Benício, British Council, Recife. Roseli Serra, Cultura Inglesa Madalena, Recife. Alberto Costa, Cultura Inglesa Olinda, Recife. Glória Luchsinger, English Learning Centre, Recife. Angela Pougy Azevedo and Márcia Porenstein Toy Centro, Rio de Janeiro. Julian Wing, British Council, Rio de Janeiro. Karla Koppe, Colegio Tereziano, Rio de Janeiro. Márcia Martins. Ricardo Sili and Janine Barbosa, Cultura Inglesa, Rio de Janeiro.
Ágnes Tisza, Ring Nyelvstúdió, Budapest. Katalin Nemeth and Edina Varga, Novoschool, Budapest. Szilvia Hegyi, Mack Alasdair, Eva Lukacsi and Katalin Jonas-Horvath, Babilon Language Studio, Budapest. Nikolett Pozsgai, Európai Nyelvek Stúdiója, Budapest. Krisztina Csiba and Anett Godó, Oxford Hungária Nyelviskola, Budapest. Zsuzsanna Tóth and Szilvia Fülöp, H-Net, Budapest. Judit Csepela, TIT Globe, Budapest. Judit Volner and Rita Erdos, Dover Nyelvi Centrum, Budapest. Ildikó Tóth and Piroska Sugár, Katedra, Budapest. Katalin Terescsik Szieglné and Magdolna Zivnovszki, London Stúdió, Budapest. Agota Kiss and Gabriella Varga, KOTK, Budapest. Rita Lendvai and Judit Szarka, Atalanta, Budapest. Péter Gelléri, Tudomány Nyelviskola, Budapest.
Maria Montanaro at IPSIA "Romolo Zerboni", Torino
Carla Mantelli at Istituto Professionale Commerciale Turistico e Grafico-pubblicitario di Stato "Tommaso D'Oria", Cirié (TO)
Luisa Salvetti at IPSIA "Birago", Torino
Professoresse Legnani, Placidi, Forbelli and Volpe at ISS "Torno", Castano Primo (MI)
Placidi, Moneechini and Rosati at IPC Marco Polo in Monterotondo.
Frau Antje Weber and Marcia Canedy-Stehlin at VHS Leinfelden-Echterdingen
Birgit Baumann-Stephan at Anglo-German Institut, Stuttgart
Karenne Sylvester at Fokus Sprachschule, Stuttgart
Uwe Fischer, Sabine Uhlig and Magnus Kristinsson at VHS Stuttgart

The authors and publishers would like to thank the following for permission to reproduce the following photographic material:

Alamy/M. Lewis (hotel), Lightworks Media p6 (bus), J.White photos p6(taxi), D.Burke p6 (police), J.Angerson p6(airport), All Star Picture Library pp15(r), 122(C), 132(tr), (b), 135(tl), 135(mr), T.Craddock p19 (c), C.Stadtler p22(l), J.Powell p24(B), Popperfoto p135(b), Nagelestock p33(A), H.Westheim p33(C), M.Dyball p33(E), Acestock p35, P.Libera p38 (L), A.Sapountzi p44(A), T. Del Amo p44(D), J.Henkelmann p44(C), Coverspot p48(l), EPH p54 (br), R.Abboud p54(tr), A. Jenny p54(l), L.Beddoe p58(t), E.Sumner p58(b), R.Harding p68 (b), S.Reddy p75(t), B.Mullennix p82(b), allOver photography p84, A.Kowalsky p104(b), R.Harding p 104(ml), A.Tsunoda p114, P.Titmus p116 (b), D.Crausby p137(bl), M.Wojtkowiak p137(ml), F.Waldhaeusl p137(br), G.Gay p137(t); Anthony Blake/D.Marsden p72(H), A.Sydenham p75(b), N.Hollands p76(mr), C.Stebbings p76(m), T.Robins p76(b); Art Directors and Trip Photo Library / Helene Rogers p108, p109, Corbis/R.Faris p24(c), A.Rod p24(A), S.Pandolfi/Reuters p132(m), W.Krecichwost p33(F), N.Fobes p33(D), B.Burkhardt p33(B), R.Sachs p34(l), B.Krist p54(mt), T.Melville p66 (t), B.Kraft p66 (m), A.Woolfitt p68(t), O.Franken p72(c), B.Luigart-Stayner p76(t), L.White p94, P.Hardy p104(t), B.Ross p104(mr), R.Watts p104(tr), J.Rotman p106(t), LWA/S.Welstead p116(m), N.Preston p122(A), Reuters p122(D), Contographer p122(B), K.James p124(t), H-J. martin p147, J.Springer Collection p152; Corbis/ RF/Andrew Banks p16, /RF/Food & Ingredients p72 (A)(B),(F),(G),(I),(J),(K); Empics/P.A/S.Dempsey p68 (J), (J);
(c) Exploratorium, www.exploratorium.edu, (composites by) David Barker, p96(t),(m); Eye Ubiquitous p16(clock), p49; Getty Images/A.Pretty p22(r), Altrendo Images p24(D), K.Black p26, M.Hamilton p48(t), B.Elsdale p48(br), Bongarts p66(bl), E.Agostini p66(br), Getty p103, C.Melloan p104(t), D.Allen p106(b), J.Rowley p124(b),Yellow Dog Productions p124(m),Getty p126-127, M.Rutz p148; J.Cole Photography p6 (hospital); Redferns/S & G Press Agency p135(t);
Rex Features pp38(r), 125, A.Dunsmore p68(mr), Eye Ubiquitous p74(t), M.Lee p76(ml); Robert Harding Worldwide p78; Stockbyte RF p97;
Royalty Free/Photodisc pp16(glasses, organiser),19(A), (B), (E), (F), p72(D), M.Parkinson p19(D); Tate Gallery p38 (floorplan); Topfoto/N.Strange/UPPA p15(l), UPP p132(t), Topham p34(r), P.A p44(A), PA p85; Zefa/A.Green p27, R.Ooms p54(bm), M.Mahovlich p72(E), D.Wilson p74(background), A.Inden p78, K.H.Haenel p82(t), LWA/D.Tardif p96(l), LWA/D.Tardif p113, D.Schmidt p116(t).
Metronap pod reproduced with kind permission of MetroNaps p42;
Phraselator reproduced with kind permission of VoxTec International p52.
Lingo Global 29 reproduced with kind permission of Lingo Translators p52.
Cape Grace Hotel reproduced with kind permission of Cape Grace Hotels p106(m).

Commissioned photography by Rob Judges pp6, 9, 62, 108, 133, 137, Haddon Davies p16(umbrella, mobile, camera), Dean Ryan p7, and David Tolley p16(newspaper).

Thank you to Ruth Bishop and Bob Swan.

Printed in Thailand

2016 2015 2014 2013
17 16 15 14